# PLATO
# AND HIS CONTEMPORARIES

# PLATO AND HIS CONTEMPORARIES

## A STUDY IN FOURTH-CENTURY LIFE AND THOUGHT

BY

### G. C. FIELD, M.A., B.Sc.

PROFESSOR OF PHILOSOPHY IN THE UNIVERSITY OF BRISTOL

**HASKELL HOUSE PUBLISHERS LTD.**

*Publishers of Scarce Scholarly Books*

**NEW YORK, N. Y. 10012**

**1974**

HASKELL HOUSE PUBLISHERS LTD.

*Publishers of Scarce Scholarly Books*

280 LAFAYETTE STREET

NEW YORK. N. Y. 10012

Library of Congress Cataloging in Publication D

Field, Guy Cromwell, 1887-1955.
    Plato and his contemporaries.

    Reprint of the 1930 ed. published
New York.
    Includes indexes.
    1. Plato. 2. Philosophy, Ancien
B393.F5 1975      180      74-30008
ISBN 0-8383-1992-0

Printed in the United States of America

TO

MY FATHER AND MOTHER

# PREFACE

THIS book is intended to serve as a preliminary or supplementary essay to a study of the philosophy of Plato. It deals with some of the problems that arise in connection with Plato, which cannot be treated fully in a work of ordinary size devoted to the interpretation of his philosophy. I have discussed in it problems connected with Plato's life and personality, and also many critical questions, most obviously the Socratic question, which are involved in such an interpretation. I have also attempted an account of the background, historical, literary and philosophical, against which Plato developed his thought and produced his writings. The presupposition of the treatment is the view, which I have expounded in the course of it, that Plato's chief interest in all his activities lay in his own age and its problems. If this is true, it is clear that some knowledge of these points is essential or at least highly desirable for an attempt to understand his philosophy.

The book is, therefore, intended primarily for the student of Plato and of Greek thought in general, for very much the same kind of public, that is to say, as that whose needs are served by Professor Taylor's *Plato*. I hope, however, that it may not be entirely without interest for the more specialized scholar, even though he would probably find little in it with which he was not already familiar. It is partly for his sake that I have added certain appendices and notes at the end of chapters, which summarize in a convenient form the sources and evidence for certain points of view that I have adopted. But for the student also it may be of interest to see how the thing is done, and not merely to be presented with results which give no insight into the processes by which they have been reached. The two last appendices are reprinted with some alterations from the *Classical Quarterly*.

In the numerous illustrative extracts that I have quoted from various authors I have, with some hesitation, made my own translation in every case, even where a satisfactory translation already existed. I made this decision partly for consistency's

vii

sake, as in a good many cases I had to make my own translation, as none existed in English.  But I was also influenced by a belief that the translator of illustrative extracts should be guided by somewhat different principles from the translator of a complete work, and might allow himself liberties to paraphrase which would be out of place for the other. With regard to the transliteration of Greek names I have followed throughout what I believe to be the main current of English literary tradition and latinized every name.  It seems to me that "Thucydides" is as much correct English for Θουκυδίδης as "Athens" is for 'Αθῆναι.

There are doubtless many omissions for which the work might be criticized.  But I may try to anticipate criticism by mentioning two of them of which I am conscious myself. I have said nothing about the religious background of Plato's time, not because I think it unimportant but because there seems so very little that can profitably be said, at any rate in a work of this kind.  The subject is still so obscure that it could only be treated in a way which would not be easy to fit in to the general lines of this book.  A more serious criticism would be that I have not dealt, except incidentally, with the scientific and mathematical background.  I omitted these because adequate treatment of them seems to me to need more specialized knowledge than I possess of these sciences themselves, particularly of mathematics.  In such allusions as I have had to make to mathematical questions, though I have consulted other authors, I have, in general, trusted to the guidance of Sir Thomas Heath.

This brings me to the question of my obligations to other writers.  I have taken ideas and information where I found them, and should probably find it impossible, even if there were any need for it, to indicate all my sources.  It is very likely that there is hardly a point made in the book which has not already been made by some one else before me.  Naturally enough there have been many occasions on which I arrived at a conclusion independently before I found that I had been anticipated in it by a previous writer.  But this is a fact of little importance.  When I was conscious of a special obligation to any particular author or authors for the subject matter of any particular chapter I have indicated it in the text.  For the rest, I must be content with a general acknowledgement of my debt to other writers, which I would couple, to a special degree, with the names of Wilamowitz-Moellendorf, Constantin

Ritter, John Burnet, and A. E. Taylor. I should like to emphasize particularly my profound sense of obligation to these last two, because on one central point, which is continually arising in the course of the book, I have been unable to follow them. Because of their well-deserved influence in English Platonic studies, the point must be prominent in any treatment of the subject by an English writer, and I have felt it necessary to revert to it on several occasions. This might give the impression that my attitude to these two great scholars was simply one of critical hostility. But if I could only put all I have learned from them by the side of the few points on which I have had to differ from them, the full absurdity of such an impression would be manifest.

It is even more difficult to single out what I owe to conversations and discussions with many friends. I cannot pass over in silence the help given me by my colleagues in the department of Classics in this university, who have always ungrudgingly put their scholarship at my disposal. My wife has read the whole book in manuscript and discussed many points in it with me, and she has, in addition, taken on her shoulders a great part of the troublesome clerical work involved in preparing such a volume for publication.

*January, 1930*                                   G. C. FIELD

*The Frontispiece is reproduced from the "Journal of Hellenic Studies" by kind permission of the Society for the Promotion of Hellenic Studies.*

# CONTENTS

## PART I

### PLATO'S LIFE AND WORK

## PART II

### THE MORAL AND POLITICAL BACKGROUND

## PART III

### THE LITERARY AND PHILOSOPHICAL BACKGROUND

### APPENDICES

xi

# PLATO
# AND HIS CONTEMPORARIES

## PART I

## PLATO'S LIFE AND WORK

### CHAPTER I

### THE LIFE OF PLATO

#### EARLY YEARS

NO philosophic writer of past ages has such permanent interest and value as Plato. We ought to read him primarily for the help that he can give to our own philosophical thinking. That is certainly what he himself would have wished. But behind his writings we get glimpses of a personality, which must arouse the interest and curiosity of the narrowest philosophical specialist. Furthermore, even for the understanding of his philosophical arguments some knowledge of his life and surroundings is essential. These arguments mean much more to us if we can form a picture of the circumstances in which they were used, and the situation that was in the mind of the philosopher himself in using them. Historical research, then, into Plato's life and the circumstances of his time, has a value for philosophy as well as a value as history, for its own sake. And time spent on it by the philosopher is not wasted, as long as he avoids two dangers. In the first place, he must reconcile himself to the fact that there is a great deal which we should like to know, but cannot possibly know, and he must learn to draw the line between reasonable conjectures and idle speculation which is merely waste of time. And secondly, and more seriously, he must stand up against the tendency to pay too much attention to history, to describe Plato and his philosophy as merely the product of the circumstances of his time, and to forget

1

how much of this philosophy arises from reflection on realities which are the same in all ages.

What do we know of Plato's life ?   It has often been noticed how the Greek idea of biography differs from our own.   It is curious that the Greeks, who invented the scientific study of history, seem to have had so little idea of applying their historical methods to the biographies of individual persons. Even the best of them seem to write for edification rather than for truth.   And in the average biography, when we are looking for an account of the events of the life, we find only strings of anecdotes and incidental comments, with little or no chronological connection and no coherent thread running through them.

This is particularly apparent in the extant biographies of Plato.   It is true that we have lost a good deal of material that might have told us more.   We should learn a good deal from the writings of the Middle Comedy if they had survived. From the few quotations that have come down to us we can tell that Plato, at any rate in his later years, was a favourite subject of theirs.   Then after his death Speusippus, his nephew and successor, wrote an *Encomium of Plato*, which might have told us something more, though the only 'fact' for which he is quoted as an authority by later writers is the story that Plato was really the son of Apollo.   Hermodorus, another disciple of Plato, wrote a book on the Socratics, which was probably of more value than the work of Speusippus.   It is quoted once by Diogenes as his authority for an interesting fact, and once at third-hand by Simplicius for information about Plato's philosophical teaching.   Yet, even if we had this and other lost material it is doubtful whether it would tell us very much more about the things that we most want to know.   For instance, one of the things that we should be most glad to have would be a single reliable date for the composition of any of the dialogues.   Yet it appears likely that not even among the writings of his immediate successors was such information to be found.   For later writers, who had access to these works, on the one or two occasions on which they mention such a matter at all, can only quote popular opinions based on inferences from the character of some one of the dialogues.   And very foolish inferences they are.

We have, of course, one great piece of good fortune in the preservation of some of Plato's own letters.   From the most important of these, we are very well informed about even the details of one chapter in Plato's later life, his second and third visits to Syracuse. And in one of them there is a brief piece of autobiography, describing the growth of Plato's opinions on certain matters and his impressions of certain events in his earlier life. This is of inestimable value, and affords almost the only certain basis of our knowledge. For the rest we have to turn to the biographers. The earliest of those is Apuleius, better known, as he would probably be horrified to hear, as the author of the *Golden Ass*. He dates from the middle of the second century A.D. At the end of that century or at the beginning of the next comes Diogenes Laertius, whose *Lives of the Philosophers*, third-rate production as it is, still remains one of our most important authorities for many points in the history of Greek philosophy. From the sixth century A.D. comes the life by Olympiodorus, and an anonymous life is probably of about the same period. These various lives have a great deal in common and were probably based on much the same authorities. That by Diogenes is the fullest, and is also of more value than the rest in that it often quotes the earlier authorities for the statements made. Added to these we have a few anecdotes in Cicero, Plutarch, Aelian, Athenaeus and other late authors, and that is all.

Even the date of Plato's birth is not entirely certain. Apollodorus, the chronologist of the second century B.C., put it in 428–427 B.C. And that date has been generally accepted, though Apollodorus' methods of calculation are not always above suspicion. There was, however, another version preserved by later writers which put the date two or three years earlier. The discrepancy, however, is not of great importance. The date generally given for his death is 347. The disputes about his precise age at his death, referred to by Diogenes, probably arose from the different versions of the date of his birth. All his earlier life was thus passed under the shadow of the Peloponnesian War. He saw the downfall and partial recovery of his own city, the rise and fall of Sparta, the rise of Thebes, and his death came just as the growing power of Philip of Macedon was beginning to concentrate on itself the hopes or the fears of far-seeing men.

About his family we are more certainly informed. He was the son of Ariston and Perictione, both of whom traced their descent back to distinguished ancestors. Ariston, evidently of an extremely ancient line, traced his descent to Codrus, who was, according to the legend, the last king of Athens.

Perictione's family came down from Solon, who as an ancestor, if some centuries later than Codrus, had at least the advantage of having really existed.  Thus on either side Plato was of ancient and noble lineage.  He was not the only child.  Of his two brothers, familiar to readers of the *Republic*, Adeimantus and Glaucon, certainly one and probably both were considerably older than Plato.[1]  There was also a sister, Potone, whose son, Speusippus, afterwards succeeded Plato in the headship of the Academy.  It would be natural to place her birth in the considerable interval between that of Plato and that of his next brother, so that we are probably justified in thinking of him as considerably the youngest member of the family.  We are safe in dismissing as a fiction the story, which still finds its way into some modern writings, that his name was originally Aristocles and that Plato was given him as a nickname on account of some distinctive physical feature.[2]  The evidence for it is of the slightest, and Plato was a regular Athenian name.  Of the brothers we know practically nothing beyond the attractive picture given of them as young men in the *Republic.*  We know that Adeimantus, at any rate, was alive in 399.  But there is no other record of what happened to them or of what they did.  Perictione married a second time and lived to a very great age.  Plato writes as if expecting her death in a letter dating some time about 366.  If the view adopted here of the age of Plato's brothers is correct, she must have been over ninety then.

There is a slight impression left from reading Plato's own writings that some of his other relations, such as his uncle Charmides and Critias, stood for more in his life than either his parents or his brothers.  These were among the men who became notorious as the 'authors of the oligarchic *coup d'état* and the White Terror which followed the close of the Peloponnesian War.  It has been argued from this that Plato's birth and family connections would from the first incline him to the anti-democratic side.  As against this,

[1] The evidence is conflicting.  Xenophon certainly speaks in the *Memorabilia* as if Glaucon were younger than Plato.  But he is often careless about such details.  And if Burnet and Taylor are right— and to me their arguments seem absolutely decisive—in placing the dramatic date of the *Republic* somewhere about 421, it is evident that Glaucon, who had already seen service in the field by then, must have been at least thirteen or fourteen years older than Plato.

[2] It is amusing to note that the authors who gave currency to the story could not apparently agree as to what the feature was.

Burnet has pointed out that the earlier affiliations of his family appear to have been rather with the Periclean democracy and that it was only late in the war that Critias and Charmides became prominent members of the oligarchic party. Such a development was characteristic of the time. The rich and noble families which had accepted the Periclean régime and been proud to serve it, seem to have been driven in increasing numbers into the ranks of the extreme opponents of democracy by the financial oppression to which they were subjected to pay for the war policy of the democratic party. At any rate it is clear that during the susceptible years in which Plato was first coming to manhood those most near to him were becoming more and more hostile to the democracy and ready to go to any length to overthrow it.

We have, naturally, no reminiscences of Plato's childhood, though from his own dialogues we can get glimpses of what a boy's life in Athens could be like. There are stories of an early interest in painting and poetry, which are probable enough, though not based on evidence of any value. The well-known story of how on meeting Socrates he burnt the plays that he had been writing and from henceforth devoted himself to philosophy may be safely rejected. There is too much of the story with a moral about it, and incidentally it does not altogether tally with what we can conjecture of his relations with Socrates. What these were we must consider directly. But there is one more occupation of his youth and early manhood which it is worth while mentioning. From the age of eighteen till the end of the war about five years later he must have been fairly continuously occupied in military service. It is a probable conjecture that a youth of his wealth [1] and family would be qualified for service in the cavalry, and, as a corollary of this, that most, if not all, of these years of service were passed in Attica. For the special duty of the cavalry during the last years of the war was to watch for and when possible repel the Spartan raiding parties from the fort at Deceleia.

It is very unlikely, however, that this was Plato's last experience of military service. For when Athens was once more involved in war in 395 he was still of an age which might make him liable to be called up if required. Service at this time would be beyond the boundaries of Attica. We can read

[1] The question of Plato's financial position is disputed. But on the whole the evidence is in favour of regarding him as a rich man.

in the speech that Lysias wrote for a certain Mantitheus of how the cavalry were ordered to reinforce their new allies, the Thebans, at Haliartus, where Lysander met his death, and of how again the same troopers had to ride to Corinth a year later to make head against Agesilaus. There is an account that comes from Aristoxenus and is recorded, though certainly in a garbled form, by Diogenes,[1] which would lead us to suppose that it was precisely in those expeditions that Plato took part. It was said, even, that on one of these occasions he was decorated for valour in the field. This, however, is to anticipate. What is important to remember is that an Athenian philosopher in Plato's time could not be a mere cloistered scholar but had to know what it was like to be a man of action too. The present generation of scholars in our own country who gave service in the great war will be able to estimate the difference that this must have made to their understanding of many problems.

To return to the earlier years of Plato's manhood, there still remain the two most important influences in his life, upon which we have not yet touched, his political interests and his friendship with Socrates. And it is on these points that we are in a position to call Plato himself as evidence.

'As a young man,' he tells us in the Seventh Letter written when he himself was well over seventy, ' I went through the same experience as many others ; I thought that, the very moment I became my own master, I should devote myself to public affairs. And by the hazard of politics a chance of this offered itself to me. For the existing constitution became an object of abuse to many people so that a change took place . . . and thirty rulers were set up with supreme powers. Some of these happened to be relatives and friends of mine, and they at once called on me to join in this as my proper work. And, as was not surprising for one of my age, I felt that they would lead the city from an evil to a righteous way of life and govern it accordingly. So I paid great attention to what they would do. But I saw that in a little time their behaviour had made the former constitution seem a golden age by comparison. For among other crimes, there was their treatment of Socrates, a dearly-loved older friend of mine, whom I should not hesitate to call the most righteous man of his time.

---

[1] Diogenes mentions three expeditions, the first and the last being in Boeotia. This is impossible. Athenian troops were not serving in Boeotia again until after Plato had passed military age. Aelian, who mentions the same fact, gives more plausibly the two expeditions only. He does not quote his authority.

[Here follow the details of their unsuccessful attempt to force Socrates to implicate himself in their evil activities.] When I saw all this and much else like it, I was indignant and withdrew myself from contact with the evils of that time.

' Not long after this the thirty fell and their whole constitution was upset. And once more, but this time with less urgency, the desire to take part in politics and public work began to draw me. Certainly in those troublous times many things were done at which one would do well to be angry. Indeed, it is not to be wondered at that amidst all these reversals of fortune some people managed to revenge themselves too severely on their enemies. But in general those who returned to power then showed the greatest fairness and moderation. By some chance, however, certain of the ruling men of that time happened to bring this friend and associate of mine, Socrates, to trial, on a most monstrous charge, which, of all people, was the least applicable to Socrates. For they accused him of impiety, and he was condemned and executed for this. . . .'

This is a definite statement, and one which cannot be disregarded. It warrants us in assuming that, whatever interest he may have felt from time to time in philosophy or the arts, his chief interests and ambitions were, at any rate till the death of Socrates, political. Not, of course, that that was incompatible with a lively interest in other matters. We can see from Plato's own dialogues how some of the most politically ambitious young men were ready on occasion to plunge most deeply into a philosophic argument. Indeed, we know incidentally that Plato's philosophical studies at this period extended even beyond what he learnt from Socrates. For we are told by Aristotle, who had every opportunity of being well informed on such a point, that in his youth Plato learnt the doctrines of Heraclitus from a follower of these doctrines, Cratylus. How deep his studies in this philosophy went and how much impression they made on him at the time we cannot tell. He certainly realized to the full the importance of the doctrines taught then at the later period of his life when he was thinking out his own philosophy. But from the picture of Cratylus given in the dialogue called by his name it does not seem likely that his personality made a very deep impression on Plato at the time he knew him.

With Socrates, of course, it was very different. Plato's association with him is one of the best known things about him. And from the account just quoted we can see that at least on two occasions the attitude of the ruling powers of the time to Socrates was the decisive factor in determining Plato's attitude towards them. What was the nature of Plato's association with Socrates, and what was the effect that it produced on him ?

The position of Socrates in Greek thought and the nature of his influence has been a fruitful source of controversy. Some, at any rate, of these controversies can be avoided if we confine ourselves to the question of his influence on Plato, and if, in trying to answer that question, we take as our chief evidence the impressions that we get from Plato's own writings. Of these we find that very few represent Socrates as ever developing a positive and systematic doctrine on any particular point. The great majority represent him as primarily a critical influence, helping others to think out their own views but not producing a positive contribution himself. In a famous passage, he is made to compare himself to a midwife, who can help others to bear their children, but cannot bear herself. The positive lesson that we can draw from his arguments is the absolute necessity for a rigid standard of clear and exact thinking and precision in the use of words, a lesson which is constantly being driven home by a merciless exposure of the confusion and ambiguity of current thought. These first lessons in criticism might well prove a heady wine for young men, and the danger was always present that they might carry away from them nothing but an ability to criticize, which would develop into a contemptuous scepticism about the possibility of any kind of truth or knowledge at all. From this danger those who really understood Socrates were saved by the influence of his personality. His intellectual honesty and clear-sightedness, which made him so dangerous in criticism, were only possible because of the strength with which he held to his ideals and standards of thought. Absolute scepticism could never really move anyone to take the trouble to apply these standards so thoroughly. That could only be the result of a faith that there was a truth to be discovered and that nothing could be more important to us than its discovery. It was the same in the sphere of conduct. His criticism of the confusions of ordinary moral judgements might make some faint hearts begin to doubt the reality of any moral standard. But if anything could still such doubts it would be the spectacle of the very man who first taught them this criticism setting in his own person such an example of how a life could be ruled by an ideal of conduct in the face of all possible difficulties, dangers and temptations. It is perhaps more than anything else as his ideal of the righteous man that Socrates impressed himself on Plato. It is much the same picture that is drawn, though with a far inferior art, by Xenophon. He adds an aspect on which Plato does not touch to any extent, namely the extraordinary shrewdness and insight that Socrates showed in the practical affairs of life. He represents it as the regular thing to apply to Socrates for help or advice in any of the ordinary difficulties and problems, professional, personal and even domestic. And those who did thus apply were seldom disappointed. Both accounts emphasize his other qualities, his humour, his kindliness, his imperturbable good temper, his friendliness and *bonhomie* to those who knew him. It is altogether a picture that leaves nothing to surprise us in the fact that he was the centre of a circle of devoted friends, who all came in a greater or lesser degree under his influence.

What was the nature of this circle? Perhaps the nearest modern parallel would be the circle that centred round Dr. Johnson. Johnson, indeed, though neither intellectually nor morally quite on the level of Socrates, seems to be the figure with which one would most naturally compare him. At any rate, it seems clear that Plato had no intention of representing this circle as a group of disciples who came to learn any particular doctrine from their master, nor indeed, with one or two very significant exceptions,[1] is there any indication that there was any kind of doctrine or belief that was common to this circle. Nor is it represented as being in any sense a closed body with defined membership. The impression we get is that, as one would expect, there were all sorts of degrees in the intimacy between Socrates and his friends. And yet, once more as we should expect, there are indications that certain people had become tacitly recognized as being to a special degree his intimate friends. Thus, if we can judge from the *Phaedo*, it is noteworthy that certain particular names are mentioned as being among those that one would expect to

---

[1] The chief exception is the Theory of Ideas, which is spoken of in the *Phaedo* as being a familiar doctrine to all present. This, of course, is one of the chief points on which controversy rages about the extent to which Plato has gone beyond historical fact in the views ascribed to Socrates. On the other hand, it is noticeable that the arguments for the immortality of the soul, though Socrates is represented as producing them on several different occasions, appear on each occasion to come as something new to his hearers, who have to have it proved over again for them from the beginning.

find present at the death scene, and an explanation is evidently thought necessary of why they were not present.

The group seems to have included very different kinds of people, both Athenian citizens and foreigners, and its members seem to have been led by very different motives to their friendship with Socrates. It is possible that some may have been led primarily by a philosophic interest, hoping to get light on the philosophic views and problems that interested them by putting them under the searchlight of Socrates' keen critical mind. Without doubt in every case the motive of personal affection and admiration played a large part, and there seem to have been some for whom this was the main tie that bound them to Socrates. Among these is probably to be numbered his oldest and most intimate friend, Crito, whose picture in the dialogues is one of the most beautiful and delicate pieces of portraiture that Plato gives us. Apollodorus, who narrates the story of the *Symposium*, may have been another such. And, besides these, Socrates seems to have exercised a great attraction on men who were preparing to enter, or had already entered, public life. We can readily imagine how stimulating such men would find a Socratic discussion of the subjects to which they were going to devote their attention. Socrates paid dearly for this influence of his. It is by no means all politicians who like having the foundation of their beliefs examined critically. And, though among Socrates' intimate friends there were men of all political faiths, it was chiefly remembered against him afterwards that they included Alcibiades, Critias and Charmides, who of all men of their time did most evil to their city.

There seems little reason to doubt that, at any rate in Socrates' last years, Plato was in the most intimate circle of his friends. His absence has to be explained in the *Phaedo*, and in the *Apology* he is mentioned as one of the young men who would be likely to have been corrupted by Socrates, if anyone had been. And when he speaks of Socrates in the passage quoted from the Seventh Letter, he speaks of him as his ἑταῖρος (translated above, perhaps rather clumsily, as ' friend and associate '), a word which generally implies a rather special relation. It is, indeed, used by Plato himself in the Letters to describe the members of his own school. It therefore seems possible that, so far as there was an ' inner circle ' of Socratics—and I have explained above the only sense in which I believe there to have been one—Plato was certainly a member of it. Further, it is probable, in view of what he tells us of his own early ambitions, that it was to the last-mentioned class of Socrates' associates that he belonged. And Socrates' influence on him, at any rate at this period, seems to have been chiefly moral. It was the righteousness of Socrates that gave him a touchstone by which to judge of politics and institutions and the behaviour of politicians. It was, perhaps, only at a later period and in reminiscence that the intellectual methods and ideals of Socrates began to appear to him as the standard by which to judge of theories and philosophies.

For an account of the mood that he was in after the death of Socrates and the state of mind that developed from this we must turn once more to the Seventh Letter.

' I considered these events,' he writes, ' and the kind of men that were engaged in politics, and the existing laws and customs, and the more I considered and the older I grew, the more difficult did it seem to me to conduct the affairs of the State properly. For it was not possible to effect anything without the aid of friends and associates. And it was not easy to discover such men, even when they existed . . . and it was impossible readily to acquire fresh ones. The laws and customs, also, went on deteriorating to an extraordinary degree. And the effect of all these things on me was this. Whereas at first I had been full of enthusiasm for public work, now I could only look on and watch everything whirling round me this way and that until it made me completely giddy. I did not cease to investigate all possible means of improving these points, and indeed of reforming the whole constitution, while as far as action went I went on awaiting a favourable opportunity. But in the end I came to the conclusion that all the cities of the present age are badly governed. . . . And I was forced to say, praising the true philosophy, that it is from it that we can come to recognize what is right both in public and private affairs. Therefore the race of men will not have respite from evils until either the race of true and genuine philosophers comes to political power or those who exercise power in the cities become by some divine chance real philosophers. This was the idea in my mind on my first arrival in Italy and Sicily.'

This visit, we have been told earlier, took place when he was about forty.

There is thus a period of about ten or twelve years in which Plato's state of mind was as described in this passage. The political interest was still uppermost. But any hopes of immediate action were dead, and buried deeper and deeper as the years went on, and disillusionment grew, not only with his own State but with all others of which he knew anything. And yet this still seemed to him the most important aim that a man could set before himself, and he never ceased studying and reflecting to see if a way out could be found from these evils. It is profoundly to be regretted that he has left us no record of the form this study and reflection took and the friends who joined in it with him. We can guess something about the material that he found for his study. He would have every chance of watching the political developments in his own city. Though he took no part in politics, that does not necessarily mean that he refrained from attending the Assembly or from filling the ordinary routine offices when his turn came round. We have seen that he probably went abroad at least twice on military service, and doubtless he would have used this opportunity to make what observations he could of the ways of other cities and their citizens. And this was not the limit of his journeys. We have it on good authority (that of Hermodorus, a disciple of Plato himself) that immediately after the death of Socrates, many of his friends, Plato among them, went to visit one of the circle, Euclides, at his home in Megara. There is no reason to doubt the truth of this statement. And we can well imagine that to the friends of Socrates an opportunity at that moment of leaving the city which must have been so full of memories of him would be welcome.

We have no means of knowing how long he stayed in Megara. It is not likely that he was there for long. The account quoted above gives rather the impression that most of his political investigations at this period were carried out in his own city. And certainly he must have been back by the outbreak of war in 395. It is this period, also, which saw the beginnings of his literary activity, and the publication of many of his dialogues—how many, is a disputed point which will come up for discussion later. It does seem probable that normally his literary work would be more congenially undertaken when settled down in his own home. So that the greater part of these years, at any rate, may be regarded as being spent in Athens.

As far as Plato's own account in the Letter goes, we should suppose that the next change of importance in his life was his visit to Italy and Sicily when he was about forty. But there is a very strong later tradition which ascribes to him at some time during this period much more extensive journeys than this.

We find the stories in Cicero, which means that they can be traced back at least as early as his Greek originals ; that is, they were current, very probably in the Academy itself, about two hundred years after Plato's death. The most strongly attested is a journey to Egypt, where the house in which he was supposed to have lived was shown to Strabo over three hundred years later. If he went to Egypt, there is nothing unlikely in the story, which was also current, that he visited Cyrene too. There are some very late stories of visits to Phoenicia, Babylonia, Persia, Thrace and elsewhere. But these are certainly pure myth. They are entirely incompatible with the accounts given by other writers, and they bear witness to the fashionable craze of certain periods, which is still not altogether unknown, for looking to the East as the source of all wisdom.

This tendency is also observable with regard to Egypt. We see it as early as Herodotus, and it was no doubt encouraged during the Alexandrian period. This serves to throw a certain degree of suspicion on the story even of the Egyptian journey. On the other hand, the evidence for this is much stronger than for anything else. Plato's own silence on the matter is not decisive, as there was no particular reason for him to mention it. And in his writings he clearly shows signs that he had an interest in Egypt and knew something about it. On the whole, the wisest attitude seems to be a suspension of judgement with a slight leaning towards acceptance of the story. The date of the Egyptian journey, if it took place, must either have been immediately after Megara or immediately before Italy and Sicily. Our authorities give little help here as their accounts are too confused. Either date would be equally possible as far as the political circumstances of the time went.[1] The later date is perhaps more in accord with the general picture that we have formed. Plato would no doubt have been free to leave Athens at any time from 391 onwards, from which date, according to Xenophon, no more large-scale expeditions of citizen forces were sent out by Athens.

[1] I cannot understand why Constantin Ritter thinks that an Athenian would only have found a welcome in an Egypt in revolt from Persia at the earlier period. By the later date Athens was already becoming estranged from Persia, and her friend and ally, Evagoras, of Cyprus, was already drawing near to the last independent rulers of Egypt.

# CHAPTER II

## PLATO'S LATER LIFE

### PERSONAL CHARACTERISTICS

WE are on firm historical ground once more when we come to the visit to Italy and Sicily, which took place when Plato was 'about' (σχεδòν) forty, a phrase which allows a margin of perhaps as much as two or three years on either side. Italy was naturally visited first, and from Plato's Seventh Letter we should gather that the chief impression that he received there was of a life of unrestrained and unashamed luxury, both public and private, a state of things from which nothing healthy could arise, either in the way of personal character or of stable laws and institutions. But, though no doubt in the letter he is describing what he actually saw, there must have been another side to his experiences there. At Tarentum, which may well have been his first stopping-place, he made the acquaintance of a remarkable man with whom he was to enjoy a long friendship afterwards. This was Archytas, a Pythagorean philosopher, a mathematician of real eminence, and, added to that, a statesman and general. He seems to have established a pre-eminence in his own city, comparable to that which Pericles had enjoyed in Athens. We are told by writers of a generation or so later that in his favour the Tarentines suspended the laws limiting the number of re-elections to the chief office of the city that were allowed. There is no suggestion that his authority rested on anything but his own personality and abilities. Further, we are told, that he was a uniformly successful commander in war. It is quite likely, though the exact dates are unknown,[1] that he had already

---

[1] We are very badly informed about the details of the life of Archytas. But he was probably more or less of the same age as Plato. It is certainly the impression given by later writers, who record the journeys, that this journey was made in part to make the acquaintance of Archytas. And it is clear from the letters that the friendship was already established by the time of Plato's second visit.

14

reached his dominating position in the city at this period. As a mathematician he made contributions of real importance to the development of the science. He is said, also, to have taught, at one period, Eudoxus, one of the first mathematicians of the age, whom we shall meet again in Plato's Academy. We can see that such a man would naturally exercise a profound attraction on Plato. We know that their friendship was close, though we know but few further details about it. We have one, and possibly two, of the friendly, intimate letters that Plato wrote to him. And many years later he was able to intervene decisively on Plato's behalf at a very critical period. But besides this, if we are to believe the unanimous tradition among the writers from whom Cicero drew his information, this friendship marked a very special influence on Plato's philosophical development. For Tarentum at this time was one of the chief centres and Archytas one of the chief representatives of what survived of the school or society of Pythagoras. And, we are told, it was here, and perhaps to some degree elsewhere in Italy,[1] that the influence of Pythagoreanism first began to work on Plato's mind. What exactly that influence was will have to be discussed more in detail later. According to the information contained in Cicero [2] it accounted for the interest that Plato's writings show in almost any subject beyond the problems of conduct. In particular we are told that the belief in the immortality of the soul and the interest in mathematical questions— ' numeros et geometriam et harmoniam '—and the conviction of the importance of mathematical knowledge came to Plato from this source. It is further hinted that his attempt to construct a systematic positive philosophy at all was largely due to this, and that in this he was beginning to go beyond anything that he had learned from Socrates. We may, of course, like some modern scholars, reject or ignore all this evidence. But if we do not, we can combine it with what Plato tells us himself, to form a consistent picture of his state of mind during this period.

We have seen him gradually losing faith in the practical politician, even of the best type, and we have seen the con-

[1] Probably in Locri. This city, by the way, must also have formed an exception to his general strictures on Italian conditions. Both in the *Timaeus* and the *Laws* he pays tribute to the excellence of its laws and institutions.

[2] For details see Appendix III.

viction gradually strengthening itself in his mind that the mere study of practical politics by itself can never bring about what is needed. It is necessary to go beyond this to a systematic study of the foundations of conduct. But not even here is it possible to stop short. For the principles of conduct themselves seem to demand, before they can be regarded as established, that they should be followed back to something more fundamental still. Ethics and Politics demand a metaphysic. We may conjecture that Plato was feeling in this direction when he came to Italy. And in the Pythagoreans, particularly at Tarentum, he found men who had developed a metaphysic of their own and applied it in practice to the conduct of their own lives and of the affairs of the city. Doubtless Plato knew something about them already : there were Pythagoreans among the friends of Socrates. And there is therefore likely to be truth in the suggestion of the later writers that his chief motive in going to Italy was to see and hear more about them in their own country. At any rate, we can hardly fail to accept the general conclusion that this journey had an effect of great importance on Plato's thought.

After Italy Plato proceeded to Sicily, and in particular to Syracuse. The later lives give as his chief motive for this journey a desire to see the volcanoes. We do not know what authority there is for this statement. But it is quite likely that he was interested in such strange natural phenomena. It is hardly likely, however, that this was his sole motive. It is true that there was little of philosophical interest there, of the kind he had found in Italy. But the political situation was of first-rate interest. The tyrant of Syracuse, Dionysius, was in the process of establishing what became the most powerful dominion of the contemporary Greek world. And Plato was certainly alive to the importance of these developments. We can guess from his writings, both from the dialogues and the letters, what impressions he received from Dionysius' rule, on the one hand of the evils of absolute despotism and on the other of the great achievements of this particular despot.

His impression of the general standard of private and public life in Sicily seems to have been no more favourable than of Italy. But here, also, he made a great friendship, fraught with significance for the future. In Syracuse he met a young man of about twenty, named Dion, whose sister had recently married the reigning tyrant. The two seem to have been naturally attracted to each other. But this time it was Plato who was the teacher.

' I became friends with Dion, who was then a young man,' he tells us, ' and I used to expound to him my beliefs about what was needed for mankind. I advised him to act himself on these principles. I never thought at the time that I was thus, in a sense, arranging the future overthrow of the tyranny. Dion was a ready learner in everything and particularly of the views I then put forward to him. And he responded to these views more quickly than any young man I have ever met. He resolved in future to lead a very different kind of life from that of the ordinary Italian or Sicilian, and to love goodness more than pleasure or luxury in general.'

This mode of life, we gather, did not make Dion very popular at the tyrant's court. But Plutarch tells us that he was still trusted by the tyrant himself and employed by him for various public services of importance.

That is all that we know from Plato himself about his Sicilian visit. But there is a story about the end of it which was widely known in later antiquity and appears in almost all the writings about Plato that we have. It is no doubt a reasonable inference from his acquaintance with Dion that Plato came into contact with the tyrant himself. The story runs that he infuriated Dionysius by his outspoken condemnation of tyranny. That, we may add incidentally, is a regular motive of Greek literature and some incident of this kind would surely have been invented whether it actually took place or not. But the story goes on that in revenge the tyrant handed him over to a Spartan envoy who was just returning home from Syracuse with instructions to sell him into slavery. According to one version he was not openly seized by Dionysius, but secret instructions were given to Pollis, the Spartan envoy on whose ship Plato took passage, to sell him as a slave. In any case, the sale is said to have taken place at Aegina. He was saved by the timely arrival of a friend from Cyrene, one Anniceris, who ransomed him and sent him safe home to Athens.

The story may be true. But, although there is no passage in the letters in which Plato need have mentioned it, one would expect, considering how predominantly they deal with Sicilian affairs, that some hint of it would have been dropped. Further, the extant versions of the story are not always consistent

2

with each other.  There seems to have been a version in which the Aeginetans seized Plato on their own initiative and, after debating the proposal to put him to death, decided to sell him into slavery.  The story of the sale and the ransom at Aegina appears in the earliest authority which mentions the matter, and there is no mention of Dionysius as prompting to it : this by itself is not necessarily decisive since the passage in question is only a mutilated fragment.[1]  But this part of the story is in itself highly probable.  For we know that between 389 and 387 Athenian commerce was being regularly preyed on by raiding parties from Aegina.  And the seizure and sale of an Athenian traveller at this period would be quite a normal event.  So we should probably be safe in following Eduard Meyer in accepting the story of the sale and ransom at Aegina, but rejecting the complicity of Dionysius as a later invention.  If we do accept it, it enables us to date within a certain period the return home of Plato, which in all probability is to be put towards the end of 387.

And so by the time the King's Peace had come into force Plato was once more settled down in Athens.

After these years of reflection and investigation, Plato at last saw clearly what his real work was to be.  At some date, probably almost immediately after his return, he purchased a property at a spot just outside the city walls known as the Academy, and there he started the famous school to which that name was applied.  For the remaining forty years of his life he was before anything else a teacher.  For us who know him directly only as a writer it is of the first importance to realize, whatever view we take of his writings, that in his eyes they would certainly have appeared as of very secondary importance by the side of his teaching activity.  Both these activities, writing and teaching, which filled the greater part of the latter half of his life, will call for a special treatment by themselves.  Of the actual events in Plato's life for the next twenty years we know absolutely nothing.  We can only conjecture with reasonable certainty that it was passed in Athens, and devoted to the organization of the school and the development of his own philosophy, a life busy and absorbing enough, but not of a nature to provide much material for the biographer.  It is not till twenty years later that the

[1] This is the *Index Academicorum* by Philodemus which was discovered at Herculaneum.

veil is lifted once more. For the events that took place then
we have a more detailed account than for any other period
in Plato's life. In 368 the elder Dionysius died after a long and successful
reign in which he had extended his power, direct or indirect,
over the greater part of Hellenic Sicily and Italy. This great
realm passed on his death, apparently without any question
or difficulty, to his son Dionysius II. We can derive a clear
picture of the character of the young man from Plato's letters.
He had apparently been kept in the background by his father,
for reasons which do not appear, and no special pains had
been taken over his education. The results were what might
be expected. It is clear that he impressed Plato as having
a quick and ready natural intelligence above the average.
And he seems to have possessed the rudiments of other amiable
qualities. Part of his trouble with Plato came from his
constant jealousy and complaints that Plato preferred other
people's friendship to his. This suggests the rather pathetic
longing of a man, who knew that his position set him apart
from most of those around him, for the real affection of
someone whose motives could never be suspected. On the
other hand, much though he may have desired Plato's friendship, he was not willing to take any trouble to deserve it.
He appears in Plato's correspondence as being almost entirely
lacking in any concentration of purpose or any power of balance
and self-control. He was a weak character, and he was
conscious of it. And this had the usual effect of making him
timid and suspicious of stronger men around him, and always
apt to try to show himself a strong man by ill-timed acts
of arbitrary violence. In his later life, this developed into an
extreme cruelty. But this hardly appears at the time Plato
knew him.

From the first there appear to have been two parties
struggling for the control of the mind of the young despot.
His uncle, Dion, who would naturally enjoy considerable
prestige, represented a reforming party which aimed at so
influencing the ruler as to lead him gradually to transform
his power into a legal authority over a State organized on
the lines suggested by true philosophical principles. But
there was another party, led apparently by the historian
Philistus, a faithful minister of the despotism, to which
philosophical principles made no appeal. For one motive or
another they felt their own future to be bound up with the

maintenance of arbitrary rule, and could be relied upon to
oppose by any means in their power the direction which Dion
sought to give to the policy of the State.  For the moment
Dion seemed to have the upper hand, partly perhaps through
his family connections, partly, too, through the attraction
that the presentation of a noble ideal would naturally exercise
on a mind like that of Dionysius, before he discovered that
it involved taking some trouble and even perhaps sacrificing
some things that were pleasant to him.  Dion no doubt felt
that his own influence was precarious.  And the idea came to
him that he might definitely secure it if he could have the
aid of the man whose conversation twenty years before had
had so much effect on his own life.  He wrote to Plato and
urged him to come to Syracuse.  ʻ Now, if ever,ʼ he wrote,
ʻ is there a good chance that your own ideal can be realized,
and true philosophy and power over a great dominion be
united in the same persons.ʼ

Plato gives us a clear picture of his state of mind on receiving this appeal.  To his personal feelings the idea of such
a journey was very distasteful.  He was no longer a young
man, and his time and attention were fully taken up by what
he speaks of as his own ʻ by no means contemptible interests ʼ.
A tyrant's court was of all places the least likely to be con-
genial to him.  And he had no confidence that the sudden
enthusiasms of a young man such as Dionysius were likely
to be very lasting.  On the other hand, he felt a strong
obligation to Dion.  It was not only a question of reinforcing
his influence, for he knew also that under a despotism a loss
of influence might mean more serious consequences to follow.
What, however, really decided him was the thought that
here at last he was being called on to help to put his own
teaching into practice.  And if there was any chance, however
doubtful, of this, it would be a piece of cowardice which he
would never be able to forgive himself if he let it slip through
his own personal distaste for the task.  ʻ And so ʼ, as he says,
ʻ I followed reason and justice as far as a man may, and
went.ʼ

His impressions on his arrival were not very favourable.
He found himself in an atmosphere thick with palace intrigues
and cabals, directed in particular against the influence of
Dion.  For the moment he held his position.  And he and
Plato took the opportunity of trying to instil some of the
true principles of politics and education into the mind of

Dionysius. They did not go very far in this. It was impossible to touch on the more ultimate principles on which these depended. Plato states quite definitely that Dionysius absolutely refused any philosophical discussion or instruction during the whole of this first visit. They tried to insinuate into his mind, as openly as was safe, the idea that perhaps arbitrary power was not the best basis for personal happiness. Further, one or two points in practical politics were discussed between them. Plato had some suggestions to put forward about the recolonization of the cities which had been laid waste in the Carthaginian wars. They discussed also some suggested pieces of legislation. And it was perhaps at this period that Plato was influential in bringing together Dionysius and Archytas of Tarentum and establishing friendly relations between them. But the plotters on the other side were busy. They succeeded in playing on the tyrant's fears and in making him believe that Dion was plotting against him. And four months after Plato's arrival, Dion was seized and expelled from Sicily on this pretext.

The breach was not yet final. Dion for some years was allowed to enjoy the income from his very considerable property. And Dionysius exerted himself to show every consideration to his friends. With Plato his relations became more and more friendly as the time went on, though he could never bring himself to submit to any instruction in philosophy. But Plato himself felt increasingly uncomfortable in those surroundings, and finally persuaded the tyrant to send him away. A new war with Carthage was just breaking out, and an agreement was come to that when peace was re-established both Plato and Dion should return once more to Syracuse. In 366 Plato returned to Athens.

During the next four years he doubtless resumed his full activities as head of his school. But he also kept constantly in touch with Syracusan affairs. His personal relations with Dionysius continued to be friendly. We have a letter of that period which shows them in a very pleasing light. It was written partly to recommend friends of Plato's to the favourable notice of Dionysius, and partly to arrive at some understanding about financial arrangements. Plato, it appeared, had incurred considerable expense through his visit to Sicily, and was also constantly being called on to execute small commissions in Athens on Dionysius' account. It was naturally understood that he should be reimbursed for all this, but it was not always easy for him to arrange for payment when he required it.  He makes a very careful estimate of his own probable expenditure in order to explain why he has to trouble Dionysius about money matters,[1] and takes the occasion to give a little fatherly advice about the importance of keeping exact accounts and knowing just what is being spent and received.  There are many pleasing little bits of personal gossip.  One of the Syracusan ambassadors has hurt his hand.  Plato's eldest great-niece is going to be married shortly—to her own uncle, Plato's nephew Speusippus.  Perhaps a few sentences may be quoted in full.

' Now about the commission you asked me to do for you.  I have had the Apollo made and Leptines is bringing it to you.  It was done by a very good sculptor, a young man called Leochares.  There was another piece of work at his place which I thought very clever.  I bought it because I should like to give it to your wife.  She looked after me when I was well and when I was ill in a way both you and I may be proud of.  So give it to her, if you don't mind.  I am sending also twelve jars of sweet wine and two of honey for the children.  We got back too late to lay down figs to dry.  The myrtles that we did lay down had gone bad.  We shall have to look after them better another time . . . Goodbye.  Go on with philosophy, and encourage the younger men to do so, too.  Remember me to your tennis partners [2] . . .'

But there was, for Plato at any rate, something more important than these personal matters.  For Dionysius had at last awakened to a realization of the opportunity that he had lost when Plato was with him, and had begun in earnest to study philosophy.  The progress he made and the ability he showed were attested by all who came in touch with him : even so good a judge as Archytas, who visited Syracuse about this time, was impressed and wrote to Plato to say so.  Finally

---

[1] It seems to me clear that this is a correct description of what the letter is intended to convey.  Some writers have discussed it as if Plato were simply begging for money from Dionysius for his own use, and the genuineness of the letter has been doubted in consequence.  The phrase (361. e. 8) ἀνάλωμα διὰ τὴν παρὰ σε ἄφιξιν shows that it was a question of expenses incurred through Plato's journey, and, of course, of those subsequently incurred on behalf of Dionysius at his own request.  Not that Plato had any scruples about receiving money from friends like Dion, any more than, we must suppose, he would have hesitated to offer what was required to friends less fortunately situated than himself.

[2] I think a permissible modernization of συσφαιρισταί.

Dionysius himself wrote to Plato a long letter urging him to come once more, and his request was backed up by several of their friends. It seemed to Plato ominous that the invitation was not extended to include Dion, who was urged to remain a little longer away from Sicily, though Dionysius insisted that this was not to be regarded as an exile. And Plato at first refused the invitation. But it was repeated again and more urgently, and Dion himself, who had by now, it seems, joined Plato's school as a regular member, pressed Plato to accept it. And this he finally did, on the clear understanding that if he did come, Dion's affairs should be arranged as he wished. And in 362 he was once more back in Sicily.

This visit was even more of a failure than the last, and it broke down on the same point. Plato began his philosophical instruction with a brief account of his general principles, and then proceeded to sketch out a scheme of preliminary study of some length which it was necessary to go through before these philosophical doctrines could be really grasped. The readiness to submit oneself to these preliminary studies was an essential test that should be passed by anyone who wished to be regarded as a serious student of philosophy. Many modern writers have ascribed what happened next to the natural laziness of Dionysius and his unwillingness to submit to serious study. But that is not at all Plato's account. He makes it perfectly clear that what alone prevented any further attempt at philosophical instruction was the question of Dion which once more came between them.

Dionysius, for the first time, began to tamper with Dion's property. Plato protested at once and declared that friendly relations were impossible if this kind of thing was to be done. Dionysius, jealous and irritated and perhaps genuinely afraid of Dion, could not bring himself to give way, and yet remained pathetically anxious to keep on friendly terms with Plato. He half-promised, withdrew again, made alternative proposals, to which Plato seems to have listened with commendable patience, and, finally, without daring to face Plato until it was already done, seized and sold up the whole of Dion's property. This was the final breach, though relations were still outwardly courteous. Things grew worse when the mercenary soldiers mutinied against a reduction of pay. Dionysius scented a plot of Dion's, and attempted to arrest one of his friends, who only just escaped. Plato once more protested, but without much effect. By this time he was practically a prisoner. No ship would take him away without permission from Dionysius. The unruly mercenaries, who were stationed near his house, threatened to cut his throat. At last he succeeded in letting Archytas know of his situation. Archytas acted promptly. He made up some excuse for sending an embassy to Syracuse. And the ambassadors managed to persuade Dionysius to allow them to take Plato back with them. Nothing further was said about Dion or his property. In the summer of 360 Plato returned to Athens.

It has often been discussed whether a different result could in any way have been brought about. Some writers have suggested that Plato was to a certain extent lacking in tact, and that with more skilful handling Dionysius could have been brought to a different state of mind. But our existing evidence hardly justifies this impression. It is difficult to see how and at what point Plato could have acted differently. He does not seem to have shown any too uncompromising an attitude to Dionysius. On the contrary, he listened with patience to some of his suggestions, which he tells us in reality disgusted him. On the other hand, he could hardly have acquiesced in such a gross act of injustice as that committed by Dionysius against Dion. To have done so might have raised his influence as a courtier, but would have been fatal to any influence he might have had as a teacher and philosopher. He obviously could not have abandoned Dion's cause. And there is not the slightest sign that at any point he could have assisted this cause by seeming to acquiesce in Dionysius' action. The tragedy seems inevitable. And it is all the greater because, from the evidence at our disposal, there seems to have been at least a chance that Plato might have eventually made a real philosopher out of Dionysius, if the affairs of Dion had not come between them.

This was the last time Plato left Athens. But he was not yet free from Syracusan affairs. Dion took Dionysius' final action as a declaration of war, and devoted himself to preparations for a revolutionary expedition to Syracuse. Plato found himself in a painful dilemma. Some of his closest associates were co-operating actively with Dion. And there was no denying that in strict justice Dion had every excuse for violent action against the tyrant. And yet, as Plato tells us, he could not forget that when Dionysius had had him

completely in his power and when he was being urged by many
people to put him to death as a conspirator, he had not done
so, but sent him away unharmed. This was enough to prevent
him taking any active steps to help or encourage Dion. But,
on the other hand, he did nothing to restrain him, though he
believed afterwards that he could have done so if he had
chosen to exercise his influence. And several of the members
of his school took an active part in the expedition. Dion
sailed in 357.

Into the sordid story of intrigue and violence which makes
up Syracusan history in the next few years we need not enter.
Plato rejoiced at Dion's first successes and wrote him a letter
of encouragement and wise advice, warning him among other
things against the dangers of a too unconciliatory temper.
He wrote also an open letter to Dionysius, now established
at Locri, protesting in a tone of considerable asperity against
certain insinuations that had been made against himself. It
is the least agreeable in tone of Plato's letters. But there is
no reason for doubting its genuineness. The assassination
of Dion, four years after he first set out, was a crushing blow
to Plato. He had faith in him till the last in spite of his
undoubted blunders, and his death was far more of a blow
to his hopes of seeing the rule of philosophy established than
was ever his disappointment in Dionysius. There is a touching
tribute to him at the end of the Seventh Letter. He still
kept in touch with Dion's friends, and his two longest and
most important letters are really pamphlets in the form of
letters addressed to them. Whether the advice he gave
them and the suggestions he made were at all practical has
been a matter of dispute. The truth probably is that there
was really no satisfactory way out of the confusions of that
time at Syracuse. We cannot tell what impression the
restoration of Dionysius would have made on him. It took
place in the year of Plato's death. He had kept some kind of
hope for Dionysius all the time, and in one letter even suggests
an attempt to bring him into a kind of coalition government.
The restoration only lasted three years, and the final expulsion
by Timoleon, who would have seemed to Plato a man really
after his own heart, took place in 344.

But these incursions into politics were certainly not the
main interest of the last thirteen years of Plato's life. The
school probably occupied his full attention. And some of
his profoundest and most important writings are to be assigned

to these years. Even the latest of them show no diminution
of his intellectual powers. He died in 347, and was buried
in the grounds of the school which he had created and served
for forty years.

Is there anything to be gathered from our evidence about
the character and personality of Plato ? We know nothing
certain of his physical appearance. There is no undoubtedly
authentic portrait,[1] and the few remarks of later writers are
without value. But we can see something of his personal
characteristics from his own writings and to some extent, if
the material is used with care, from the mass of anecdotes
that have come down.

Of his intellectual power it is unnecessary to speak. It
would be hard to point to any other thinker who has surpassed
him, or perhaps even equalled him in this. But it is not
alone the mere intellectual ability which impresses us. There
have been other men quite as clever as he. He stands out
even more for the intensity of his single-minded desire for
truth, in the service of which his abilities were used, and his
absolute freedom from irrelevant passions and prejudices.
We cannot find a single piece of mere captious criticism or
obvious unfairness in Plato's writings.

It is the same quality which shows itself in his actions, as
far as we know of them, as a simple and direct governance
of his conduct by what he thought right, quite regardless
of any dangers or temptations that might lead him aside
from it. His courage in the face of danger and his unflinching
loyalty to his friends are the expressions of this spirit which
perhaps most impress us. We can see plenty of instances
of it in his behaviour in Sicily. And later writers recount
a not improbable story of how he went out of his way to
stand by the general, Chabrias, when he was on trial and in
danger of his life and deserted by most of his friends.

It is natural that these qualities went together with a
certain austerity and even intolerance. Fragments of contemporary comic poets suggest perhaps a somewhat aloof and
intimidating manner, though one, in particular, which will

---

[1] The bust of which a photograph is reproduced as the frontispiece
was discovered by F. Poulsen among the classical busts at Holkham
Hall, and is discussed by him in *The Journal of Hellenic Studies*, Vol.
XL. It is quite possible that it is a genuine portrait of Plato, but
this certainly cannot be taken as proved.

be quoted at length later, indicates that he had nothing but sympathy and courtesy for the efforts of his students. And, of course, his advocacy of a strict censorship and suppression of undesirable views is well known. Yet absolutely strict standards of judgement both for himself and for other people seem to have been combined with real kindliness and charity towards individuals. He seems to have been able to condemn the sin uncompromisingly, while still seeing that something may be said for the sinner. His attitude towards the younger Dionysius is typical of this. He knows that there is nothing to be said for many of his actions. But he knows too that, brought up as he was, he had really very little chance of being anything better, and he gives him all the credit possible for the occasions on which he might have done worse than he did. He had, we are probably right in supposing, a natural generosity and kindliness of disposition towards human beings in general. And, of course, towards intimate friends and associates he felt the profoundest depths of loyalty and affection, and aroused the same in them.

As far as we can judge, Plato was no Puritan. He was perfectly ready and able to do without comfort and pleasure and security, if the situation demanded it. But he did not, as some of his contemporaries were beginning to do, regard these things as in any sense evil in themselves. Everything points to the fact that he had a real human enjoyment of good food and drink and good society. There are indications from the comic poets that the tendency among the members of his school, for which he was doubtless responsible, was towards a noticeable niceness and care in dress. We could tell from his writings that with his fondness for social intercourse there must have gone a keen sense of humour. If he talked as well as he could make the characters in his dialogues talk, he must have been a brilliant conversationalist, more so, perhaps, in his earlier years than later in life.

We can tell from letters and dialogues alike that he was a man of profound religious feeling. But so far as the forms of religious observance went, like many men of his time, he seems to have been ready to accept without question the conventional customs of his city. In this, as in less serious things, he saw no point in defying convention merely for the sake of defying it. The observance of the customs of his city may have been made easier for him by his strong feeling of loyalty for that city. His unsparing criticism of many of

its institutions ought not to blind us to the obvious strength
of his patriotism.    The fiery words with which, in the Seventh
Letter, he defends Athens from the shame that might seem
to be cast on her by the fact that an Athenian was responsible
for the murder of Dion should make that sufficiently clear.
And hardly less strong, as we can see from many passages
in his letters, was his feeling for Hellenic civilization as a
whole.

Perhaps a word ought to be said, considering the fashionable interest in the subject, on Plato's sexual life.    But we
really know very little about it.    The more scandalous gossip-
mongers among ancient writers had many stories of early
amours, but they are quite worthless.    They can be shown
to be inferences, often entirely impossible inferences, from the
dialogues.    All such inferences in any case are without foundation so far as they depend upon the assumption that Plato
must have experienced any feeling that he knows how to
describe.    We cannot thus fix limits to the powers of artistic
imagination.    Equally worthless, in the absence of all material,
are the efforts of some modern writers to apply the method
of psycho-analysis to Plato's mind.    Definite statements by
other writers of antiquity that Plato had no sexual experience
at all are almost certainly part of the propaganda of the
ascetic movements which arise at certain periods.    In any
case they are late and quite unsupported by any evidence.

Any opinion we can form on this subject can only be very
uncertain impressions.    The fact that Plato never married
tells us nothing.    Marriage for most Greeks was thought of
primarily as a way of founding a family rather than of satis-
fying sexual impulses.    But it is difficult not to derive some
impressions on the subject from his writings, though we must
admit that they are necessarily very uncertain.    Two such
personal impressions may be recorded.    One is the impression
that any sexual impulses that he did feel were aroused by
members of his own sex.    We know, of course, that Plato
strongly condemned homosexual vice, though he certainly did
not feel the special and peculiar horror for it which is generally
felt in modern times, and which leads us to put it in a place
by itself quite apart from any other kind of vice.    But it is
probable that he knew at least what the impulse towards
this was like.    If the second impression, however, is correct,
we are justified in supposing it unlikely that he ever yielded
to such a temptation.    For the second impression received

is that his sexual impulses, though felt, were never of very great strength. Such an impression is derived mainly from the discussion of sexual temptation and control in the *Laws*, where the effect is certainly of someone discussing it, as it were, from outside, from observation rather than from experience. Of course, the memory of such feelings would tend to weaken in extreme old age. But, on the whole, the impression given seems a little stronger than could be accounted for by that. But these are conjectures only. And beyond this there is no material on which to base even conjecture.

# CHAPTER III

## THE ACADEMY

IT has been claimed for Plato that, in founding the Academy on its distinctive lines, he really brought something new into the world. And as a general statement the claim is justified. So far as we know, there was nothing quite like the Academy before. But, on the other hand, most if not all of its individual characteristics could be paralleled in one or other of the previously existing institutions. And an examination of the various affiliations of Plato's educational foundation will help us to understand what it did and what it did not do.

The idea of organized groups of philosophers had long been familiar. It is probable that the earliest school of philosophy, that at Miletus which produced Thales, Anaximander and Anaximenes, was organized into some sort of corporation. Of the details of the organization we know nothing. It is, indeed, only a guess, though a likely one, that it was organized at all. Later we hear of Heracliteans and Anaxagoreans and Eleatics. But, of course, the words may imply no more than a merely personal connection of common belief in the teaching of the same philosopher, as we speak of Hegelians or Bergsonians now. On the other hand, the Pythagoreans were certainly an organized body, though once more we know little of the details of their organization. But they seem to have resembled a church rather than an educational foundation. They had certain common beliefs, and common religious observances and taboos. At times, also, the organization acted together for political ends. But it never seems to have concerned itself much, except incidentally, with the development of a system of education. Even the scientific and mathematical researches, to which the Pythagoreans so largely devoted themselves, seem to have been left to the initiative of individuals and not organized or controlled by the society as a whole.

The more purely educational movements came from a

different direction. They were particularly the product of the later half of the fifth century, the period in which Plato was born and grew to manhood. The demand for something more than the conventional school education seems to have been, in the first place, the result of the democratic movements which marked that period. And the first form it took was a demand for professional training in oratory, which was one of the most obvious roads to success in a democratic State. This began first, we are told, in the Greek cities of Sicily, where the fifth century saw the downfall of a series of despotisms and the general establishment of democracies. But it was the rise of democratic Athens to a leading position among Greek States that gave the great stimulus to the movement. Throughout the greater part of this period Athens was probably the most powerful and certainly the most interesting city in Greece. Her vivid and intense life attracted the attention of the whole Greek world, and men of ability everywhere found it specially worth their while to try to cater for what Athens and the Athenians wanted. The Athenians of that period, as was natural in citizens of a democracy at a time of great political activity, wanted before all else something that would help them to success in public life. And this demand was met by the class of men who came to be known as the sophists.

Much has been written about the sophists, and many different views about them have been at different times maintained. These need not be discussed here. It is now generally recognized that they were a profession, not a school of thought, although certain of them put forward definite philosophical views, while undoubtedly the practice of the profession tended to encourage the development of a particular point of view. As a profession they have been variously compared to University professors, extension lecturers, and journalists. But the real modern parallel is rather with those institutions like the Pelman Institute which claim by some more or less defined method to teach the art of success in life. That, indeed, was essentially the claim of the sophists. Some of them, indeed, such as Gorgias, professed to do no more than teach the art of public speaking. But they urged, at the same time, with a considerable degree of justice, that this itself was one of the surest means to success and power, at any rate in a democratic city. Others of them, however, of whom Protagoras was the best known, put forward a more extended claim. For they professed to teach ἀρετή, a word which we usually translate ' virtue ', though it has in Greek a clear suggestion of capacity and efficiency in the conduct of life which is not brought out in the English translation. We feel, perhaps, even more in a modern atmosphere when we find that Hippias of Elis had developed an elaborate system of memory training.

Plato is sometimes described as treating the sophists with extreme hostility in his writings. Such a description, however, is not accurate. He could handle some of them severely enough. But his picture of the two best known figures, Protagoras and Gorgias, particularly the latter, is kindly and favourable. He was, however, undoubtedly fundamentally at variance with their ideals. This will emerge clearly enough in the course of the discussion. But he also marked a very great advance on what we may call their administrative methods. None of the sophists ever started an organization. Their relation with their pupils was purely personal. Nor in general did they have a single centre where their pupils might come to them. It was rather a case, as Plato would say, of the doctor waiting at the rich man's door. They travelled from city to city, giving instruction, at a regular fee, wherever they could find an audience. There are indications that towards the end of his life, Gorgias settled down in one place and waited for his pupils to come to him. But the facts are obscure, and at any rate the greater part of his professional life was not spent thus.[1]

A definite move in this direction was made when Isocrates, himself a pupil of Gorgias, set up his school of oratory in Athens a few years before the foundation of the Academy. In some points this school resembled the system of the sophists. It seems to have been a purely personal connection, without any permanent organization. And the pupils paid fees, sometimes very large ones, on which Isocrates lived. But the great difference was that the school was permanently settled in one place, and that pupils came there, in later years from all over Greece, to study. The importance of this

[1] Of course there must have been plenty of men teaching particular subjects, oratory very likely among them, in the cities in which they were resident. But probably their pupils were confined to that area also. At any rate, if we can trust Plato, the statement in the text is true of all the well-known sophists, those who could really describe themselves as the educators of Greece.

change was great. It gave the head of the school an established position and prestige among serious people, which the sophists in general, in spite of their meteoric popular successes, lacked. But what is more important from the educational point of view is that it enabled a prolonged and systematic course of instruction to be organized, instead of the cramming system to which itinerant teachers, however brilliant, necessarily tended.

The difference comes out clearly when we read what Isocrates himself has to say in criticism of the sophists and their system of teaching oratory.[1] His constant complaint is that they pretended to give their pupils a ready-made system of rules which they could apply at once, whatever the circumstances, without effort on their own part. He regards such a claim as a sham. What he thought he could do was to develop, by long training, certain general abilities in his pupils which they would then have to use themselves and apply to circumstances as they arose. Indeed, even this capacity could not be developed at all without natural endowments and, what was perhaps even more important, continued effort on the part of the pupil. He is never tired of insisting that the learner must himself contribute as much as, or more than, the teacher.

All this would have been absolutely after Plato's own heart. Many stories were told about the rivalry and even this hostility between the two men. But the best ancient tradition represents them as being personally on friendly terms throughout. We can see that in their views, too, they would have much in common. But, for all that, Plato could not rest content with Isocrates' contribution to education. He would have thought that Isocrates exaggerated greatly the value of the art of oratory, though no doubt the latter's claim that the ability to express one's ideas clearly and convey them to other people was essential for right thinking would have aroused a sympathetic echo in Plato's mind. But where they would really part company would be over Isocrates' scepticism about the value of scientific and philosophical research. He thought of this not as a possible instrument for attaining the truth, but at most as a kind of mental gymnastic which might be of value at some stage in the course of education, but was not worth wasting any further time over.

[1] These are to be found chiefly in the fragment *Against the Sophists* and in several passages in the *Antidosis*.

3

Besides all this, Plato was probably somewhat unfavourably impressed by the introduction of the financial element into a relation which should really be a disinterested partnership in the search for the truth.

The result was that, when he came to establish his school, he turned rather to the Pythagorean societies for his model than to the school of Isocrates.[1] What he founded was an organized society, a college. There can be little doubt that the Academy existed as a legal entity, with a definite membership and constitution. Plato was, of course, the first head or principal officer. But his successors, as we know from reasonably reliable later evidence, were elected by the votes of the members. The legal form that the society took was probably that of a θίασος or religious corporation, founded for the observance of the cult of some deity or deities. In such foundations it was really the deity which provided the permanent legal personality : the members of the society, as it were, administered the property for him. One would like to know more details about the membership. And on certain points, though we have no definite information, it is possible to make conjectures.

Were there, for instance, any tests or conditions for membership ? When Plato is describing his last visit to Syracuse he tells us how he resolved to test the reality of Dionysius' alleged devotion to philosophy. And he speaks of the method he adopted—the preliminary exposition and the insistence on a period of hard preparatory studies—as a method that he was accustomed to use in such circumstances. It is natural to suppose, then, that there was, if not an entrance examination, at least a probationary period of membership. This probability may throw some light on another question. Were there different grades of membership, any distinction corresponding to that between graduate and undergraduate members of a University, or between students and staff ? General

---

[1] I say nothing about the school of Euclides at Megara, which some writers have supposed to have influenced Plato, because we know nothing about it. We do not know whether there was an organized society, like the Academy, at all. In fact the account in Diogenes rather suggests that there was not. There is no mention of a regular succession, and of the various pupils ascribed to Euclides each seems to have gone his own way. Even if there was an organized society, we have no knowledge at all of when it was founded. It might well be later than the Academy. And the dates make the influence of the Pythagoreans much more probable than the influence of the Megarians.

probabilities, as well as such slight evidence as we have, suggest that there must have been. We can hardly suppose that Speusippus or Xenocrates after twenty or thirty years' association with Plato were regarded as on exactly the same footing as the latest joined student. There is a fragment of a comic poet, which will be quoted at length in discussing the teaching methods of the Academy, which is one of our most valuable bits of information, bearing as it does all the marks of intimate knowledge. From this we certainly get the impression that Speusippus and others were thought of as associated with Plato as teachers, and distinguished from the crowd of youthful students under instruction. It is possible, though there is no definite information on this point, that actual membership of the society was normally restricted to those who had gone through a complete course of preliminary studies, and who seemed likely to devote themselves seriously for the future to the work of the Academy. If so, the society would have resembled even more closely than was previously suggested a modern college with its Master, Fellows and Scholars.

In any case, whether there was such a legal distinction or not, there were clearly in fact great differences among those who worked in the Academy. Some, we know, spent the greater part of their lives there in study and research. Others seem rather to have treated it as a place of education, and left it after a relatively short period there to devote themselves to a more active life. Later on, at any rate, when other schools on the model of the Academy were founded, it seems to have been not uncommon for a student to pass from one school to another, just as German students of the present day attend at two or more Universities before finally taking a degree. And lastly it is possible that, besides the permanent members and the regular students, certain lectures or courses of instruction may have been open to the general public. This is more doubtful. We should not expect from what Plato himself has to say in his letters and elsewhere that he would be very anxious to provide anything of this kind. On the other hand, from the comic fragments we gather the impression that his methods and mannerisms in his school were familiar to a good many people who could hardly have been serious students. And there is a well-known and amusing story recorded by Aristoxenus which bears on the point. When Plato lectured on the Good, he says, his audience came expecting to gain some valuable hints on how to get hold of one or other of the recognized good things, money or health or happiness in general.  But their disappointment was profound when they heard him talking about geometry and astronomy and numbers and the Definite and Indefinite. He quotes Aristotle, whose pupil he was, as his source for this story, so, though Aristoxenus himself is a most unreliable witness, it is probable that something of the kind really happened.  But the picture rather suggests the presence of a considerable proportion of people who were not well acquainted with the sort of thing that might be expected from Plato.

About any events in the history of the Academy during Plato's lifetime we know extraordinarily little.  We do not even know with any certainty the date of its foundation. It is extremely probable that Plato began teaching almost immediately after his return to Athens in 387.  Later tradition associated the purchase of the land at the Academy with the money that he raised to repay his ransomer at Aegina, and which the latter refused to accept.  Further, so far as one can reconstruct a coherent story from the obscure and confused account given by Diogenes of the life of Eudoxus of Cnidus, he was attending courses by Plato in or about the year 385.  But the actual establishment of the college as a corporate body may have taken place some time later than this.

The only other dates that we can even conjecture anything about are connected with the entry of some of the better-known members into the Academy.  One of them was the Eudoxus, just mentioned, who was among the most brilliant mathematicians of antiquity.  So far as it is possible to straighten out the story of his life, he seems, after studying under Plato and other distinguished teachers as a young man, to have returned to his own city and started a school of his own there.  At some unspecified date later, perhaps in the middle or late 'seventies, he returned to Athens, bringing the bulk of his pupils with him, and rejoined the Academy. It has been conjectured from an obscure phrase in a late life of Aristotle that he was left in charge of the school during Plato's first journey to Sicily.  The conjecture is not improbable.  It might help to explain the great respect that Aristotle shows for Eudoxus and his familiarity with his views.  For, if the conjecture is true, he must have found Eudoxus at the head of the Academy on his first arrival there. This was in 367, when he was seventeen years old, an interesting indication of the age at which it was possible to begin study there. Aristotle remained in the Academy till Plato's death. Eudoxus predeceased Plato, dying, we are told, in the year 355. Another pupil, afterwards fámous as a mathematician, joined the school probably about the same time as Aristotle. This was Heraclides, a wealthy citizen from Heraclea on the Pontus. He also is said, by Suidas, to have been left in charge of the school during one of Plato's journeys. If the story is true, it was no doubt on the second journey. What dictated the choice we have no means of guessing. It does not on the face of it appear as natural as the choice of Eudoxus. But Heraclides evidently rose to a position of influence in the Academy. He was a candidate for the headship on the death of Speusippus, when Xenocrates was elected by a small majority in a three-cornered contest.

More interesting and more easy to answer are the questions which naturally arise about the methods of teaching and the studies pursued in the Academy. On these points we have a fair amount of information. The ultimate object of all the activities of the Academy was, at any rate for Plato, to arrive at final philosophical truth. And he tells us in the Seventh Letter what he considers the only way in which the ultimate truths of philosophy can be grasped. They can only be learned, he says, ' by devoting every effort and a great deal of time to them. All these different things must be, as it were, rubbed against each other, words and statements and visual images and sense perceptions ; they must be tried and tested in friendly disputation by the ungrudging use of questions and answers. Only then, if even then, when the mind has been strained as far as is humanly possible, does the understanding of each thing shine out.'

From this one would gather that the true method of teaching for him was by argument, discussion and question and answer. There is other evidence, which will be given directly, that this was a prominent method in the Academy. And there is, of course, the very powerful indirect evidence of the fact that he chose the dialogue form as the most appropriate for his own writings. But, as we know, in the dialogues there are occasions when this method of exposition ceases to be found altogether suitable. Sometimes it seems to be retained merely as a formality, and in the latest writings it almost

disappears.  Similarly there can be no question that Plato
did give systematic and continuous expositions in lecture
form, on some of the most important points in his doctrines.
These are quoted by Aristotle as the ' Unwritten Opinions ', and
Aristotle himself and other members of the society are said
by later writers to have published versions of these lectures
from notes taken by them at the time.  It has been conjectured
that we can find a specimen of the kind of exposition given
in the lectures in the long philosophical passage in the Seventh
Letter, in which Plato says that he is repeating what he has
often said before.  The conjecture is a plausible one.  And
though it has been objected to, the objections do not seem
very weighty.[1]

There is a lively picture of a seminar or discussion class
for the junior students of the Academy given in a well-known
fragment of the comic poet, Epicrates.  There is no doubt a
considerable element of caricature in the picture.  But it is
not unsympathetic.  And the vividness and convincing detail
in it might reasonably incline us to believe that it was drawn
from direct acquaintance or at least from a first-hand description.  The fragment is worth quoting in full.

' A.  Tell me about Plato and Speusippus and Menedemus.
What are they working at now ?  What deep idea and what great
argument is being examined by them ?  For the land's sake tell me
truly, if you know anything about it.
' B.  I know all about it and will tell you plainly.  At the
Panathenaea I saw a group of boys [2] in the gymnasia of the
Academy.  And there I heard strange and indescribable things.
' They were defining and dividing up the world of nature, and
were distinguishing the habits of animals and the natures of trees
and the species of vegetables.  And there in the middle of them

---

[1] The conjecture is made by Professor L. A. Post in his translation
of the Letters.  It was objected to by Professor A. E. Taylor, in a review
of this work in *Mind*.  His sole objection was that we knew from
Aristotle that Plato's Lectures were not written down : he speaks of
them as ἄγραφα δόγματα.  But this seems to lay rather undue weight
on a phrase.  Plato may have written them out, or at any rate made
notes, for his own use, and this would have been enough to enable
him to reproduce the substance of a passage from a lecture in the
letter.
[2] μειράκια, more usually translated by the objectionable word
' youths ' or the archaic ' stripling '.  It suggests, roughly, the ages
fifteen to eighteen.  But no doubt in a passage like this it might be
extended to include a greater age than that.  But it certainly suggests
youthful students.

they had a pumpkin and were inquiring of what species it
was.
' A.  And what did they decide that plant to be, and of what
species is it ?  Tell me, if you know.
' B.  Well, at first they all stood silent and bent over it for some
time considering.  Then suddenly, while they were still bending
over it and examining it, one of the boys said that it was a round
vegetable, and another said it was grass, and another that it was a
tree.  On hearing this a Sicilian doctor who was there exploded
with wrath at the nonsense they were talking.
' A.  I should think they must have been very angry at that and
shouted him down as a scoffer.  For it was a rude thing to do in the
middle of such talk.
' B.  It didn't worry the boys.  But Plato, who was there, told
them very kindly, without being in the least disturbed, to try again
from the beginning to define its species.  And they went on with
their definitions.'

We ought, perhaps, to make a distinction between Plato's
methods as a teacher of the younger students and as a director
of research collaborating with the more senior members of
the society.  This scene obviously refers to the former situation.  In which connection the continuous lectures are more
likely to have been used, it would be hard to say.  They
probably had their place at both stages, in rather different
forms.  It goes without saying that there must have been
continual discussion on philosophical problems at all stages.
Plato seems to have done a good deal in the way of directing
research and suggesting problems for investigation.  The
*locus classicus* in this connection is the statement of the very
well-informed Simplicius [1] that Plato used to set it as a
problem to all serious students of the subject to find the
simplest possible mathematical formula for the motion of
the heavenly bodies consistent with the observable facts.
And there are other stories, which are probably apocryphal,
but which serve to indicate the general impression that the
· Academy was a place to which problems involving complicated
mathematical work might be sent for solution.
There was, however, undoubtedly a good deal of independent
research initiated by the individual members themselves.
And this sometimes involved the development of different
and even opposed theories within the society itself.  We must
never think of the Academy as a kind of church with an

[1] Simplicius, *De Caelo*, 488. 16-24.

established orthodoxy of opinion. Aristotle tells us incidentally something about the views that were developed and the differences of opinion that arose within the Academy itself.[1] There was a controversy between Eudoxus and Speusippus about the place of pleasure in the good life, Eudoxus maintaining that pleasure was the only ultimate good and Speusippus denying it any place in the good life at all. Plato's own contribution to the controversy is undoubtedly to be found in the *Philebus*. Eudoxus suggested developments in the Theory of Ideas which would certainly not have commended themselves to Plato. And it is probable that Aristotle's own first tentative criticisms of the theory, in works no longer extant, may have been written before Plato's death.

What were the subjects studied and taught in the Academy? Philosophy, of course, in all its branches was the ultimate interest of the members. But, besides this, the great glory of the society was its contribution to the development of mathematics and mathematical astronomy. Plato himself was evidently a mathematician of ability. But his own personal contributions to the growth of the science seem to have consisted mainly in suggestions as to methods and in the general inspiration that he gave to his associates. But among these associates were the most brilliant mathematicians of the age, and an account of the progress of mathematics in this period is mainly the story of what was done in the Academy. The two names that stand out are those of Theaetetus, the hero of the Platonic dialogue, probably one of the original members of the society, and Eudoxus, with whose name we are already familiar. It was Theaetetus who practically created solid geometry, and he is also known as the first who arrived at a general theory of incommensurables. Eudoxus, among his many other services to the science, is known as the inventor of the theory of proportion and of the method of exhaustion. But probably his most brilliant exhibition of mathematical genius was that which is of least significance for modern thought, namely his theory of concentric spheres by which he answered Plato's problem, quoted above. There are many other names of men who, as Proclus tells us, associated with each other in the Academy and worked together. There was Heraclides Ponticus, already mentioned, who may have discovered the axial revolution

[1] *Eth.-Nic.* 1172b 9. *Metaph.* 991a 17.

of the earth, and certainly discovered the revolution of Venus and Mercury round the sun. There were Menaechmus, the discoverer of conic sections, Theudius, the author of the most popular mathematical textbook of his time, Hermotimus, Philippus, and others who are but names to us. But they serve to show that in the fourth century the Academy was the real centre of mathematical study in Greece. Archytas is about the only name of the first rank which is not to be found among its members.

There were many other subjects which we can guess from the dialogues to have aroused Plato's interest at one time or other. But it would hardly be safe to infer that they were all studied seriously in the Academy. The *Cratylus*, for instance, is not sufficient evidence for supposing that the science of philology was studied and advanced there. There is one line of study which we are justified in supposing to have originated there. We know that Plato, no doubt inspired by Socrates, attached great importance to the investigation and working out of correct definitions. There is a list several pages long of definitions, which appears at the end of the manuscripts of Plato's works. There can be no reasonable doubt that this list is the record of the results of these investigations arrived at in the Academy. And in it we may see the first development of the idea of a dictionary. So the science of lexicography takes its rise in the Academy.

It is a matter of doubt how far the more empirical sciences and the minute observation of natural phenomena were pursued or encouraged in the Academy. That Plato himself was acquainted with contemporary developments in some of these sciences, at any rate, is clear from the *Timaeus*. But in the scheme of education in the *Republic*, which must surely have some connection with his plans for the Academy, the only scientific studies prescribed are the purely mathematical sciences. On the other hand, the fragment of Epicrates quoted above is evidence that in practice there was at any rate some study and observation of the world of organic nature required. But it is not clear that this was any more than a propædeutic pursued chiefly for the practice it afforded in arriving at clear ideas of definition and classification. If, as scholars of all ages with very few exceptions have done, we take the *Timaeus* as representing Plato's own views, it is clear that the empirical study of nature was by him regarded as a mere game or recreation in comparison with the more rational studies of mathematics and philosophy. It does not follow from this that there may not have been other members of the Academy who devoted much more time to it than Plato himself would have thought ideally desirable. It has been known in other educational institutions that some members have devoted the greater part of their energies to what those in authority regarded as mere recreation. But it is hard to believe that Plato would have encouraged this, except as one stage in the process of education.

Nor are there many signs that in fact this line of research was followed to any great extent. Aristotle is clear that the main interest of the Academy was mathematical and indeed makes it somewhat of a reproach to them. It is significant that his own serious biological work began after he had left the Academy : it has been shown that the great bulk of his observations of natural life must have been made during his stay at Atarneus and Mytilene. Speusippus certainly wrote on plants and animals. From the fragments of his book *On Resemblances* quoted by Athenaeus he appears to have attempted a systematic classification of these, and he seems to have acquired a considerable knowledge of existing species. But his mathematical and philosophical studies appear to have been much more prominent. Eudoxus and Heraclides are said to have written on medical or physiological questions. But in their cases most certainly this can never have been more than a very subsidiary interest. Altogether it is difficult to believe that Plato really encouraged the devotion of very much time and energy to the work of empirical observation. No doubt this appears shocking to the predominating ideas of modern times, and it has been made a reproach to Plato by some writers. Some of the greatest modern scholars, Wilamowitz-Moellendorff, Burnet and Taylor, have felt moved to defend Plato against such reproaches. And they have certainly made the most of their scanty material in this effort. But it is difficult not to suspect the intrusion of a certain emotional element into their motives for speaking to this brief. Anyone who has devoted much time to the study of Plato will recognize how easy it is to slip into a state of mind which takes for granted that Plato must have been right in whatever he did and that any criticism of him must be unjustified. But such a feeling is not an infallible guide. And it may well be questioned whether a more successful line of defence would not have been to suggest that a corrective to excessive empiricism was just as essential a service to the progress of science as any development in the opposite direction.

If our information stopped short here we should get a picture of the Academy as a kind of research institute for scholars, scientists and thinkers, who were little concerned in what was going on in the outside world. But such an impression would be an error of the first water. Plato, though none knew better the attractions of a life of pure thought, always held to the conviction, expressed in the *Republic*, that this by itself was only a second best, unless it could be brought about that the city in which the philosopher worked was ordered as he would wish it to be. Indeed, the inspiration for the foundation of the Academy at all came from the belief in the necessity for the union of philosophical thought and political power in the same persons. And, in obedience to that call, the Academy became a training ground in statecraft as well as in science, and by the end of Plato's life it had become a real political influence in the Greek world.

It was probably in its own city that its influence was least felt. And the habit in modern times of concentrating attention on Athens may account for the common impression of Plato and his followers as impractical theorists with little real influence upon politics. The history of Dion and Syracuse ought to be enough to dispose of that idea. For, though Plato did not bring about there what he hoped to bring about, it is evident that his influence made an enormous difference to what did happen. It worked to some extent on Dionysius, it worked far more obviously through Dion and the many friends of Plato who acted with him. Of most of these it may be said that, at some point or other, they would not have acted as they did if it had not been for Plato's influence on them. They recognized this. And even after Dion's death, if we can trust the opening passages of the Seventh Letter, we find his friends appealing to Plato for advice and for his support. They recognized the value of his influence and the importance of gaining it on their side. As for the final collapse, it was probably inevitable from the start. It is not easy to see at what point Plato could have acted differently. There is no evidence at all that if he had been more ' practical ' and been content to aim at much less, he would in fact have effected anything more than he did.

All over Greece his pupils were playing their part in the

life of the different states.  Even at Athens more certain
information might show that they were not without influence.
Most of the stories in later writers about the association of
this or that famous man—Demosthenes, for instance—with
Plato bear the mark of mere gossip.  The one case in which
the assertion of a connection with Plato does seem to ring
true is that of Phocion.  But even this has been doubted.
We do know, however, that Plato was in touch with the
relatives of some of the leading men of the time.  In the
Thirteenth Letter he speaks of a brother of Timotheus who
was a member of the Academy.  Beyond this, however, the
letters are full of recommendations of pupils and friends of
Plato to this or that foreign correspondent.  Some of them
were Athenians, some foreigners.  Euphraeus of Athens took
a letter of introduction—the fifth in the collection—from
Plato to Perdiccas, king of Macedon.  Various stories are told
of his influence there.  We know of his final fate from
Demosthenes.[1]  He became a political leader at Oreus in
Euboea and eventually fell a victim to the intrigues of Philip
of Macedon.  Again, Erastus and Coriscus, both citizens of
Scepsis, went from the Academy to the court of Hermias,
tyrant of Atarneus, with whom they seem to have been
eventually on terms of close friendship.  The Sixth Letter,
written jointly to the three, shows us how Plato concerned
himself to keep in touch with his old pupils and their friends.
It is interesting to notice the warnings that he utters of the
need for a philosophical training to be supplemented by
practical experience of the outside world and all its wicked-
ness ·  ' They are inexperienced ', he says,  · through having
passed the bulk of their lives with honourable men like us
in whom there is no guile.'  This connection was made use
of later by Aristotle and other members of the Academy
who migrated to the court of Hermias after Plato's death.
   But Plato's influence was felt more directly than that.
For his society had become recognized as a school of legislation, and there is the best of evidence that many cities naturally
turned to the Academy for advice, when it was a question of
drawing up a new code of laws.  There is a well-known
passage in Plutarch which speaks of this.  ' Plato ', he says,[2]
' sent from among his associates Aristonymus to the Arcadians
to organize the constitution, Phormio to Elis and Menedemus
to Pyrrha.  And Eudoxus drew up laws for Cnidus, and

---

[1] 3rd *Philippic.* 59–62.         [2] *Adv. Colot.* 1126 c.

Aristotle for Stagira : both these men were companions of Plato.' There are other more doubtful stories of help being asked by different cities and refused on various grounds. It was at one time common for sceptical critics to doubt the whole of these statements. But, with the growing recognition of the genuineness of the letters, this scepticism has become more difficult. For in the Eleventh Letter we have a reply to a request of just this nature which had been sent to Plato. Laodamas of Thasos, himself an old pupil and a mathematician of distinction, was concerned in the foundation of a new colony by his city. And he had written to Plato asking for help in drawing up a code of laws for this new city. If Plato could not go there himself it had been suggested either that Laodamas should come to him at Athens or that the younger Socrates, by this time one of the senior members of the Society,[1] should go to Thasos in Plato's stead. Unfortunately none of these arrangements were possible, and the invitation had to be reluctantly refused. But it is significant that it should have been made and that Laodamas should have been in a position to make it.

This is sufficient evidence to show that in the Academy we have an attempt to realize Plato's ideal and to produce philosophers who could rule and rulers who were capable of philosophy. And, one may add, the evidence shows further that the attempt had met with no little degree of success.

### NOTE TO CHAPTER III
#### SOME CONTROVERSIAL DETAILS
I. *Eudoxus.*

The account here given of the life of this man depends on a number of constructions and combinations from very obscure testimony. It must not be regarded as historically certain. Some scholars, for instance, would not admit that he was ever a member of the Academy.

Diogenes says that when he was about twenty-three he came to Athens ' because of the fame of the Socratics ', that he stayed in the Piraeus and came up every day to listen to ' the sophists '. If this part of the story is true at all, it must refer to Plato at least as included among the other Socratics. This visit is stated only to have lasted

---

[1] He is the interlocutor of the Eleatic Stranger in the *Politicus*. He is thus approximately a contemporary of Theaetetus, which would make him about ten or twelve years younger than Plato. The letter is probably to be dated about 360, so that Socrates would have been between fifty and sixty at the time.

for two months.  Later in the account he says that, after having made
his reputation as a teacher elsewhere, ' he came back to Athens bringing
with him many pupils.  Some say that this was to annoy Plato, who
had sent him away at the beginning '.  This statement is followed by
a story which represents Eudoxus as on terms of friendly social intimacy
with Plato and helping him to arrange his dinner-parties.

He further quotes Sotion (of about 200 B.C.) as saying that Eudoxus
' heard ' Plato.  Plutarch (loc. cit.) and Strabo (XIV, 656) speak of
him as a συνήθης or ἑταῖρος of Plato.  This, of course, is not necessarily independent evidence.  It may all go back to the same source,
though that source might be a good one, such as Theophrastus.  The
two latter phrases imply rather more close connection than is suggested
by the story of his first visit to Athens ; but, of course, their use may not
have been warranted.  It is perhaps of more weight that Proclus in
his commentary on Euclid says that Eudoxus was associated with
Plato, and mentions of some of the men whom he describes as
working in the Academy that they were also pupils of Eudoxus.
It fits in with this that Simplicius (De Caelo, 488. 16–24) describes
Eudoxus as giving his theory of concentric spheres in response to the
problem set by Plato.  But it is not absolutely necessary for this that
he should actually have been a member of the Academy.

The phrase on the strength of which he is supposed to have been
appointed head of the Academy in Plato's absence, occurs in an anonymous life of Aristotle, in which he is spoken of as coming to Plato
ἐπὶ Εὐδόξου.  The conjectural explanation of this was made by
Jacoby (Apollodor's Chronik, p. 325), who also points out that it
explains why Apollodorus puts the ἀκμή of Eudoxus in 368–7.  This
certainly gives an intelligible meaning to an otherwise incomprehensible
phrase, though it is not really safe to assume that all phrases used
by writers of this class necessarily had any intelligible meaning.  But
the theory finds a certain support in the attitude to Eudoxus revealed
in Aristotle's writings, as described above.

II. *The juristic position of the philosophical schools.*

The account given above is that generally adopted.  But it has
been disputed by Gomperz in two articles in the *Sitzungsberichte der
kaiserlichen Akademie der Wissenschaften in Wien*, for 1899 and 1901.
He bases his conclusions largely on an examination of the wills of
the philosophers preserved in Diogenes, and he asserts that the philosophical schools had no legal personality and could not own property.
The property was the personal property of the head of the school and
disposable by will.  He certainly seems to prove his case for the
Lyceum, which probably only became a legal corporation after the
death of Theophrastus under the terms of his will.  But his conclusions hardly seem to apply to the Academy.  There is no mention of
the school buildings or property in Plato's will, and the obvious explanation was that he had already made them over to the Society, and that
the will dealt only with the private property that he retained.  Gomperz rejects this, without giving any explicit grounds for doing so.
But he can only prove his case by quite gratuitously inventing a lacuna
in the text of the will and inserting conjectural words suggesting that
Plato was trying to create a trust and leaving some of his property
to his heir (' the child Adeimantus ', probably a nephew or great-

nephew) only on condition that it was applied to the upkeep of the school. But the argument seems very unconvincing. There seems to have been no juristic difficulty about the Academy taking the form usually supposed. Vinogradoff (*Historical Jurisprudence*, Vol. II, vi, 4) considers it certain that at this period it was open to citizens to form self-governing societies for almost any purpose (at any rate, non-political purpose), as long as they did not positively infringe some law. On the other hand it must be admitted that the actual form the corporation took is necessarily a matter of conjecture. A perusal of the material collected in B. Laum's *Stiftungen in der griechischen und romischen Antike*, though most of his material comes from a later period, shows that the form suggested here was not the only form the organization might have assumed. Laum himself would rather assimilate the philosophical schools to the family associations of which there are numerous instances. And of some of the later ones at any rate that is probably correct. In these the will or deed of gift would name (I) a group of persons either by a common description or by the name of each one, and (II) an object or purpose. The group of persons might then become self-governing and control future admissions. But the purpose was permanent. In later times there were certainly foundations established avowedly for educational purposes.

III. *The Library of the Academy.*

In the earlier of the two articles mentioned Gomperz attempts to combat the common assumption that there was a library in the Academy, the property of the Society, and in particular that Plato's own works were carefully preserved there. He maintains instead that what books there were in the philosophical schools were the personal property of the head, and could be left by him to any one in the school or out of it. Here again he is certainly right as regards the Lyceum, at any rate in its beginnings. The terms of Theophrastus' will prove that, and it is confirmed by the fate of the MSS. of Aristotle's writings as described to us by Strabo. This is part of Gomperz' case, that what happened there was probably what happened in the Academy.

The other part of his case rests on a passage in Diogenes, in which he describes the critical marks—the obelus, etc.—used in a critical edition of Plato's works. Gomperz identifies this edition, on grounds which are not stated, with that of Aristophanes of Byzantium at the end of the third century B.C. And he demands what would have been the necessity of such a critical edition, with marks indicating inter-polations, corrupt passages, etc., if there was an authorized text in the Academy. This argument seems of curiously little weight.

As against it we have general probabilities for the existence of a school library. There is also the fact that there must have been books there, and there is no mention in Plato's will, as there is in Theo-phrastus', of books to be bequeathed to any one. But the considera-tion of chief weight is the testimony of those concerned with textual criticism that the condition of the text of Plato's works is far superior to that of other writers, even those edited in Alexandrian times. This argues that from the beginning they must have been preserved with peculiar care, and it would be natural to suppose that that must have been in the Academy.

There is a statement by Antigonus of Carystus quoted by Diogenes that when the works were first published, if anyone wished to read them they had to pay a fee to their owners.[1] Wilamowitz-Moellendorf in his *Antigonus von Karystos* infers from this that the Academy acted as a kind of publishing firm, and owned what corresponded to the copyright of these works. It is not impossible, though the statement rather suggests a circulating library. We cannot, however, suppose that the books could only be read in Athens. There is a story in a fragment of Aristotle of a Corinthian farmer who read the *Gorgias* and was so moved by it that he sold up his property and came to Athens to join the Academy, so that the books were evidently procurable in Corinth. One would be glad of more information on methods of publishing in Greece.

We may conclude then that there was probably a library in the Academy and that Plato's works were preserved there from the first. But some modern scholars certainly seem to exaggerate its importance. It does not seem to have been very well kept up in later times. It is instructive to look at the references given for quotations by that careful and accurate scholar, Simplicius. It is noteworthy how often he has to quote important works of the earlier period at second or even third hand.[2]

---

[1] Mr. R. D. Hicks must, I think, be mistaken in translating this passage, in the Loeb Diogenes, as if it referred to the first publication of the edition with the critical marks. If by this edition is meant the work of Aristophanes—we know of none earlier that could be referred to—it would probably be too late in date to be mentioned by Antigonus. Though their lives seem to have overlapped Aristophanes was very much the junior. But it seems to me far more likely that the critical marks referred to appeared in some very much later edition. This, if true, would go a long way to overthrow Gomperz' argument.

[2] Thus Hermodorus' book on the Socratics is quoted by him at third hand from Porphyry who takes it from Dercyllidas. Again (in a passage previously quoted from the commentary on the *De Caelo*) he does not quote Eudemus directly, but through Sosigenes.

## CHAPTER IV

## THE WRITINGS OF PLATO

IT is perhaps hardly necessary to state that Plato's writings consist of dialogues and letters. The question of the genuineness of the letters deserves a treatment by itself.[1] The development of critical opinion on the subject forms an interesting chapter in literary history. They were accepted without question earlier : even Bentley after the Phalaris controversy entertained no doubt of their genuineness. Then followed a period of extreme scepticism ; and throughout the nineteenth century they were rejected wholesale by the great majority of scholars. During the present century, after a vigorous literary battle, opinion has gradually swung round to the earlier view. And it is safe to say that by now they are generally accepted, either entirely or with small reservations on particular letters or even particular passages. About the dialogues, in spite of occasional individual eccentricities, such scepticism has never been possible. And it is as certain as anything in the history of Greek literature that the great bulk of them are Plato's own work.

There are, of course, non-Platonic dialogues, like the *Axiochus* and the *Eryxias*, which are included as spurious in the Plato manuscripts. But there has never been any question of accepting them, and they do not concern us here, though they are not entirely uninteresting in themselves and might repay more attention than they have generally received. But besides these there are a few dialogues among those handed down to us as Plato's own, which even the most conservative scholars have found themselves unable to accept. The most generally rejected are the *Theages*, *Hipparchus*, *Amatores*, *Alcibiades I* and *II*, *Minos*, *Clitophon*, and perhaps the *Hippias Major*. Philosophically these are unimportant. But their presence in the Platonic corpus is of interest. It is generally recognized that nearly all of them are, as far as can be judged from the language, fourth-century work. And there is no

[1] See Appendix I.

4                                                            49

reason to suppose that they were deliberately intended to pass as Plato's work when they were written. The great age of literary forgeries begins a little later than this. The most natural explanation is that it had become the fashion in Platonic circles to compose Socratic dialogues, after the manner of Plato. If they were written and preserved in the Academy it is very easy to see how, a little later, some of them might have got mixed up by mistake with Plato's own writings.

In this chapter we are concerned with the genuine dialogues. And for the student of Plato and the student of philosophy alike it is of the first importance to arrive at a clear conception of how the dialogues are to be regarded and what is to be looked for in them. The student of philosophy, in particular, who is accustomed to expect from his authors a continuous exposition of some philosophical problem, may well ask what he is to make of this series of conversations, cast in dramatic form, in most of which the chief part is taken by Socrates and in none of which the author appears at all. Unfortunately he will look in vain to the specialists in the subject for a definite and unanimous explanation. He will find himself at the outset faced with one of the most troublesome controversies in the history of philosophy, the controversy about the exact significance of the introduction of Socrates as the principal figure in the dialogues. Does it mean that the author is throughout merely trying to reproduce the point of view of Socrates without any reference to his own? Or is Socrates merely the mask for the expression of his own opinions? Or is there any intermediate position possible between these two extremes? The question must be discussed at length here, even at the risk of introducing yet more confusion into an already sufficiently confusing controversy.

It may help to clearness if one distinction is made at the outset. If we were primarily concerned with the life and views of Socrates, it would no doubt be necessary to try to arrive at a conclusion on every point as to whether what Plato ascribes to Socrates is historically correct. On the other hand, if, as here, our chief interest is in Plato, we may hope, in some cases at least, to evade this tiresome obligation. At any rate it is not with that aspect of the problem that we must begin. The first necessity is to try to guess what Plato's interests and intentions were in writing the dialogues. And it would be well to remember that, however careful our investigation is, its conclusion will at the end still remain a guess.

We may think that the cumulative evidence makes it a very probable one. But, whatever the evidence, in judging it a large element of personal impression must come in. So that it would be foolish to be disappointed if, in spite of all our discussions, differences of opinion still remain.

Perhaps the clearest way of treating the question would be to state, in the first place, the view of the matter adopted in this work. The reader will then be able to arrive at a first impression of its apparent general probability. But after that it will be necessary to give more in detail the positive evidence that we have. And at each point the question can be raised how far that evidence tells in favour of the view put forward. It would be out of place here to enter into detailed controversy with the advocates of rival views. And no direct mention will be made of these.

As a first point, it does not seem probable that Plato would have entirely changed his intention in the use of the dialogue form at any particular point. If he did, he would surely not have retained the same form. At the least we must say that if there was such a change of intention it must have been gradual and almost imperceptible to Plato himself. That probability must be borne in mind in any attempt at constructing a plausible theory. And full allowance is made for it if we suppose, in the first place, that from first to last Plato's main object in writing, as in all his other acitivities, was to do something to meet the needs of his own time. He wrote primarily to help people to think rightly. That means that any views definitely advocated in a dialogue and any views towards which the arguments of a dialogue inevitably led were views that Plato regarded as certainly or probably true. If a dialogue did not come to any positive conclusion, but opened up certain questions or suggested certain lines of thought, it means that Plato regarded work on these lines as likely to be fruitful. What our theory does not mean will have to be explained later. But it maintains that in this sense the dialogues express Plato's own views throughout. And that is their chief object.

How, then, does Socrates come in ? A natural explanation of his position in the dialogues is, that when Plato first began to write, he felt that what his world chiefly needed was a dose of the Socratic spirit. It was by being taught to discuss its problems by the methods and in the spirit of Socrates that it had the best hopes of solving them. So his first writings are attempts to clear up the meaning of certain moral concepts by the methods that he had learnt from Socrates. The actual words used are of course his own. But he doubtless believed that he was being absolutely faithful to Socrates' spirit and that they were simply the sort of arguments that Socrates would have used on the subject. And so they may well have been. But however faithfully a man of ability tries to reproduce the point of view of some one else, he generally puts something of his own into it. So that from the beginning we may suspect that there is a touch of Plato about even the most Socratic arguments.

It is to be noted that the intention here ascribed to Plato would easily, at this stage, have fused with another intention, that of preserving the memory of his friend and defending it before the world. We can be sure that to Plato the best defence and the best memorial of Socrates would have been to persuade other people to think and act like him. This would have seemed much more worth while than to labour to make his portrait of him absolutely historically accurate on every point.

If he was at all moved by such considerations, and much more if they were his main object, he would very soon find himself applying Socratic methods of argument to subjects that he may never have heard Socrates explicitly discuss. And at the same time he would begin to draw out the implications of arguments that Socrates had used, without troubling himself if this involved going beyond anything he had ever actually heard him say. It is doubtful if he himself would have been able to say exactly at what point this began. Most students of philosophy must have had experience of this difficulty. Even when it is merely a question of trying to interpret some one else's views, especially when we have only learnt these by word of mouth, we know how hard it often is to draw the line between ' This is what he said ' and ' This is what he must have meant.' And when we have developed views of our own under the influence or inspiration of some other thinker, we know that it is absolutely impossible to draw a sharp line at the point at which what we have learnt from him ends and what we have thought out for ourselves begins. Indeed, the distinction itself is not a real one, if taken absolutely. For in philosophy we can never simply take over another person's beliefs. We have to think them over again and make them part of our own thought. No disciple can ever really literally

reproduce his master's teaching in its entirety, even if he believes
that he has done so.

If Plato's attitude has been guessed at correctly, he would
not have hesitated to let the discussions that he wrote about
go on wherever the wind of the argument carried them, without allowing himself to be restricted by merely historical
considerations. And even when he realized, which he would
probably only do long after the thing had really happened,
that he had gone a good way beyond anything that Socrates
ever actually said, he would not be seriously disturbed. Nor
would he see any reason to change the literary form that had
served him so well. He would still feel that he was either
developing a hint that Socrates had let fall or drawing out
the logical implication of some view that he had expressed,
or at the least conducting his investigations by the method
and in the spirit of Socrates. And, as a matter of fact, most
of the philosophical views expressed in the dialogues could
be looked at in that light, even on the most restricted view
of the extent of Socrates' actual contribution of positive belief.
When he does change the literary form it is not necessary to
suppose that it is merely because he has realized that he has
gone beyond Socrates' views, nor even, I think, because he is
discussing a subject that Socrates never actually discussed.
It would be most naturally because he realized that he was
discussing subjects to which the Socratic method was not really
appropriate. Such would be the processes of physical nature,
discussed in the *Timaeus*, where the dialogue form is dropped
altogether, or—though less obviously—the details of legislation in the *Laws*, where the dialogue form is only formally
retained. The choice of some other character than Socrates
as the chief figure in the *Sophist* and *Politicus*, where the
dialogue form is preserved—though it does not seem to add
much—may possibly be because he felt, not that he was
himself going further than Socrates, but that on these questions his thought had been specially influenced from some other
direction.

There are one or two important points in the views expressed
in the dialogues on which there is definite evidence, which
has seemed to most people reasonably convincing, that Plato
was consciously going beyond anything that could be attributed
to Socrates. But it is only a happy accident that we know
of these. In most cases we cannot expect to reach any definite conclusions in the matter. Nor need that trouble us in

our present investigation. It belongs rather to the study of Socrates than to the study of Plato. The important thing is to be assured that, so far as we can find any views inculcated in the dialogues, they are those of Plato. And these views are of value for themselves. It is only of secondary interest to trace their sources.

This view does not commit us for or against a belief in the accuracy of the historical facts about Socrates and other people that are mentioned incidentally or implied in the dialogues. But as it would be difficult to suggest any motive for falsifying them, they may probably in general be safely accepted. About the historical reality or possibility of the meetings described in the dialogues, the case is a little different. There might possibly be reasons for imagining a meeting which did not or perhaps even could not have taken place. But Plato would hardly have gone out of his way to do this. Each case would have to be considered on its merits. And the same would apply to the general historical setting of the dialogues. Certainly many of the supposed anachronisms that critics, from Athenaeus onwards, have thought they detected, prove on closer examination to be without foundation. But there still remain a few which seem hard to explain away.

One more estimate of general probabilities may conclude this exposition, It is difficult to see any satisfactory resting-place between some such view as this and a view which would hold that the dialogues were wholly biographical in intention and had no connection at all, except accidentally, with Plato's own views. It is difficult to imagine Plato trying to serve the two aims at once, and limiting his philosophical arguments to what might correctly be attributed to Socrates, while at the same time he was limiting his historical account to what he himself found philosophically acceptable. Either interest might be well served by the dialogue form. But one or other would surely have to become predominant.

Assuming this general point of view, can we, it may be asked, simply substitute Plato for Socrates in the dialogues, put down everything he says, and present the total result as the Platonic philosophy ? That is what those who do not accept the biographical theory of the dialogues are sometimes supposed to believe. But, as a matter of fact, it is doubtful whether anyone ever actually has maintained such a crude view. If it has been held, it is certainly a profound error. An inspection of the dialogue form itself ought to be enough to prevent anyone falling into this absurdity. For absurdity it is, and would be just as much even if Plato actually were substituted for Socrates as the principal figure in the dialogues.

Plato may be regarded as the real inventor of the dialogue. It is true that Aristotle is said, according to a second-hand quotation by Diogenes from a lost work, to have ascribed the invention to an obscure person, Alexamenus of Teos, whom no one else ever seems to have heard of. But he cannot be taken very seriously. This literary form may have been suggested to Plato in part by other established literary forms, like the drama or the mimes of Sophron, which he is said to have admired greatly. But the obvious source of inspiration for the choice of the dialogue form must have been the originals which were represented in it, namely the conversations of Socrates. And if we ask what it was in the way of ideas that Plato would naturally choose the dialogue form to present, the answer must be found by asking what would be most easily treated in a conversation of this kind.

It is obvious that it would not be suitable for the systematic presentation of a complete philosophy. Nor in fact is anything of the kind ever attempted in the dialogues. The nearest approach to it that we have is to be found in the account of the physical world given in the *Timaeus*, the construction of a legislative code in the *Laws*, and the development of a theory of the state in the *Republic*. In the two first mentioned the dialogue form practically disappears, and in the *Republic* there are many long passages where it is not really appropriate. Socrates states his views, and the other characters merely say yes or no as he requires. Two conditions seem to be needed for a favourable field for the use of the dialogue form. The discussion must be, not of a general philosophical position, but of a specific point or problem : the distinction here is, obviously, one of degree, but none the less real for that. And, secondly, there should be real differences of opinion and alternative views to be expressed and discussed. The first condition is always fulfilled, with the partial exceptions just noted. The second is not so invariably fulfilled, though it is the general rule, particularly in the earlier dialogues. We must also remember, in this connection, that the dialogues were written at intervals over a long period of years. They are not, except in one or two special cases, even intended to have any direct connection with each other.

In this they differ from modern examples of the use of a similar form. Berkeley's three dialogues, for instance, are really all chapters of the same work, and the discussion follows continuously from one to the next.

We have to regard the dialogues in general, then, as a series of occasional essays written at different periods, and dealing with different special problems of thought. Each is a dramatic whole, with a plot and a unity of its own. And they must be read as such.

We shall have to discuss in detail later the precise significance of the other characters in the dialogues. All that needs to be said here is that the questions discussed must be supposed to have some reference to the movements of thought, philosophical or popular, in Plato's own time. In general the more strictly philosophical views are discussed in the later dialogues, while in the earlier ones Plato is interested rather in bringing out the confusions and contradictions of the ordinary assumptions of the ' plain man '. We need to remember this, by the way, when, on first reading one of the dialogues, we feel inclined to criticize the inadequacy of the demonstration. We feel that the other characters allow themselves to be refuted too easily, that we could have done better ourselves by avoiding certain contradictions, and that Socrates has not established his position against every possible objection. But this is to ask of a dialogue what it could not possibly do. The whole point is to bring out the fact that these confusions and contradictions did actually exist in current thought. And we can demand no more than that.

We still want to know how we are going to get at a philosophy of Plato from all this. Some great scholars have held that the demand is an impossible one, and that all we can do is to consider the argument of each dialogue by itself on its merits. But this is surely an exaggeration. Plato may not have arrived at a complete system of thought. Indeed, it is natural to suppose that he always realized that there were many problems that he had not solved. But he was a serious thinker, and we are therefore bound to assume that he was aiming at a system, and that at all times he had a considerable degree of clearness and consistency in his views. There must have been behind the treatment of particular questions in particular dialogues a general point of view which inspired and coloured this treatment. And that is what the philosopher will want to discover. He need not despair of attaining a considerable degree of success in this, if he will avoid certain dangers. Above all, he must remember the independent dramatic unity of each dialogue. Each has its own subject and its own situation. And the appropriate treatment in each case will, therefore, at some point be different. It is a common fault in Platonic exegesis to look for some deep significance in comparatively minor differences of outlook or even of mere wording. It is particularly dangerous to try to extract such significance from a silence in one dialogue about a subject or belief mentioned in another. Only if we have considered fully the special object of the particular dialogue and made it clear beyond a doubt that this ought necessarily to demand a mention of this belief, can we deduce anything from the fact that it is not mentioned. We have to be very careful, then, before we can conclude that there is any real difference of view from the mere fact that different language is used or even that a different aspect of some reality is emphasized.

On the other hand, it must equally be remembered that the dialogues were written at intervals over a long period of fifty years. It would certainly be curious if there was no point on which Plato's views were developed, modified or even perhaps changed altogether in the course of that long period. So it would be absurd to take it as a dogma that his views were exactly the same in every dialogue, and to labour to reconcile passages if no reconciliation appears possible. It is the task of the philosophical interpreter of Plato to bear in mind both these considerations and to steer a course between the two dangers.

Of the system of beliefs which lies at the back of the arguments in the dialogues we have sometimes a general mention in a dialogue itself, though never a complete exposition and never more than a sketch of the kind of arguments with which it was demonstrated. It is thus with the famous Theory of Ideas, which was regarded by later generations, and if we can believe the Sixth Letter [1] by Plato himself, as his greatest contribution to thought. It is mentioned in dialogues like the *Phaedo* and' the *Republic*, but only as the foundation or presupposition of a particular argument in the discussion of the subject of the dialogue. Nobody could imagine that it was

[1] 322 d. 5. πρὸς τῇ τῶν εἰδῶν σοφίᾳ τῇ καλῇ ταύτῃ. This is mentioned as summing up the philosophical gifts of his pupils, in addition to which they need knowledge and experience of the world.

supposed to be conclusively demonstrated in these or any other dialogues. And the countless controversies that have arisen on the subject are sufficient proof that it is nowhere expounded in detail. This is really what we should have expected. We know from Plato's own words both in the letters and the dialogues, that he did not believe that the profoundest and most important truths could be properly expounded, much less demonstrated in the course of a single argument.

Sometimes we can only infer by examining what seem to be the assumptions of the particular arguments what Plato's views on certain points would be, and how he would connect them with the views, which he expresses or implies, on other points. We cannot even assume that Plato himself had arrived at perfect clearness about all his beliefs or that he had thought of all the further difficulties and problems which occur to us now. Even if he had arrived at a clear conviction himself we cannot always hope even to be able to guess what it was. It is only when the point that we want to be clear about happens to be important for the subject of a particular dialogue that we can hope to get some light on it. The task of extracting a system of philosophy from Plato's dialogues must always be something like tracing the course of a submarine mountain chain by the occasional peaks which emerge above the surface of the sea.

We are not entirely without information about Plato's philosophy from other sources. We have the account and the criticisms of Aristotle which are clearly and naturally mainly based on what he learnt from Plato personally in the Academy. Unfortunately this tells us very much less than we might have hoped. It only touches on a limited range of subjects. And even these are handled in an unsympathetic spirit, which is more anxious to criticize than to understand or explain. A good deal of the reference to Plato is merely by way of allusions often hopelessly obscure. And, even when there is more than that, the account is sometimes very difficult to understand, and its interpretation has led to the widest differences of opinion. Yet with all faults the information is of first-rate value, and the work that has been done on it in recent years has opened up most suggestive lines of interpretation. But it is quite unnecessary to regard it as a rival or alternative method of interpretation to that provided by the dialogues. The two should be used to explain and supplement each other. And of course the warnings that have been given about the interpretation of differences of expression between one dialogue and another apply with greatly increased force when it is a question of differences between dialogues and reports of oral teaching.

What motive must we ascribe to Plato in the publication of the dialogues, if it was certainly not to present the whole of his philosophy systematically to the public? One might answer that it was to present as much of it as he thought they might grasp. And that would no doubt be true as far as it went. But it hardly tells us what we want to know. For whom did he write the dialogues? What aim did he hope to achieve in them? What was their relation to his oral teaching? Some answer must be attempted, though it can only be a conjecture.

For most of the earlier dialogues the answer is not very difficult. They were directed to the ordinary educated public of Athens, and Greece generally. And they aimed at stimulating them to think clearly and examine their assumptions. Even when a semi-philosophical view is discussed, as in the *Gorgias*, it is one which would probably be familiar to every educated man. In other cases, the answer is not so easy. What of the *Republic*, for instance? The greater part of the political exposition ought to have been capable of appealing to any thoughtful and educated person. Indeed, the *Ecclesiazusae* suggests that the proposals put forward were much more ' in the air ' and much less a new and startling invention of Plato himself than we are sometimes apt to assume.[1] But, if it was intended for the general public, why are there passages which discuss the Theory of Ideas, a doctrine which Plato himself believed could only be rendered intelligible by long and careful study?

It is sometimes suggested that the main object of the dialogues written after the foundation of the Academy—which those were is a matter of dispute—was to interest the outside world in these questions and so attract suitable students to the Academy. There may have been some such motive at times in Plato's mind. And if the story from Aristotle quoted above [2] is true, it was certainly on occasions the result. But

[1] I take for granted, what seems to me certain apart from views of the date of the *Republic*, that Aristophanes is not alluding to Plato's writings. If he were there is no reason why he should not have mentioned him : there are plenty of references to contemporaries in the *Ecclesiazusae*. But he does not even suggest that the schemes were the work of any particular person. See the discussion in Adam's edition of the *Republic*.　　　　[2] See page 48.

one difficulty about accepting it as a general explanation is
that in the latest dialogues as a whole the popular appeal
becomes less and less, and they become more technical and
difficult to understand without special study. Two possible
motives may be suggested as having been at work.
In the first place, Plato had doubtless many purely philosophical connections outside his own society. It was not a case
merely of the Academy on the one hand and the general
public on the other. There were many other philosophical
schools and individual philosophers at work, and there must
have been relations, friendly or polemical, between them and
the Academy. Indeed, there is evidence that many of Plato's
philosophical views were the subject of vigorous discussion
beyond the bounds of his own school. It may be suggested
that some of the later dialogues were written as a contribution
to these discussions. They were directed beyond the limits
of the Academy, but they would hardly be expected to have
much appeal except to trained philosophical thinkers. Probably the *Theaetetus*, the *Parmenides* and the *Sophist* would fall
mainly into this class.
For other dialogues a rather different motive may be suggested. There were doubtless many subjects discussed in the
Academy on which Plato felt very varying degrees of interest.
And it might happen from time to time that a question arose
which Plato did not regard as being of such central importance
that it was necessary to deal with it in his own teaching work.
And yet he may have felt that it was of sufficient interest for
him to say something on it, and that he had opinions on the
subject which had arisen as a sort of by-product of his main
work and interest. He might, then, write a dialogue on the
subject, which would be, of course, accessible to the general
public but mainly of interest to the members of his own society.
Such would perhaps be the *Philebus* and the *Timaeus*. We
must not, however, attempt to fit one exclusive explanation
to each dialogue. No doubt these two motives, mingled with
others also, were present in varying degrees in most cases.
Such is the general view here maintained of the nature
and purpose of the Platonic dialogues. We are not without
certain detailed pieces of positive evidence, by means of which
this view might be tested, particularly in connection with the
Socratic question. A summary of these may therefore be of
interest, and is given as a separate study. But the real test
must come from a careful reading of the dialogues, with this

view in mind. Some sort of conviction would then probably emerge as to whether it rang true as an account of them.

## NOTE TO CHAPTER IV

### Summary of Evidence on the Socratic Question

This may be classified conveniently under the following heads :—
I. *Evidence from Plato.*
1. Direct statements in the letters. Besides the general account of his state of mind there are three passages which bear on this.

(i) The passage from the Seventh Letter (325c–326b) already quoted, in which Plato describes his gradual disillusionment about all existing constitutions and his growing conviction that philosophers must become rulers or rulers philosophers before things will be better. This is, of course, the central thesis of the *Republic* expressed in the same words, and a similar point of view, both in its despair of existing conditions and its conviction as to where help must be looked for, is characteristic of the *Gorgias*.

It is here, therefore, clearly stated that the point of view expressed in these dialogues is Plato's own point of view arrived at as the result of his own experience several years after the death of Socrates. This is the strongest piece of direct evidence that we have.

(ii) Another passage in the Seventh Letter (344c) in which he says that ' if any one sees a written composition of any one, whether by a legislator on laws, or anything else on any other subject, he must know that these are not that man's most serious interests, if he is a serious man '.

This has no special reference to the Socratic controversy, and it looks as if Plato had his own *Laws* in mind. But in any case it may be permitted to believe that there is a certain amount of exaggeration about it, as it is a part of a polemic against Dionysius for having claimed to write on Plato's philosophy. Further, Plato's ideas on such a point may not have always been exactly the same. I have attempted to do justice to what is seriously meant by the statement in the account given above of the relations of the dialogues to Plato's general philosophical system.

(iii) A passage from the Second Letter (314c). ' There is no written composition (σύγγραμμα) of Plato nor will there ever be one. What are now called such belong to Socrates become young and beautiful.'

The Second Letter is the one on which I feel least certainty about the genuineness. But it may be accepted as genuine for the purposes of the argument. This passage again would have to apply equally to a work like the *Laws*. How exactly it is to be interpreted depends mainly on the exact weight attached to the phrase καλοῦ καὶ νέου γεγονότος. It obviously does not imply a very close adherence to historical fact. On the theory given above it should mean ' Socrates brought up to date ', i.e. the Socratic method and spirit applied to modern problems. But the whole phrase is quite naturally taken as a half-playful exaggeration, warning against the danger of looking for a systematic presentation of the Platonic philosophy in the dialogues.

2. Indirect inference from the dialogues.

(i) The general form of the narrative. Plato is never present at any of the conversations recounted, and some of them are represented as taking place at a time when he was an infant or before he was born. This is obviously deliberate, and is certainly incompatible with a *purely* biographical interest in the dialogues. It implies some degree of readiness to depart from strict historical fact, and some degree of invention by the author. But, of course, it tells us nothing of how much of this he allowed himself.

(ii) The views expressed in the dialogues. If a definite development, still more a definite change, could be detected in the views expressed by Socrates in the earlier and later dialogues it would be very difficult to deny that Plato at some point was using him to express his own point of view. To decide whether this was so would need an exhaustive discussion of all the dialogues. I can only say here that, though many of the supposed changes of view in the dialogues do not really exist, it seems to me there are some points in which the difference between one dialogue and another is most naturally explained by the supposition of a change or at least a development of view on the part of the author. There is also an undoubted change in the picture of the manner and method of Socrates as between the earliest and the latest dialogues.

(iii) References to contemporary conditions in the dialogues. These will be the subject of a separate discussion, with special reference to the criticisms of political conditions. It will be argued there that all those conditions apply just as well to the fourth century as to the fifth, and that some apply far better and more naturally to the fourth.

II. *Evidence from contemporary sources.*

This is very slight, and almost entirely a matter of doubtful inference, but two points may be mentioned.

1. The other Socratics.

(i) How did these writers, who used the Socratic dialogue, regard it ? The scanty evidence that we have on the subject will be discussed later. But it is clear that at least in one case—Xenophon's *Oeconomicus* —it was regarded as an appropriate vehicle for the presentation of the author's own view. Further, these presentations of Socrates do not always coincide, which suggests at least that there must have been a good deal of subjective element in it.

(ii) So far as we know the different people who claimed to be disciples of Socrates and devoted themselves to the study of philosophical problems, all developed philosophies of their own, differing from and sometimes strongly opposed to each other. This is very difficult to explain if Socrates adopted and taught such definite philosophical views as are ascribed to him in some of Plato's dialogues.

2. Aristophanes. He shows in the *Ecclesiazusae* that he was acquainted with current speculations which had some resemblance to those of Plato's *Republic*, and that he thought them a fit subject for caricature. We also know that he was well acquainted with Socrates and that he loved to have a hit at him in his plays. Is it credible that, if Socrates had really put forward proposals like those in the *Republic* (which he is represented as having done quite openly to a large and mixed audience), Aristophanes would not have heard of it and connected them with him ?

III. *Evidence from later writers.*

1. Plato's immediate successors. Aristotle is practically the only witness in this class available. His testimony on the most important point, the theory of Ideas, will be discussed elsewhere, and it will be argued that, except on a very strained and unnatural interpretation of his words, he ascribes to Plato, as expressly distinguished from Socrates, views which are put into Socrates' mouth in some of the dialogues. Exactly the same conclusion would emerge with regard to ethical views, if we could regard the *Magna Moralia* as a genuine work of Aristotle.

2. Later writers. These are also discussed at length elsewhere and two conclusions emerge. (i) They all without exception believe that we can look for Plato's own philosophy in the dialogues. (ii) While they differ about the relation of them to Socrates' teaching, the earlier writers definitely give expression to a tradition that Plato introduced a good deal into the dialogues which goes much beyond the historical Socrates.

## CHAPTER V

## THE CHRONOLOGY OF THE DIALOGUES

IF the dialogues are to be used in this way in order to extract Plato's philosophy from them, it becomes of the first importance to discover the order in which they were written. It would be of the greatest help and interest if we could discover also some definite dates for the composition of the more important dialogues. But that is not so essential as a knowledge of the order. It follows, also, if the dialogues are as described, that we cannot hope to work out a logical order of the development of the thought contained in them, and then apply this as a proof of the chronological order. Since the dialogues were not written as a connected exposition of a system of philosophy, it stands to reason that they cannot give us the information necessary for such an arrangement. And earlier scholars who attempted to work out an order by this method alone revealed its impotence by the startlingly divergent results at which they arrived.[1] It is indeed a method which is foredoomed to failure. For it involves not merely trying to impose a system on Plato, but each one of us trying to impose his own system. On the other hand, it is clear that, if we could arrive on other grounds at an ordering of the dialogues, our results would receive a welcome confirmation if they provided a reasonable picture of the logical development of Plato's thought.

A method which, when it is available, is the most certain of all, is a reference in one dialogue to another. But this is a very rare occurrence. All that we can say with certainty by the use of this method is that (1) the *Sophist* is later than the *Theaetetus*, and the *Politicus* than the *Sophist*, (2) that the *Timaeus* is later than the *Republic* and the *Critias* than the *Timaeus*. There is also a possible allusion in the *Theaetetus*

[1] See the instructive tables in Ritter's *Platon*, Vol. I, showing the very different orders ascribed to the individual dialogues by scholars who did not use linguistic tests, and comparing their results with the comparative agreement among the scholars who did.

to the *Parmenides.* Another method which would infallibly give us at least an upper limit of possible dates would be references to an actual historical event in a dialogue. We have to be very certain about these before we can use them in evidence, since the majority of the dialogues are supposed to take place in the lifetime of Socrates, and any allusion to a historical event must normally be supposed to apply to an event that occurred during that period. We have to be sure beyond a doubt that it cannot be such an event that is referred to before we can suspect Plato of an anachronism. In any case there are only very few of such references even suggested. Supposed references to other published works that appeared during the period of Plato's literary activity are even more dubious. Short of an actual quotation by name, which never occurs, there can be no certainty about them in view of our vast ignorance of the great bulk of the literary productions of that period. This source of information had better be dismissed altogether. Finally the very few statements on the subject in later writers prove on examination to be almost entirely worthless. There is a foolish story in Diogenes, of just the kind that later gossip-mongers invented, implying that the *Lysis* was published during the lifetime of Socrates. There is also a more definite statement, ascribed to ' some people ' unnamed, that the *Phaedrus* was the first dialogue written. But it is apparent on reading further that this is a mere inference from the supposedly youthful character of the subject treated.

There is, however, one statement from this source which bears more of the stamp of truth on it, and has been generally accepted by modern scholars. This is the statement that the *Laws* was left unpublished at Plato's death, and was copied out and published by his disciple, Philippus of Opus. It is therefore the last, or among the last of Plato's writings. This is borne out by the condition of the text, which bears the marks of incomplete revision. It is further confirmed by an allusion (638*b*) to a conquest of the Locrians by Syracusans, which is naturally to be taken as referring to the exploits of Dionysius II somewhere about 356. This shows that it was at any rate begun when Plato was well over seventy. Add to this the fact that the Athenian Stranger who conducts the argument, and who can hardly be taken to be other than Plato himself, is represented as an old man, and the tone of the discussion throughout is characteristic of an advanced age, and

5

it will be seen that there is plenty of justification for taking the *Laws* as at any rate representative of the work of Plato's latest years, and probably the last work on which he was engaged. Of course, however, it is quite likely that the composition of some of the other later works overlapped that of the *Laws*. Opinion on the order' of Plato's dialogues was, with these few exceptions, in an absolutely chaotic state, when it occurred to some scholars that a more definitely objective method might be looked for in an examination of the details of Plato's language and style. Of course, here, too, there was a certain degree of merely personal and subjective impression. But there were many points on which it was possible to collect definite facts and present them in a statistical form. Among such facts were changes in vocabulary, the use of different words and the use of the same words in a slightly different meaning. Allowance had to be made for the special subject and character of the dialogue. But, after subtracting what was due to this, there remained a large residue which indicated a real change or development of language. Particular attention was paid by some scholars to the smaller words, particles, conjunctions, etc., where changes could hardly be explained by the subject of the dialogue. To take one among many instances, there is a marked division between different groups of dialogues according to their preference for either μέχριπερ or ἕωσπερ in the sense of ' until '. It is the same with καθάπερ and ὥσπερ. Or again the particles used to indicate affirmative or negative answers to a question differ noticeably in different groups of dialogues. For instance, τί μήν; as indicating an affirmative answer, is very frequent in some dialogues and entirely absent in others. Then there are grammatical peculiarities, order and arrangement of the words in a sentence, the rhythm of sentences, and tricks of style like the avoidance of hiatus. No single one of these things by itself might be very significant. But when a large number of them seemed to point in the same direction, it did indicate a probability that a method had been found which would serve to group the dialogues in some sort of chronological order.

The pioneer in these investigations was a British scholar, Lewis Campbell of Oxford and St. Andrews. We may still see one of the best illustrations of the kind of work that was involved in the use of this method by looking at the Introduction to his edition of the *Sophist* and *Politicus*. His work ·remained unknown on the Continent. And twenty years later

Dittenberger in Germany began researches quite independently in the same direction. Since then a large number of researchers have followed on these lines. A Polish scholar, W. Lutoslawski, in his *Origin and Growth of Plato's Logic*, gives the most complete account of the] results, of [this research that has been produced in the English language. Unfortunately the exaggerated claims that he made for the method tended to throw discredit on it. He supposed that, taking the *Laws* as admittedly the last work, it was possible to give an exact mathematical formulation of the chronological relation of each individual dialogue to the *Laws*, so that each one could be put in its place in the series. It is obvious that the use of the method could never allow of this degree of detailed accuracy.

The great master of this method, Constantin Ritter, makes much more modest claims for it. And the conclusions to which he is prepared to commit himself may be safely accepted, particularly as they are confirmed, with small exceptions, by all workers in this field. He considers that we may take as proved beyond doubt the existence of three definite stylistic groups which can be placed in chronological order. The differences between them suggest either the lapse of an appreciable time or the occurrence of some event which might be expected to influence the author's style. Within the groups, however, the order is always very doubtful and in many cases there is no material for a judgement at all. Starting once more from the *Laws* as the last or among the last dialogues, we find that the latest group consists of the *Sophist, Politicus, Philebus, Timaeus, Critias, Laws*. There is then a well-marked middle group of which the *Republic* is probably the earliest. The First Book of the *Republic*, however, has more stylistic affinity with the earliest group, and was therefore very probably composed earlier and then used later as the introduction to the larger dialogue. This middle group also includes the *Phaedrus* and the *Theaetetus*, and in all probability the *Parmenides*, though the peculiar form of the latter dialogue makes it difficult to be absolutely certain. All the rest go into the first group, within which it is difficult to assign any particular place to individual dialogues. Probably, however, the *Phaedo* and *Symposium* come at the end, and it is not likely that the *Gorgias* or the *Meno* are among the very earliest. It may be noted here that these stylistic investigations lend no support at all to the hypothesis, beloved of certain scholars, of second editions or revisions or rewritings of particular dialogues.

It must be insisted that this idea is in every case a purely gratuitous invention, introduced to bolster up the pet theory of some particular scholar which would otherwise be too much at variance with the evidence to be maintained.

These conclusions may be confidently accepted. But there are still some people to whom the idea of dealing with the works of a great writer by such methods seems too strange and unattractive to be really convincing. It may therefore be worth while to summarize briefly the arguments in favour of accepting these results.

In the first place it is clearly probable on general grounds. A great writer, with a highly individual style, does not change this style lightly and capriciously from one passage or one work to the next. His style becomes part of his nature, and is changed, if it is changed, by the slow and largely imperceptible working of different influences upon him. That by itself ought to be enough to convince us that these inquiries, if carefully used, should be capable of throwing light on the chronological relations of the writings. That there is nothing personal or subjective in the use of these methods is proved by the fact that different scholars working quite independently have reached substantially the same results. Further, the results arrived at accord very well with such information as we get from other sources, with one possible exception which will be considered shortly. In particular, they give a very reasonable picture of the philosophical development. Finally, in response to a challenge put forward by Zeller, Ritter in 1903 undertook the laborious task of applying these methods to the works of a modern author, where the dates of composition were already known. He applied them to certain selections from the works of Goethe, and the results succeeded, he tells us, beyond his highest expectations. The details that he gives amply confirm this claim. So altogether the method of stylistic investigation has met fully all the tests applied to it, and its results may well be regarded as having passed into the realm of established fact.[1]

So much for the order of the dialogues. This does not, however, give us anything in the way of more precise dating, though if we could fix the date of one or two important dialogues it would provide an approximate measure of the distance of

[1] For a fuller discussion see Ritter, *Platon*, Vol. I, and the same author's report on recent Platonic literature in *Bursian's Jahresbericht* for 1921–22.

the others from it. But this is just the difficulty. Most of
the indications that have been suggested for dating this or that
dialogue prove on examination to be without foundation.
Thus, for instance, scholars of the greatest eminence have
thought that they had found such an indication in a passage
from the *Republic*. In the Seventh Book the age of fifty is
fixed as the age at which the guardians are released from
practical administrative duties and allowed to devote themselves to the study of philosophy and the ordering of the state
in the light of that study. It is urged that Plato would hardly
have fixed this age unless he had himself reached it, or rather
would hardly have ventured to undertake the construction of
a scheme for an ideal commonwealth unless he had reached
the age at which on his own showing such speculations were to
begin. Now if Plato had said that it was impossible or unwise
for anyone to attempt to speculate on these subjects before
that age, the argument would undoubtedly be strong. But,
be it noted, he does not go as far as this. The guardians
only reach this point at the age of fifty, because they are
forced to spend fifteen years in practical work. And they
have to do this partly in order to gain practical experience,
—and this in the circumstances of the time Plato recognized
that he had to forgo anyway,—and partly because the city
needed their services. We cannot therefore conclude anything certain about Plato's own practice from what he thought
the right arrangement in an ideal state.

It is the same with other similar arguments. The scheme
of education in the *Republic* might be, it has been suggested,
a sort of prospectus issued at or just before the opening of
the Academy. But it might equally well be a record of the
conclusions arrived at after a number of years of teaching
experience. Again, some references to general political conditions have been thought to be more appropriate to one date
than to another. But this must necessarily be very uncertain,
though it might suggest a conjectural dating, if it were used
within a chronological framework established by more certain
methods. This is, of course, putting aside—as the view here
adopted would put aside—the supposition that the political
conditions discussed were those of the age of Socrates rather
than of Plato. Apart from this it is clear that all such methods
could only be used at all if we had some more definite and
certain indication to start from. And the only direction in
which we can look for that is in some direct statement or

allusion connecting some dialogue with a known historical date.

The most hopeful instance of such an allusion is the prologue to the *Theaetetus*, in which Euclides describes Theaetetus as being borne back from the camp at Corinth at the point of death from wounds and dysentery. The only two recorded expeditions to which this could refer are those of 395 and 369 respectively. And the great weight of authority at the present time is in favour of the latter date. At the earlier date Theaetetus could be little over twenty, judging by the age ascribed to him in the dialogue at a date shortly before Socrates' death. And he is spoken of by Euclides as already a distinguished man by this time. Further, it is clearly implied, though not actually stated, that Theaetetus died at this time, and the dialogue reads most naturally as a posthumous tribute to his memory. But later writers speak of him as a distinguished mathematician, who made important contributions to the subject, an associate of Plato, and himself subsequently the head of a school. All this would be impossible if he died in 395, particularly if, as is certainly implied in some of the later accounts, a great deal of his work was actually done in the Academy. So we are probably justified in putting this dialogue in 369 or 368.

It is true that there are difficulties in the way of this dating. But they are not nearly strong enough to outweigh the arguments in its favour. Thus, Terpsion tells Euclides that he has always been meaning to ask him for his account of the conversation. But apparently it has taken him thirty years to come to the point of actually doing so, surely a record in procrastination. This is probably, however, a convenient literary device, which we ought not to criticize too pedantically. There is also a story in Aulus Gellius, according to which Euclides was already an associate of Socrates at the time of the passing of the Megarian decrees. This would make him at least eighty by 369. And yet he says that he walked a good part of the way with Theaetetus ; in fact, altogether, he must have covered about thirty miles, which would hardly be possible for an octogenarian. So that this story must be given up. And indeed it rests on no real authority, and the circumstances in which it is told suggest that it was quite possibly invented to convey a moral lesson.[1]

[1] The story is that when the Megarians were forbidden on pain of death to enter Athenian territory, Euclides took the trouble and risk

The *Theaetetus*, then, was composed just before Plato's second journey to Sicily. And the other dialogues of this group, the *Republic*, *Phaedrus* and *Parmenides*, must come within reasonable distance of that date and at a definite interval from any possible date for the limits of the other groups. Their composition might be spread over ten years, but the interval is more likely to have been less. So, on these grounds, one would suggest a date somewhere about 375 for the *Republic*, and the other two would be inserted somewhere between these two dates. But, it has been argued, this is contradicted by another piece of definite evidence which proves the *Republic* to have been composed much earlier than that. This is the familiar passage from the Seventh Letter, already quoted and discussed in other connections. The use of the same phrase as that used in the *Republic*, about philosophers and rulers, and the way in which it is used, have been thought to indicate that the *Republic* must have been already composed before Plato's first journey to Sicily, at least twenty years before the composition of the *Theaetetus*. If this were true, it would certainly shake our faith in the results of stylistic research. If change of style indicate anything at all it would be quite impossible to believe that in the middle of the first ten years of his literary activity, which would have to be fairly continuous to get in all the works that must be ascribed to that period, there should be a sudden and marked change of style. And that then, after twenty years of travel and teaching, with little or no writing activity, there should be no change of style at all. If we must accept this evidence as decisive, it means giving up a good deal of our belief in stylistic method.

But need we accept it so implicitly? A more careful consideration suggests doubts. If we look at the letter carefully, we see that, though Plato says he was eventually driven to make use of the phrase in question, he does not actually say that he used it before he went to Italy and Sicily. What he does say is that the point of view expressed in it was already in his mind by the time he went there. And we can tell from

of coming disguised to Athens to consort with Socrates. This is contrasted, of course, with the attitude of modern students to their lectures. (Aulus Gellius, VII, x.) Euclides' successor in the school, Eubulides, appears to have been contemporary with Aristotle. At any rate, he is said to have attacked Aristotle, which implies that the latter was already known as head of his school in Athens. This makes it difficult to think of Euclides as very much older than Plato.

the *Gorgias* that that point of view was already present at any
rate in germ before it was expressed so clearly in the *Republic*.
As for the phrase itself, Plato may well have coined it and used
it in conversation long before he put it into a published dialogue.
And in any case we must not fall into the error of talking as if
Plato wrote the Letters to enable us to date the dialogues.
Nothing in the argument of the Letter depends upon the use
of the actual words at any particular time, as long as it is clear
what his general state of mind was.   So, considering that he
was writing thirty-five years after the events, he might well be
forgiven certain inaccuracies about the exact chronology of
the use of a particular phrase.   Altogether there does not seem
sufficient definiteness about the evidence to warrant a complete disregard of that derived from other sources.

For there is evidence from other sources to re-enforce these
conclusions.   It will be argued later that some of the political
allusions in the *Republic* refer to Syracuse in a way that strongly
suggests they must have been written after Plato's visit.   But
besides this there is another apparently definite allusion to a
historical event in the *Symposium* which would help to place
other dialogues in relation to it.[1]

In the speech of Aristophanes in the *Symposium* (193a 2)
when he is describing how human beings in their original form
were split into two, he uses the words διῳκίσθημεν ὑπὸ τοῦ
θεοῦ, καθάπερ ᾿Αρκάδες ὑπὸ Λακεδαιμονίων.   ' We were broken
up (or dispersed) by the god, as Arcadians were by Spartans.'
This had long been taken as a reference to the action of the
Spartans in 385, when Mantinea as a city was destroyed and
split up into five separate villages.   And it was regarded as a
definite anachronism, and was supposed to date the dialogue at
some time after this event.   Some scholars, however, in their
anxiety to defend Plato against the charge of anachronism,
have urged that the real reference was to the events in 418,

---

[1] I have said nothing about the supposed references to Ismenias
the Theban and his reception of Persian gold in the *Republic* (336a)
and the *Meno* (90a), because I am by no means convinced that the
reference is necessarily to the events usually supposed.   There may
have been some other occurrence of which we know nothing.   Even
if there is such a reference it only tells us that both dialogues were
written later than 395.   There are certain difficulties for the dramatic
dating of the dialogues in the fact that an event which is referred to
as having taken place ' lately ' in the *Meno* is referred to as a familiar
fact in the *Republic*, which should be referring to a time about twenty
.years earlier.   But with this we are not now concerned.

two years before the dramatic date of the dialogue. After the Spartan victory at Mantinea in that year, a league of Arcadian cities under the leadership of Mantinea appears to have been dissolved, and it is to this that reference is made. It has, however, been objected that the word διοικίζειν could hardly be used to apply to the dissolution of a league or confederacy. And this argument has been thought conclusive by the great majority of modern scholars who have dealt with the point.

When scholars of eminence differ, he would be a bold man who ventured on a positive assertion. But an examination of the use of the word elsewhere certainly tends to support the latter position. It invariably seems to imply something much more drastic than anything we know to have taken place in 418.[1] Demosthenes, for instance, uses it of the absolute destruction of the Phocian cities by Philip. But what is much more significant is that it is the regular word used to describe what happened in 385, and that it is applied more frequently to that than to any other occasion. Thus Xenophon and Isocrates (in the *De Pace*) use it to describe this event, and among later writers it is used in the same connection by Polybius and Pausanias. It is difficult, therefore, not to believe that Plato had this event in his mind when he used the word. Whether he deliberately intended the anachronism is another matter. We cannot say with certainty that he might not on occasion for some purpose of his own introduce a striking reference to a contemporary event in the middle of a description which in general remained true to the period of the scene described in the dialogue. But it is also quite possible that the anachronism was unintentional, that he intended the reference to be taken as applying to the events of 418, but used a phrase that was not really applicable to them, because he had

---

[1] We really know very little about what happened in 418. Coins were struck before that with the inscription 'Ἀρκαδικὸν and they appear to cease after that date. Thucydides tells us that the Mantineans were forced to give up their claims to supremacy over part of Arcadia after the battle of Mantinea. But there is no suggestion of the physical break-up of any one city, no pulling down of walls or distribution κατὰ κώμας, which seems to be an essential part of the meaning of the word. What did happen then was rather parallel to the break-up of the Athenian Empire in 404 or 355, or to the enforcement of the autonomy of the Boeotian cities against Thebes at the Peace of Antalcidas. To none of these occasions, so far as I can discover, did any writer ever apply the word διοικίζειν.

the events of 385 so strongly in his mind.  In either case the reference, if it is taken as it appears it must be taken, enables us to date the dialogue after 385, and in all probability not very long after.  Let us say 384, or 383 at latest.

This gives us a lower limit for the first group.  The upper limit must surely be the death of Socrates.  It really seems impossible, in spite of the opinion of some undoubted authorities, to make any convincing account of motives that could lead Plato to compose any of them while Socrates was still alive.  It was clearly the effect of Socrates' death which turned Plato from ambitions for an active political life to the state of mind which would find its expression in writings of this kind. Added to which is the fact that some of the dialogues which imply the death of Socrates—the Crito, for instance—bear all the marks of being among his earliest productions.

His writing activity, then, appears to have been suspended for a period beginning two or three years after the foundation of the Academy.  We may take the *Symposium*, the *Phaedo* and probably the *Cratylus* as being the work of those years immediately after the return from Sicily.  We may note how this is confirmed, for what it is worth, by the indications of Cicero, who seems to connect the systematic attempt to prove the immortality of the soul, as in the *Phaedo*, with the acquaintance with Archytas and the other Italian Pythagoreans. There are indications which have suggested to some scholars that the *Gorgias* rather than the *Phaedo* represents the first-fruits of Plato's visit to Italy and Sicily.  There is the belief expressed there in personal immortality, though rather as a religious faith than as a philosophical doctrine susceptible of proof.  This, however, proves nothing : there were plenty of sources from which some knowledge of such ideas might have come to Plato.  There is a little more significance in the quotations from Epicharmus and the reference to Sicilian cookery books.  But these cannot really prove anything. On the other hand an examination of the political comments in the *Gorgias* suggests that they were made with Athenian conditions chiefly in mind, and they have no special reference, as have some of those in the *Republic*, to the conditions of Italy and Sicily.  And in general the philosophical atmosphere of a dialogue like the *Phaedo* shows such differences from that of most of the earlier dialogues, even the *Gorgias*, that the interposition of the Italian and Sicilian visit in between comes ·as a natural explanation of these differences.

We may imagine that with the growth of the Academy Plato very soon found it impossible to give time for writing. There would then be a period of about eight or nine years solely devoted to the work of teaching and organizing the college. It would be very natural that such an interval should be followed by a marked change of style, though of course we can have little idea of what influences can have given this change, the direction it actually took. This period ends with Plato's second departure for Syracuse. To account for the change which is particularly marked when we come to the third and last group of dialogues, we must suppose another interval of some years without writing. This would be plausibly accounted for if we supposed that Plato was too much occupied with Syracusan affairs to give any time to writing until after his final visit. This gives another interval of eight or nine years. And the last period extends from 360 until Plato's death. Within this last period we know that the *Politicus* follows the *Sophist*, and the *Critias* the *Timaeus*. We know, too, that the *Laws* was the last work that occupied Plato's attention. But on any other point—for instance, the relative position of the *Timaeus* and the *Philebus*—we have really no material on which to base even a conjecture.

## NOTE TO CHAPTER V

The *Philebus* has been associated by Wilamowitz with the death of Eudoxus, which probably took place in 355, on the ground of the discussion in that dialogue of the theory of pleasure as the chief good which Eudoxus is known to have held. The date is likely enough, though the particular grounds given for it are very uncertain.

I mention only to dismiss the suggestion, originally made by Christ and accepted recently by Apelt, that the mention of the sending by Plato to Dionysius of τὰ Πυθαγόρεια καὶ αἱ διαιρέσεις in the Thirteenth Letter is a reference to the *Timaeus* and the *Sophist* or *Politicus*. The letter, if genuine, is written about 365, and it is absolutely impossible that these dialogues were written then. For it would mean that the *Sophist* and the *Timaeus*, which means the *Politicus* and possibly the *Philebus* as well, were all written in the space of about two years between the composition of the *Theaetetus* and the date of the letter, and that in those two years must have been included as well Plato's eventful visit to Dionysius II. This is absolutely incredible. But as a matter of fact there is no reason at all to identify these dialogues with the writings mentioned in the letter. For Plato does not even say or imply that the writings mentioned are his own work at all.

Another piece of evidence that has been suggested looks promising at first sight, but unfortunately does not survive a closer scrutiny.

It has been argued that it is contrary to the spirit of the dialogues to introduce into them a living contemporary by name. And therefore if anyone is mentioned we can always date the dialogue after his death.

If this could be relied on it would give us valuable information. Thus, it would definitely confirm the date suggested above for the *Symposium*. Aristophanes was certainly living some little time after the production of the *Plutus* in 388. Again, we know from the Eleventh Letter that the younger Socrates was alive somewhere about 360, but was too ill to travel. The *Politicus* would therefore have to be put later than this date, but, if we suppose Socrates succumbed to this illness, not very much later. It is true that we should have to suppose the curious coincidence that Euclides died very soon after recounting the last scenes in the life of Theaetetus. But perhaps we ought not to apply the test to the characters in these preliminary introductions to the dialogues.

On one crucial point, however, the test breaks down altogether. For the Thirteenth Letter certainly writes of Cebes as if he were still alive in 365, though it is true it does not actually say so in so many words, a date far later than the composition of the *Phaedo*, which is indeed referred to in the letter.

# PART II

# THE MORAL AND POLITICAL BACKGROUND

## CHAPTER VI

## THE GENERAL MORAL AND POLITICAL BACKGROUND

SO far we have been occupied with Plato's own activities. But these activities took place in a world which was itself very active. And certainly his teaching work, and, if our interpretation is correct, his literary work also was undertaken in direct response to the stimulus of the activities which were going on about him. The rest of the book, therefore, will be devoted to a sketch of some of the most important of these activities—political, social, literary and philosophical.

The value of a study of contemporary conditions for the interpretation of a philosopher's thought is particularly obvious when we are dealing with moral, and even more with political speculation. To understand any of Plato's thought, it is doubtless necessary to know something of the speculations of other thinkers who preceded him or were contemporary with him. But there is this difference to notice. The most important part of the material with which he had to deal in his metaphysical or logical investigations does not vary from age to age or from one country to another. The fundamental characteristics of the processes of rational thinking are the same always and everywhere. So are the processes of sense-perception. So are the physical processes of the material world ; ' fire burns both here and in Persia ', as Aristotle says. So is the nature of numbers and figures, which the science of mathematics investigates. Much more, of course, is known about these things in some periods than in others. But the material from which the investigations start is the same at all times. Not so with moral speculation, and even less with political. For here we have to start our investigations from an observation of the moral and political ideas and institutions which we see before us. And these vary indefinitely from one age and one nation to another. We could, therefore, understand with little preliminary explanation the beginnings of Greek mathematical speculation, because we know what number is, or at any rate, what the first perception of it is, and it is the same for us as for them. But we cannot understand the beginnings of Greek political speculation until we know what the Greek political conditions of the time were.

The present work is neither a geography nor a history of Greece. And it must be assumed that the reader is acquainted or can easily make himself acquainted with the general situation of Athens and other Greek states, and with the main facts in their history. We are concerned here with the special aspects of this history which seem to throw a light on Plato's thought, and with the mental and spiritual characteristics of the age and place in which he grew to maturity and began his speculations. We may distinguish certain special features which are of importance in this connection.

(1) The internal history of Athens from the earliest times of which we have historical knowledge down to the fifth century B.C. is marked by one feature of special importance. That is the gradual assertion of the unity of the city-state and of its supreme claim, as against the minor associations, the ' lesser loyalties ' as they have been well called, within it. There is, of course, at this stage of history no question of conflict, such as modern thought has made us familiar with, between the rights of the individual and the rights of the State. In early society, as Maine pointed out long ago, the unit of thought and action is the family, and the individual as such is hardly realized to exist. Property, law, religion, moral responsibility, are all matters which concern the family as a whole. And as soon as a state of settled society is approached, the family begins to extend itself into larger aggregates, the clan, the tribe, the brotherhood, or the order.[1] The exact relation-

---

[1] I have not attempted to translate exactly the Greek terms γένος, φράτρια, φύλη, which are strictly untranslatable, nor have I always taken care to distinguish their relative positions in what follows. It would, indeed, be irrelevant to my purpose. When nothing depends on which particular division is referred to, I have used the word ' clan ' as a general term. For the Highland clans are the only instances familiar to us in modern times of such large associations, with some territorial signification, but resting in the main on a fiction of common descent.

ship of these different divisions is complicated and need not be discussed here. Suffice it to say that, at the time of which we are speaking, the Athenian citizen found himself a member of a series of different bodies of this kind, which interposed themselves between him and the State and which probably represented to him something much more intimate and influential in his life than the city which embraced them all.

The first impulse towards a correction of these tendencies appears to have been given by a realization of the evils which this division caused. These showed themselves in two directions. On the one hand, the city was weakened as against other states : the citizens had, for instance, to look on while the island of Salamis, which barred the entrance to their own harbour, remained in the possession of a neighbouring power. On the other, an even more pressing evil was the constant internecine conflicts which divided the whole State. These conflicts took different forms, which need not be described in detail. In general we can detect both a horizontal and a vertical line of division. We have a sharp division between the limited number of the noble families who alone had any political rights and privileges on the one side, and the great mass of unprivileged citizens on the other. This was aggravated by the fact that the privileged classes used their political power to increase their wealth at the expense of the rest, and to establish the most ruthless economic tyranny over them. So that a social and economic struggle was added to the fight for political rights. Besides this, however, we have plenty of instances of fierce struggles between the different noble families, in which each was doubtless supported by the mass of the unprivileged clients and dependants who were members of the same clan or district.

The evils of this state of things came to a head at the end of the seventh century. Athens was on the verge of a violent civil war and Solon was appointed with supreme power to deal with the situation. Of his economic reforms we need not speak here. What is of chief interest are the measures that he took to weaken the hold of the old-established groups over their members, and to bring the individual into more direct contact with the State. Thus, alongside the old divisions, he introduced a new classification of the people according to their wealth. But more significant than this were two measures which almost for the first time recognized the individual as a legal unit independently of his tribe or clan. For the first time a degree, very limited, it is true, of testamentary freedom was allowed to the individual owner of property : in default of direct heirs, he might bequeath it to whom he would, whereas formerly it went necessarily into the common possessions of the clan. Most important of all, the individual was recognized as a legal unit, apart from his clan. For the first time, it was established as the right of any citizen to initiate legal action against a wrongdoer, instead of, as heretofore, being the exclusive privilege of the family or the clansmen of the person wronged. So that the citizen began to look directly to the State for justice and protection, instead of being dependent upon the smaller unit. Finally, the introduction of the first element of democracy into the constitution tended to break down the distinction between classes, and to assert the equal partnership of every one in the State.

The reforms of Solon produced a temporary effect, but civil strife soon broke out again. The history of Athens throughout the sixth century is full of vicissitudes, and it is not until the end of this century that the final step seems to have been taken. By the reforms of Cleisthenes the old tribes and clans were completely broken up, at any rate as political units, and the people were divided afresh on an entirely different basis. By an elaborate scheme, the tribes, which were still retained for administrative purposes, were organized in a way which secured that each one should include citizens from all the different districts of the State. The old system was thus completely destroyed, and the sentiments and loyalties which clustered round the old groups could not be transferred to these highly artificial divisions. The measure was entirely successful. The spiritual unity of the city-state was established to a degree hitherto unknown. It is clear, in spite of many controversies and feuds, that throughout the greater part of the fifth century the unity of the Athenian State and its exclusive claim on the loyalties of its members was recognized in a way which few other states attained. The glories of the Persian Wars and the establishment of the Athenian Empire were the outward signs of the new strength which grew out of this.

(2) Closely connected with this development is the gradual growth in Athens, as in many other states, of democracy as a system of government. There, too, the first steps were taken by Solon, who gave to the whole body of citizens the right of .electing the governing officials and of calling them to account

at the end of their term of office. By this step was initiated an almost continuous process which, by the time of Plato's birth, had put complete power into the hands of the popular assembly composed of the whole body of citizens. The whole constitution was directed to securing this, and to making it impossible for any other authority to set itself up as a rival power. It is important for a modern reader to remember that to a Greek democracy meant the continued and active participation of all the citizens in the work of government. Our modern systems of representative government would have seemed to him in no sense democratic at all, because they involve the abdication to selected representatives of what should be the privilege and responsibility of each citizen. Still less would a Greek democrat have approved of our modern apparatus of parties and other political organizations. The distrust for political organizations within the State seems to have been a mark of Greek democracy. In Athens at certain periods it appears to have been a criminal offence to join a political club, and the political clubs were the chief organs of the anti-democratic movements. Organization is, of course, one of the most obvious ways by which a minority can secure political power out of proportion to its numbers. But we shall probably not be wrong in seeing in this distrust of organizations something more than considerations of this kind. It may be regarded also as one sign of the general unwillingness to allow any other object of political loyalty to be inserted between the individual and the State.

It is easy to see how the whole democratic movement may be regarded as part of the general process of establishing the unity of the State. Any special privileges for a limited class mean a cause of division and dissension between the privileged and the unprivileged. And the central idea which inspires the democratic movement is the thought that the State is the chief object of interest for all its citizens equally, and that the good of all its citizens equally is its proper aim. Both Herodotus and Thucydides record discussions of the rival merits of different forms of government, and by both the champion of democracy is represented as laying stress on the fact that the chief claim of democracy is that it includes all the citizens, while any other form of government only represents a part.

(3) We have, then, the city-state recognized as the chief object of interest and loyalty to every Athenian citizen. We

6

have to ask, now, what, in the view of the ordinary citizen, his city is supposed to mean to him and to do for him. It is necessary in this connection to beware of the danger of setting out as an explicit theory what is really only an implicit assumption in the minds of ordinary men. But we can say that to the average Greek, particularly the Athenian, his city appeared as the chief educative influence on his life and character to a degree to which our modern view of the State never approaches. 'A city teaches a man', says Simonides of Ceos at the end of the sixth or the beginning of the fifth century. And this view of the relation of the State and the individual shows itself in many ways. We find it regularly assumed by early legislators that the State is intimately concerned with the manners and morals of its citizens. It attempts to set them a standard of behaviour by the institution of sumptuary laws, of laws controlling the public appearance of women, of laws against excessive drinking, or wasting one's property, or keeping bad company, or displaying undue inquisitiveness about one's neighbours. Sometimes also there is an organ of the State which is specially charged with a general supervision over the behaviour and morals of the citizens. Such, at certain periods, was the Council of the Areopagus at Athens.

The same thing appears from another side, for the laws of the city are regarded as setting up a standard of what is right and wrong to the citizen. In most primitive societies, indeed, there is no other standard of what is right and wrong than that contained in the customs of the tribe. And the same idea, in a more refined form, is really dominant throughout the period of Greek history which is of interest to us here. 'For it is by the law,' says Euripides' Hecuba, 'that we believe in the gods and that we distinguish the righteous from the unrighteous in our lives'. And this view survives as the accepted and orthodox view of the average Athenian right down to the end of the free political life of Athens. Aristotle, who is in many ways a good representative of the ' plain man's ' point of view, goes so far as to say in the *Ethics* that the just or righteous and the legal are identical. Another ' plain man ', Xenophon, ascribes the same view to his heroes, Cyrus and Socrates. And there is a well-known statement by Demosthenes about the nature of law, which ' wants what is just and noble and beneficial ', and which is finally spoken of as ' a common agreement of the city, according to which it is right for all in the city to live '. . The assertions of the orators are good evidence of the kind of thing that would appeal to the average citizen as reasonable.

The belief is maintained for long after this period that a code of laws, in spite of aberrations in particular cases, is normally and properly a complete code of morality. And further it tends to be assumed that it owes its authority to this. A curious result of this attitude which is worth noting is that it produces great respect for the law in theory combined with great readiness to violate it in practical political action. For there is only a step from this attitude to the view that if a law does not enjoin what is right, which means in practice what appears to a particular collection of citizens at a particular moment to be right, it is not really a law and need not be obeyed. Aristotle, in his handbook for orators which we know as the *Rhetoric*, suggests that if a proposal is attacked as illegal, its advocate should reply that the law against it is not in accordance with justice, and therefore not really a law. And Athenian history is full of cases in which the sovereign people disregarded in their actions some law that they themselves had laid down.

Finally, in a democratic state the view that makes morality consist in the performance of the public duties prescribed by the customs of the tribe develops very easily into a belief that the highest form of human activity consists in political life and activities and in the work of the State. ' We alone ', says Pericles of the Athenians in the great funeral speech reported by Thucydides, ' regard the man who takes no part in public affairs not as a harmless but as a useless person '. And the whole movement towards democracy is an indication of the feeling, however vague, that political and public work is the best field for the development and exercise of the highest human qualities, and that an opportunity to take part in such work is an essential condition of the ' good life '.

Such are some of the main tendencies which we may note in the thought and political conditions of Athens up to the time of Plato's birth. But to understand the influences at work on him we must recognize that this is only a part of the truth. For 'in the later part of the fifth century we see the development of a reaction against all these tendencies both in thought and conduct, and this reaction has an important effect on the growth of Plato's thought.

(1) We have said that throughout the greater part of the fifth century Athens seemed to attain an internal unity which

few cities, in that land of fierce partisan passions, succeeded in gaining. There were many differences of opinion, but they seem on the whole to have remained differences of opinion, without developing into civil strife, and to have been settled by constitutional methods. The murder of Ephialtes is almost the only instance of the introduction of physical violence into the political disputes of the fifth century. In the Periclean democracy this unity seems to have reached its supreme point. Under the leadership of that great statesman we find men of all classes, the richest and noblest as well as the poorest, accepting the democracy and devoting themselves to the service of the State. But after the death of Pericles there came a change, probably due less to the removal of his influence than to the effect of the Peloponnesian War, which in this as in so many respects marked a turning-point in Greek history.

Thucydides has given us a vivid picture of the demoralization which the war brought to Greek society. A new note of unscrupulous brutality and fierceness made itself felt both in the relations between states, and in the relations between different groups or parties within the states. This was, no doubt, in part due to the familiarity with bloodshed and the use of force which all wars bring. But it also arose from the economic effects of the war. These were damaging in the highest degree to all states, but clearly they hit different classes of society in very differing degrees. Thus the well-to-do, who paid practically the whole cost of the war, and particularly the landowners throughout Attica who saw their lands ravaged by a yearly Spartan invasion, felt it in a very different way from the poorer elements in the city population. And we therefore find that throughout the war in Athens the extreme democracy is always the war party, and the richer citizens in general the peace party. Thus differences of opinion about policy become fixed along the lines of social division, and the constitution, which nominally gave equal rights to all citizens, but in fact gave the power into the hands of one class, is made the object of attack. The last years of the fifth century saw two attempts, momentarily successful, to overturn the democratic constitution by violence. The shock that these attempts gave to feeling in the city made itself felt for years afterwards.

The change is marked when we compare the assertion of the speakers in Herodotus and Thucydides, that democracy is government by the whole people not by any part, with the definition of democracy given a hundred years later by Aristotle, who describes it as the constitution in which the poor rule and use their power to oppress the rich. Instead of a constitution in which every one is on an equality and has an equal part in the government of the city, we find in practice that it tends more and more to a form in which the population falls into two social classes, and the larger class of the two (though it may not be necessarily very much the larger) uses its power in its own interests, and disregards the interests of the other as completely as if its members had been disfranchised. So that even in a democracy the State is no longer one in spirit. And if the democracy is overthrown and succeeded by an oligarchy of wealth, whose members in their turn consult only their own interests, the division of classes becomes more acute still. Enough has been said to show the significance of this in its effect on Plato's mind. In his boyhood and youth he saw the continued process of the break-up of an ideal unity of the State which must at one moment, shortly before his birth, have seemed almost established.

(2) With this went the development of a more and more concentrated attack on democracy. The end of the fifth century saw not only the violent revolutions, which have already been mentioned, but also the growth of an established anti-democratic theory and opinion. We are fortunate in possessing, included among the works of Xenophon, a pamphlet by an unknown author, generally referred to as the ' Old Oligarch ', directed against the Athenian democracy. It dates probably from the early years of the Peloponnesian War. And from it we are enabled to learn something of the point of view of the opponents of democracy at this period. In spite of some acute observations, it must be confessed that this work shows little sign of a thought-out anti-democratic theory. The objections to democracy, which the writer clearly feels deeply, seem to rest in the main on mere snobbishness and social prejudice. The complaint most constantly reiterated is that democracy allows the wretched mass of the population to stand on a complete political equality with the capable or the good. But as we read on we speedily find that the ' good ' are identified, without more ado, with the rich, or— less frequently—with the well-born. And no argument is ever advanced to justify this identification.

But, besides this, there are one or two shrewd hits on the

point of the practical working of the constitution. The complaints about the congestion and delay of business are probably no more applicable to a democratic than to any other constitution, but considerable acuteness is shown in the observations of the writer on the weakening of a sense of responsibility in a democracy. The Athenian democracy meant, of course, government by a mass-meeting, and it had all the disadvantages with which studies of crowd-psychology have made us so familiar. One of the most marked of these effects is the ease with which an individual can divest himself of any feeling of responsibility for what is done by a crowd. And when, as the writer points out, there is no guarantee that the same citizens will ever be present at successive meetings, it is easy to see how the sense of individual responsibility disappears altogether. As the author says, ' If any bad result comes from the decisions that the people take, they put it down to the work of a few men who work against them and spoil their plans, but if the result is good they take the credit for it themselves '.

This is only one of the many defects in efficiency which the Athenian democracy showed during the testing time of the war. If we want to hear the whole story we must listen to Thucydides, who sets out remorselessly all the crimes and blunders of the Athenian people with an effectiveness which is only increased by his self-restraint in the matter of expressed criticism. In his pages we see them swayed first this way and then that by the arts of the orator and the demagogue. We see their injustice to their officers, who are too often not given a free hand, nor properly supported, and yet are liable to the severest punishments for failing in impossible tasks. We see their unfounded self-confidence and optimism, based only on their ignorance of their own resources or of the general situation. We see the unjustified confidence with which they will follow some of their public men, and the equally unjustified suspicion or anger with which they will suddenly turn against them. Thucydides is, of course, a pessimist. He thinks that nothing could possibly go right after the death of Pericles. And he does not show us with the same clear outlines the great qualities that the Athenian democracy displayed at some of the worst crises of the war, nor does he do justice to the fact that on more than one occasion an accident might have given them complete victory. But none the less, it is clear that such strictures were in the main justified. Democracy had lost its prestige. Its failure to rise to the occasion became more and more apparent, and as early as his first exile Alcibiades could speak of it with plausibility as an admitted folly.

(3) Such were some of the subversive influences which were tending to undermine the orthodox beliefs of the Athenian citizen towards the end of the fifth century. We have still to deal with perhaps the most interesting of all. For about this time we find the development of a systematic body of doctrine, about which we know very little except from the writings of its opponents, which challenged the whole of the orthodox conception of the State and its relation to the individual citizens. For the first time, we find an attempt, almost unintelligible to the average Greek, to set a limit to the claims of the State in the interests of the individual. It is clear that ideas of this order remained a heresy in Athens, at any rate, until long after the free life of the Greek city-state had been destroyed, and it is doubtful whether they had any widespread practical effect on conduct before that time. But they had a profound influence on philosophical thought and speculation. We meet them more than once in Plato's dialogues, where they provide the stimulus to the development of the opposed view, represented by the figure of Socrates. It would be hardly an exaggeration to say that the whole of Plato's moral and political philosophy takes its rise from the effort to provide an adequate refutation of these views, and a treatment of them in some detail is therefore necessary for our subject.

In order to understand the significance of this school of thought, we must grasp the fact that it only puts into more systematic form certain tendencies which were very much in the air at the period during which it took its rise. Many considerations must have impressed on the minds of men, who were in general quite ready to accept the orthodox point of view of their age, the idea that at some points this orthodox point of view was open to question. The notion that the laws of the city contained all that was necessary for right conduct began to be questioned from various sides. A good citizen and orthodox thinker like Sophocles revealed in the *Antigone* a vivid appreciation of the possibility of conflict between the claims of the laws of the State and the claims of a higher moral law. From another direction, also, doubts began to be raised about the supreme claim of the law and custom of any particular city. The fifth century saw a great increase in the knowledge of other countries. And this showed at once the wide differences between the laws, customs and moral standards of different peoples, so that it became increasingly easy to be sceptical about the special claims of any one set of these.   There is a familiar story in Herodotus of the horror which a group of Greeks at the court of Persia expressed at the idea of eating the bodies of their parents : while a group of Indians, who actually practised this custom, expressed an equal horror at the idea of burning them.   So that it appears clear to the historian who relates this that different people may observe and respect entirely opposite rules of conduct, merely because they happen to be their own.

All this does not yet amount to a philosophical view.   We get to this by the elaboration of a distinction which was first clearly made in the fifth century, but which became a familiar feature in Greek speculation for many future generations. That is the distinction between Nature (φύσις) and Law or Convention (νόμος).   The origin of the ideas which based themselves on this distinction is extremely obscure, but it is clear that they were widely spread and familiar in the latter half of the fifth century.   Plato represents the distinction as a feature of the views of the sophist, Hippias, who must have been a contemporary, perhaps a slightly older contemporary, of Socrates.   It is also ascribed by a late and not very reliable author to Archelaus, the disciple of Anaxagoras and the teacher of Socrates, which would take it back, probably, a little further still.   But the exact date need not trouble us : the meaning of the distinction is the important thing.

The word Nature or φύσις was, long before this period, familiar as expressing the fundamental nature of reality for which, for instance, the Ionian physicists were seeking.   The new feature is the contrast drawn between this and νόμος or law, the implication of this contrast being that law is something which has no basis in this fundamental nature of reality, but is a mere man-made contrivance.   And in law are included all the customs and conventions which form part of the guiding rules of any human society.   Even the city-state itself might easily come to be regarded as something which had no basis in the nature of reality, but existed ' by law ' only.   The tendency of this movement, as of similar movements in more recent times, was to think of man as ' naturally ' independent of organized society and free from all the restraints and limitations which life in a society necessarily brings.   Society or the city-state becomes, then, something imposed upon these naturally free and independent beings. About how it was imposed there seem to have been different views. Some seem to have thought that it was simply imposed by the brute force of the strongest, who made himself or themselves the rulers, and ruled and made laws in their own interests. In a more developed form we find the social contract theory so familiar to us in the pages of Hobbes, Locke and Rousseau. The Greek forms of the view are different in many ways from those which we know later, and they draw different conclusions. But the fundamental idea of a number of free and independent beings agreeing to limit their freedom and independence by forming an organized society is the same in both.

We shall see later how this line of thought developed in Plato's lifetime. In its earliest form its results were unequivocally bad. For without putting anything positive in its place it seems to have exercised a dissolvent effect on the moral outlook that already existed. We, in modern times, are so accustomed to make a sharp distinction between the moral law and the laws of the State that if our faith in the one was weakened it would not necessarily affect in any way our belief in the other. But with the Greek, as we have seen, this was not so. Doubts about the real justification of the claims of the law and the State would very easily, indeed inevitably, lead to doubts about the justification of any of the obligations towards others which any social life involves. In other words, the whole idea of morality and of duties towards other people was called in question, and came easily to be regarded as having no basis in the real nature of things. Plato in several of the dialogues shows clearly the working of this point of view. It is very instructive to read the remarks of Thrasymachus in the *Republic* or, still more perhaps, Callicles in the *Gorgias*, who represent this kind of immoralism. They draw the distinction between natural and conventional morality. Natural morality, which would be exercised, as they hold, by a few wise men in a world of fools, consists simply in getting as much as we can with no regard for the claims of other, people. Callicles is particularly interesting. He is not a sophist but a politician, and Plato, no doubt, means him to represent the type of self-seeking, unscrupulous politicians, who found in the new teaching the justification for the pursuit of their own selfish desires and personal ambitions.

That Plato's account was not an exaggeration or caricature

of these views was shown by the discovery a few years ago in Egypt of fragments of the work of the sophist Antiphon, *On Truth*. We are there told that the rules of nature would lead us to obey the laws and the current ideas about what is right, when there is any danger of our being caught in disobedience, and to disobey them when we can do so undetected. For the laws are artificial and imposed on us (ἐπιθετὰ), and have no basis in nature. The natural rules of conduct lead us to do whatever is advantageous to ourselves, in the sense of preserving our lives and giving us pleasure. Foolish actions like returning good for evil or refraining from injuring others when we could do so to our own benefit, are contrary to nature. The whole point of view reminds us strongly of Callicles, and the work may well have been written about the time that the meeting described in the *Gorgias* is supposed to have taken place. The theory seems to have developed strength during the early years of the Peloponnesian War. But it was evidently well established before the war began, and it continued to live for long afterwards.

# CHAPTER VII

## THE GENERAL MORAL AND POLITICAL
## BACKGROUND (*continued*)

PLATO thus grew up in a period when the established order and accepted standards seemed on the verge of dissolution under the pressure of political events and theoretical criticism. It is clear that from the first he felt himself called upon to deal with the situation in whatever way was open to him. We know from the autobiographical passage in the Seventh Letter, quoted above, that in his younger days he felt the vocation for a political career. He describes also the state of disillusionment which arose in his mind from various causes, above all the execution of Socrates, and the gradual process by which he came, some years after this event, to despair of any good coming from any of the existing states of Hellas. It was then that he turned to philosophical speculation as the only direction from which help might come. From one point of view, indeed, the chief aim of Plato's philosophy may be regarded as the attempt to re-establish standards of thought and conduct for a civilization that seemed on the verge of dissolution.

This is an important point to grasp. We shall misunderstand Plato entirely if we think of him as a revolutionary thinker breaking in on an established order of ideas and institutions with a demand for radical reconstruction. On the contrary, in all his most important contributions to moral and political theory he is on the direct line of orthodox Greek thought, and in strong opposition to the new and subversive tendencies that we have noticed. It is true that no one criticizes more strongly the behaviour and the confusions of thought both of the average citizen and the leading statesmen of his period. But he criticizes them rather for falling short of the ideals which he and they shared in common. And it is for the ' advanced thinker ' of his time that his most uncompromising opposition is reserved. Thus the tendency towards the establishment of unity within the city-state by setting up the State itself as the supreme object of loyalty, which is characteristic of the history of Athens, finds its most complete and logical development in Plato's proposals in the *Republic*. He is in sharp opposition to those who regard the State as not ' natural ', but imposed from without, as a restriction on our free activities, rather than as an occasion for the exercise of activities which would be impossible without it. He maintains, as against this, throughout his work, that life in a society like the State is the essential condition of complete self-development, in fact that, instead of restricting, it enlarges our lives and personalities. He is, therefore, emphatically in favour of the view of the city-state and its laws as the chief educative influence in the character of the citizen, and maintains as his main thesis the idea of this as their proper aim. It is true that he criticizes democracy. But his real complaint against it is that it fails to attain its own ideal of uniting all the citizens in appropriate service to their common city. And his criticisms have nothing in common with the attacks of the oligarchic parties, and lend no support to any pretensions of one class to seize power and use it in its own selfish interests. This point does not, then, form an exception to the general statement that Plato's real aim is not to overturn the ordinary ideas and modes of thinking of his fellow-citizens, but to refine them, to develop their logical implications, and to work out explicitly the ideal that was implicitly assumed in them.

This impression is confirmed if we compare some of the most marked characteristics of Plato's thought with the general characteristics of the bulk of Greek political thought and discussion. No doubt, it is a very dangerous thing to attempt generalizations about Greek thought, or the thought of any country or age, as a whole. To any statement that could be made it would always be possible to find exceptions. Probably no statement is possible which would be true of all Greek thought and not true of any other. But for all that, it is sometimes possible, when we contrast the thought of one country or age with the thought of another, to detect certain tendencies which are markedly stronger in the one than in the other, in spite of many exceptions in both. It is only in that sense that we can speak of the general characteristics of any particular civilization. And, in that sense, we may suggest, tentatively, certain general characteristics which mark ordinary

Greek thought [1] about politics, at any rate as compared with our own at the present day.

(1) One characteristic which is worth noting is the rationalism of Greek thought, the belief, that is to say, in the possibilities of the conscious exercise of human reason in political affairs. It may seem strange to speak of their rationalism when we see so many instances in their institutions and behaviour of what appears to us to be essentially irrational or nonrational. We may think of their belief in oracles and divination, or we may recall, for instance, the superstition of Nicias who sacrificed his whole army before Syracuse rather than move on the night of an eclipse of the moon. It is clear, therefore, that their belief in human reason was confined within very definite limits, which we in modern times would not dream of imposing. Within those limits, however, it seems to have been in many ways much stronger than our own. And this applies more specially to their attitude towards questions of political organization and institutions. For they seem, here, to have been much readier than we are to think of constitutions as being constructed on a conscious and deliberate plan, with all details worked out. It would have seemed the natural course for a Greek legislator to think out what he wanted, and what were the best means of attaining this, and then apply bodily the scheme he had thus constructed.

If we want to compare this with our own attitude, we can think of our familiar modern saying that constitutions grow and are not made. As applied to the British Constitution at the present time this is strictly true. For the British Constitution has come to be what it is as a result of a series of measures taken to meet momentary needs, and, to some degree also, by a series of historical accidents, with no intention about them. When there was intention, it was generally aimed at something very different from the actual results : probably very few, if any, of the succession of statesmen who built up the constitution foresaw the form that it was ultimately going to take, or would have approved of it, if they had.

---

[1] Of Greek thought, so far as we have any record of it. About what the half-barbarian Aetolians or Acarnanians were thinking we know nothing : but among the Greek States of which we have any knowledge we do find a certain unity of outlook in spite of individual differences. See e.g., Vinogradoff, *Historical Jurisprudence*, Vol. II, pp. 3–7, for a statement of the fundamental unity of Greek legal conceptions.

And very often they persisted in an obstinate refusal to recognize the results that had actually come about.[1]  The result of our history has been to instil into us a distrust, more or less conscious, of the attempt to guide the development of political institutions by reason.  We are apt to feel that in any case the unforeseen results of our actions are so often more important and far-reaching than the foreseen results that it is not really much use attempting to foresee and control the direction in which we are developing.  We can, therefore, do little more than deal with problems and difficulties as they arise, and leave to some other power the ultimate result of our actions.  This point of view was powerfully maintained by Burke, and it has become deeply rooted in our national outlook.  Burke, indeed, had a clear idea of what this other power was.  His profound religious faith made him content to leave our ultimate destinies to the working of that ' Divine tactic ' in which he trusted.  Many of us in modern times, without the same foundation of religious faith, seem ready to trust vaguely in something that we call Progress which will ensure that these unforeseen results will in general work out for the good.

This general point of view is probably less prevalent now than it was a quarter of a century ago.  But such reaction as there is against it should not be allowed to obscure the truth that it is possible to bring forward many undeniable facts of human experience to support it.  It is, however, emphatically not a typically Greek point of view.  It has often been pointed out that there is in the Greek language no word which really corresponds to our word Progress and no idea in Greek thought which corresponds to our idea of it.  On the whole, it is true that the Greek normally preferred to see where he was going, and the idea that we are continually drifting along in a direction which we cannot foresee or control would have been abhorrent to him.  It would have seemed more natural to him to make the attempt to think out clearly what he wanted, and then to construct an organization which would secure it.  Thus Greek political thought turns naturally

---

[1] An instance of this would be the curious delusion which existed till recently that the British Constitution is based on a sharp separation of the executive and legislative powers.  An instance of the historical accidents which affected the development of the Constitution would be the fact that the first Hanoverian king could not speak English and therefore did not attend Cabinet meetings.

to the construction of ideal States, and that not in the sense of the expression of an ultimate ideal with only a distant relation to practical politics, but rather as a concrete scheme of organization, which, given certain not impossible conditions, could be put into force at once. Aristotle, who himself described the general lines of an ideal State, mentions two other makers of Utopias before Plato. And many other writers presented their theories in a disguised form, as an imaginative historical account of a constitution which had existed in the past.

In actual fact the statement that constitutions grow and are not made would simply not have been true of ancient Greece. For there were many examples among them of constitutions which had been deliberately made. When the English settlers arrived in America they thought of themselves as carrying with them the English Common Law, which is still the basis of the legal system of the United States. But when a new Greek city was founded by colonizers from some already existing state it seems to have been more usual, at any rate in historical times, to call in a lawgiver or lawgivers to construct a fresh constitution and a code of laws. We have recorded many names of such legislators. Zaleucus and Charondas, two of the earliest mentioned, may or may not have been historical personages : the weight of authority at the present time seems to be in favour of the belief that they were. But, at a later date, there is good historical evidence for the fact that, when Thurii was founded in 444, Protagoras was called in to draw up the laws for the new colony. So natural did this procedure appear to the Greeks that, even in the case of institutions which in all probability had been the work of a gradual process of evolution, they tended to invent an imaginary lawgiver, like Lycurgus at Sparta, to whom these institutions were ascribed.

It was the same in the politics of already established states. When they did make up their minds that a change was desirable, they appear to have been ready to face a drastic reconstruction of their institutions which it would be difficult to imagine taking place without a violent revolution in any modern state. The reforms of Cleisthenes, already referred to, are typical of this, in that they involved a drastic and elaborate reconstruction of established institutions, which was accepted peaceably and was apparently quite successful in attaining its object. On the other hand, in spite of their readiness on

occasion to face radical changes, the Greek attitude in general
was extremely conservative.  Legislation is not a normal
function of Greek states, and change in laws or institutions
was not regarded as natural and inevitable, but rather as an
occasional necessity to be avoided whenever possible.  This
is only another aspect of the rationalistic point of view, which
we have been describing.  To such a point of view it would
seem the natural thing to think out the best possible institutions, to establish them, and, when once established, to maintain them in being.  It would seem clear that, if the best
institutions were once attained, any change must be for the
worse.  All serious thinkers saw many evils in the existing
state of things.  But their proposals for remedying these were
made on the assumption that, when they had been put right
and a satisfactory state of things established, no further
change ought to be necessary.

(2) Closely connected with this, indeed another aspect of it,
is a quality of Greek thought which, for want of a better word,
we may term its Utilitarianism.  The name is used here with
reference to what is recognized as the greatest service that
the English Utilitarians of the early nineteenth century did for
political thinking.  It has often been pointed out that, when
Bentham and his followers first began to develop their special
views, political discussion was in the main carried on, as
indeed to a great extent it still is, by the assertion and counter-
assertion of different rights inherent in various persons or
groups of persons in the community.  These natural rights
appear to have been thought of as simply there, not dependent
upon anything else and not, therefore, a possible matter for
argument or discussion.  The great service that the Utilitarians
did was to bring forward the idea of one single end or object of
political and indeed of all action, and to insist that every
proposed measure or existing institution should be tried by
reference to this end.  If it helped towards it, it was good.
If it hindered it, it was bad and must go, irrespective of any
supposed rights or vested interests.  It is unnecessary to
point out what a great advance in clarity of thought is produced by the introduction of the idea of one single object and
one standard by which everything can be judged.

This attitude of mind, though we can attain it by an effort
of thought, does not seem yet, in spite of Bentham, to have
become part of our habitual assumptions.  With the Greek
. thinker or statesman it was otherwise.  He would find the

mental atmosphere of his age much more favourable to the recognition of one end of political action, by which everything was to be judged and to which every other claim must give way. This does not mean that every Greek statesman, still less every Greek citizen, started out with a clearly conceived idea of the end of the State and of political action, by which he judged everything. On the contrary, in practice they were no doubt just as confused and self-contradictory in their ideas of the end of action as we are to-day. But they did start out with the implicit assumption that there was such an end, and not a number of unrelated rights ; and when a Greek started to think seriously about politics, he would naturally begin by asking himself what this end was.

One result that this had on their practice was that they often showed a disregard of vested interests or individual rights, when they thought that the good of the State was at stake, which would probably strike modern thought as somewhat ruthless. Thus Solon began his economic reforms by the cancellation of all debts,[1] a measure which, as we learn from casual notices in the historians, absolutely ruined many individuals. And yet Solon was regarded as a moderate and conservative reformer. Or again we find at Athens in the fifth century the institution of Ostracism, by which on the vote of a certain number of citizens any one might be sent into banishment for a term of years. No crime was alleged against him : the voters merely had to consider whether it was in the general interests of the State that he should be removed from the city for a certain time, and no consideration of the rights of the individual could be allowed to weigh against this. We have only to imagine the reception that a proposal to establish such an institution would meet with in England to-day to see the difference in the points of view. The supreme example of the complete subordination of the individuals to the welfare of the State—in this case conceived of as consisting in military power—was to be found in the rigid institutions of Sparta. The clear conception of a single end and the organization of everything with that end in view which was seen there made a powerful impression on the minds of many Greeks of other states.

---

[1] Or at any rate of all debts contracted on the security of the person or real property of the debtor. This would probably mean all the debts of the agricultural population, at that time a considerable majority of the State.

7

But this is only an expression of a more fundamental characteristic of Greek thought about conduct.   All moral philosophy
begins as reflection upon ordinary ideas and assumptions.   And
the ideas and assumptions from which the Greek thinker
would naturally start show, at any rate, a marked difference
of emphasis from the ideas and assumptions of modern times.
In both cases reflection would start from the fact of moral
judgements, from the fact that we do normally think of certain things as being good or right or whatever word we use,
as opposed to others which are regarded as being bad or wrong.
Now the chief Greek moral category is expressed by the word
ἀγαθός, which is usually translated 'good'.   This translation
is inevitable, as both words represent in their respective lan-
guages this chief moral category.   But we cannot understand
the arguments of Plato or any other Greek thinker unless we
realize that the further suggestions of the two words have
important differences to those who use them.   Whereas the
moral terms in modern English suggest rather to our minds
some obligation imposed upon us, irrespective of what we want
and often in conflict with it, the Greek word ἀγαθός always
suggests to a Greek in the first place a reference of some kind
to a purpose.   One might almost say that the word means
' that which fulfils some purpose '.

We cannot, of course, ask of the vague popular meaning of
an ordinary word that it should tell us precisely what or
whose purpose.   It is in an attempt to clear up the vagueness
of ordinary ideas on that point that a great part of Greek
moral speculation consists.   It is clear that the term is applied
sometimes to actions which appear to be in contradiction
to the conscious purpose of a particular individual, and that
any particular conscious purpose may be universally admitted
to be bad.

That, indeed, is just one of the facts which set the problem
to the philosopher.   But nevertheless somewhere and somehow the reference to a purpose is always implied in the word,
and the task of moral philosophy is the development and
refinement of this idea.   We must understand these primary
implications of the word if we are to understand Plato's argument.   Otherwise, we should never see why in the *Republic*,
for instance, he gives us as a definition of the good which
hardly needs discussion—' that at which everything aims ', or
why we find him in more than one dialogue using the words
. translated ' good ' as practically synonymous with various

words which are translated by ' useful ' or ' advantageous '
(e.g., χρήσιμος, ὠφέλιμος.) We can aid our understanding
of the position if we realize that in English, too, we use the
word ' good ' in various senses which do not strike us as
specifically moral. We speak, just as the Greek would, of a
' good soldier ', meaning a soldier who does his work well and
fulfils his particular object. Or we speak of ' good wine ',
meaning wine that we like and should desire to have. We
assume that the word in these connections means something
entirely different from what it means in moral judgements.
But that is, if we think of it, a strange assumption. For
how, if the meanings are entirely different, do we come to
use the same word ? At any rate, it is clear that we have
here a question which requires further examination.

(3) A third general characteristic of ordinary Greek political
thought, which may be noted, is its limitedness. With few
exceptions, the scope of their political thinking is limited to
the city-state. From some points of view, indeed, it would
be true to say that it is limited for each man to his own city-
state. Some further explanation is needed of a statement
which lies open to the possibility of misunderstanding.

In the first place, it is clear that to the ordinary Greek
and to the philosophical thinker alike it was an assumption that
hardly stood in need of argument that the city-state was the
highest form of political organization. This was not, of
course, because they knew of no other. They were perfectly
familiar with the larger country-states, the Persian Empire,
the Macedonian kingdom, and the others which surrounded
them. But they definitely held that these were an inferior
type, and that they could not do for the individual citizens
what a State ought to do. On this last point, indeed, they were
undoubtedly right. It is only possible for a small, concentrated community to be to its citizens what the Greek city
could be. Even Athens was held by some to be too large,
and both Plato and Aristotle made their ideal States considerably smaller. Only so was it possible to get the proper
unity and the concentration of interest, which they regarded
as desirable.

Less defensible by our standards is the comparative failure
to appreciate the importance of relations which extend beyond
the limits of one particular state. This is less noticeable in
questions of the relations between states. The Greeks had a
developed idea of international law, and if it was not always

successful in restraining their actions, the same phenomenon may be observed in comparatively modern times. But what we do notice is the lack of any realization that even for the purpose of education and moral development these relations outside the limits of the State are an important factor. The tendency is for the Greek to think of his own State as, normally and properly, sufficient for all social and spiritual needs, ' self-sufficient for the good life,' as Aristotle says. And in the construction of ideal States the tendency is apparent to attempt to reduce to a minimum the dependence of the one state on the others. Of course, in fact this ideal was never realized. Not only economically but also spiritually and intellectually the life of one state was profoundly affected by influences from outside. But this seems to have been regarded, by those who thought about it at all, as an accidental and not very desirable state of things. If a state needed to get anything from outside, that could only be because of some failure to provide what was needed itself. And if the ideal State was achieved clearly it ought not to need anything from outside, and external influences, if they changed it at all, could only change it for the worse.[1]

We may notice, as complementary to this tendency, that there is little or no realization that the city or its citizens had any obligations to any one outside its own limits. The Greeks recognized, more or less seriously, certain definite duties imposed by international law or custom. But there appears to be no idea that a city had any responsibilities for the moral effect of its actions to any one except its own citizens. Except in certain heretical tendencies of thought, there seems little or no idea of a duty towards humanity, for which the particular city was only an instrument. The city is normally conceived, more or less consciously, as an association of individuals for the sake of living the ' good life ', whatever that is thought to include. And such an association only exists for the sake of its own members. To those outside it is indifferent : if they seek the ' good life ' they must look for it in a similar association of their own.

If we grasp this, we shall be helped to understand several points. We shall understand why Aristotle, for instance, devotes so much attention to the discussion of the question

---

[1] It is significant of Plato's originality that in the *Laws* (though not in the *Republic*) he shows tentative efforts towards a correction of this limited point of view.

what constitutes a citizen. He is really asking a question of great importance, Who are the people towards whom the State has a moral and educational responsibility ? Again, we shall see how it was accepted so much as a matter of course that a city might include within its boundaries a large mass of non-citizens, resident aliens and slaves, who had none of the rights of the citizens, and could not normally acquire them by any process. The resident aliens came of their own accord for their own advantage, and there seemed no reason why they should be included within the civic community.

With the slaves, however, it was different. They could hardly be said in any sense to be there of their own accord. And there is evidence that the best Greek opinion was not altogether comfortable about their position. We shall see that there were thinkers who attacked the whole institution of slavery, though there is no evidence that they ever con-templated any practical steps to put an end to it. Aristotle feels it necessary in defending the institution to argue that under certain conditions it may be to the advantage of the slave himself. There may be certain people who are naturally adapted by the strength of their bodies and the inferiority of their minds to a life of slavery, and they may find the highest good of which they are capable in a life under the control of those who are wiser than themselves. But he has to admit that in practice these conditions were by no means always fulfilled. And there was a general feeling that slaves should only be made from members of inferior races, not from other Greeks. Apart from this, a certain degree of respon-sibility towards the slave was recognized. Both public opinion and the law of Athens restricted the possibilities of ill-treatment. It was, indeed, one of the complaints that good aristocrats made against the Athenian democracy, that the slaves under it were treated almost on the same footing as the citizens.

The whole subject of slavery in ancient Greece is a difficult and complicated one. The only point on which it is necessary to insist here is the avoidance of one particular error. It has been very commonly held at some periods that the civiliza-tion of the Greek city-states rested on a basis of slavery. The citizens were conceived of as devoting themselves to public affairs or the cultivation of the arts, while the labour neces-sary to support them was carried on by the slaves. It is now increasingly recognized that this is entirely erroneous. Slavery was accepted as an institution coming down from time immemorial. But there was no idea of defending it on these lines : it was, indeed, by the vast mass of people never seriously questioned, and therefore needed no defence. As a matter of fact, in Athens, at any rate, there was no such sharp division between the work of the slave and the work of the citizen as this view implies. The poorer citizens worked as hard as the slaves, and at much the same kinds of occupation. The richer might use hired free workers as well as slaves, and might well be indifferent which they employed. We must, then, free ourselves altogether from the idea that the development of Greek civilization depended for its possibility on the existence of slavery, however much that institution might modify certain features of it.

Such were some of the main assumptions of political thought. It remains to formulate, so far as the two can be distinguished, some of the ordinary moral ideas and categories on which the Greek moral philosopher would have to begin his task of criticism and explanation. First and foremost is the fundamental moral notion of good or the good, which, as we have already seen, implies primarily in its normal Greek use some reference to a purpose. And, though it is true, as was said above, that a popular notion like this could hardly be expected to define exactly whose purpose was in question, yet it would probably be also true to say that, normally and in the absence of special qualification, each man would use the word primarily with his own purpose in mind. The good would suggest to him before anything what he himself wanted. The good man would be the sort of man that he admired and would like to be, and the good life the sort of life that he would choose to lead. The opposite to this, the word normally translated ' bad ', is κακός. Besides these two, there are numerous other words, which in ordinary speech were used more or less synonymously, but which afforded, when a close argument was in progress, many opportunities for subtle discrimination of meaning.

Of special interest is the word καλός, the primary meaning of which is ' beautiful ' to look at or to listen to. In one dialogue, when the meaning of the word is discussed, Socrates suggests at one stage of the argument a definition of it as applying to whatever gives pleasure to the eyes or the ears. But in the earliest use of it that we know we find that its meaning is already extended beyond this to anything that excites admiration, and in this sense it is often better trans-·lated by some such word as ' noble '. It is associated with the word for good in the phrase (καλὸς κἀγαθός) which is used so frequently in Greek to express the ideal of manhood. Its opposite, αἰσχρός, has the same double meaning. It means ' ugly ' in our sense, but even more readily it develops a sense of ' base ' or ' disgraceful '. Both words at times become almost indistinguishable in their meaning from ' good ' and ' bad ' respectively.

The quality in a man which corresponded to the adjective ' good ' was indicated by the word, of which we have already had occasion to speak, ἀρετή. This has been variously translated as ' goodness ' or ' excellence ' or ' virtue '. But when we use the last-named word, which is in some respects the most convenient translation, we must take care to avoid some of the implications of the English. Our word in its ordinary use seems to suggest in the first place the avoidance of wrong action. The Greek suggests much rather some positive capacity. In fact, it corresponds to the sense of the English word in which it is used by chemists when they speak of the virtue of a drug or by gardeners who talk of the virtue of a soil. It is that quality which enables its possessor to do his work well or to attain his own end.

But besides this general quality of virtue, there are, for the Greek as for us, certain particular qualities, the different virtues or parts of virtue, which also are to be regarded as good. Courage, wisdom, piety were universally admitted to be virtues. The Greek words for these are represented adequately by their English equivalents. But another quality, which is less easily translatable, is one of those most frequently mentioned. That is σωφροσύνη, which is the special subject matter of the Charmides, one of the earlier dialogues. The word is often translated by ' temperance ', and if we could get rid of the unfortunate association which the English word has developed in its more modern use, the translation is not altogether unsatisfactory. For the Greek suggests the application to all desires of the attitude of mind which by the English word is referred especially to the desire for drink. It means moderation and avoidance of excess, a well-balanced and self-controlled mind. It is the virtue inculcated by the well-known Greek motto, Nothing too much, which was inscribed over the temple of Delphi. Finally we may note the virtue of δικαιοσύνη, generally translated justice. This translation, again, is not exact ; for the word has much wider implications. It really suggests giving other people their due, and may be

used to represent the general fulfilment of one's duty towards
one's neighbour. It thus easily becomes identifiable with the
whole of morality. In fact, it is the earliest word to acquire
the significance of morality, duty or right, and is used to indicate these ideas, at a time when ἀρετή still suggested primarily prowess in battle. But at the time with which we are
dealing δικαιοσύνη had acquired a more specialized and ἀρετή
a wider meaning, and it is assumed without question that
δικαιοσύνη is an ἀρετή or a part of ἀρετή.

Reflection on the ideas indicated by these various words
would by itself be enough to start us on the work of moral
speculation. Thus the Greek thinker would find himself presented with the idea of a good, which was what he wanted
and aimed at. And at the same time he would find that it was
generally accepted that certain particular qualities or attitudes
of mind or principles of conduct were virtues and good things.
But he would soon find in practice that there were occasions,
on which, for him or for others, the observance of these principles of conduct or the adoption of these attitudes of mind
would be very far from helping to attain what] he wanted
and might, indeed, positively prevent his doing so. The first
occasion on which he found that the attainment of his own
aims seemed incompatible with a due observance of the rights
of others would have afforded the occasion for the beginnings
of reflection on the real meaning of his moral categories. This
is the problem of the double standard of conduct which is the
starting-point of all moral speculation. To us it presents
itself in the form of the realization of the truth of the statement
that what we want to do is often incompatible with what we
ought to do. And this presents us with practical problems
enough, even if the theoretical difficulties of the situation are
not at first sight so obvious to us as they ought to be. But
to the Greek the theoretical problem also leaps to the eye
at the very beginning of reflection, for by calling what we
ought to do ' good ', he finds that he has, by the use of this
word, committed himself to the assumption that we also in
some sense or in some way want to do it. And the contradiction in his ordinary assumptions is thus obvious from the
first.

This assumption that the good is in some way necessarily
bound up with what we want has another effect which it is
important to notice. If the whole problem of conduct is
. simply a question of attaining our purpose, it is a very natural

step to go on to the assumption that, if we only know what to do to get what we want, we shall at once proceed to do it. And it would appear to follow that action which is not good can only be the result of a mistake or ignorance. It is significant that the same word in successive stages of the Greek language means ' to miss the mark ', ' to make a mistake ', and ' to sin '. It is often said that the mark of the earlier Platonic dialogues is that they tend to identify virtue with knowledge. And this is quite true. In the *Laches*, for instance, where the meaning of courage is being discussed, Socrates leads Nicias to the position where he asserts that courage is the knowledge of what is good and what is bad. And he then states as almost self-evident that this would make it identical with complete virtue. If we know what is good, he assumes, nothing more is needed to make us do it. But it is important to realize that this is not a peculiarity of Plato or of Socrates, but is simply a natural development of the assumptions of Greek thought and Greek language. It is clear enough that even in the earliest dialogues Plato is not completely satisfied with it, and is anxious to work out the implications of the view more completely than the ordinarily accepted ideas had done.

Such was the situation from which Socrates and Plato set out in their examination of accepted ideas. But, we must repeat once more, they were not the originators of the criticism. The accepted ideas about conduct of an earlier generation had already been undermined by criticism of the kind discussed in the previous chapter. And it was their task to see whether by a further and deeper criticism it would not be possible to pass through the stage of moral scepticism and arrive at the other side with a firmer faith based on thought-out principles of conduct. Thus the problem of the double standard of conduct was solved, in a sense, by the views which would reduce all the claims of what we ordinarily call morality to a mere convention and would assert that the only rational principle of conduct was to follow one's own selfish desires with the least possible scruples. Socrates and Plato could not accept that solution. But the problem of the double standard had to be faced by them ,too. And the earlier dialogues are mostly concerned in one way or another with this problem. The form in which it appears to have specially interested Plato was the question of the meaning of the particular virtues or good qualities and their relation to the general idea of the good or the end of life. Most of the earlier dialogues contain a discussion of some particular moral quality, courage, piety or the like.

These, then, are some of the main characteristics which we may notice in Greek political and moral thought and practice. It is necessary once more to beware of the danger of thinking of these as universal statements which can be asserted without qualification of all Greeks. Such an idea would merely be absurd. They are never more than tendencies, which admit of many individual exceptions. And even as tendencies they are rarely, for most Greeks, conscious or explicit. We find them rather in the form of unconscious assumptions and presuppositions on which thought and action are based. Unless we remember this, to formulate them at all will give a wrong impression, just because they were never formulated by the majority of Greeks themselves. But if we do remember it, we may find that an understanding of these tendencies will help us to the understanding of a great deal in Greek history and civilization in general, and in the development of Plato's thought in particular.

# CHAPTER VIII

## THE FOURTH CENTURY

THE two previous chapters were concerned with the historical development of the situation in which Plato began his speculations, and with some general characteristics of Greek thought. So far as any period was particularly emphasized it was the closing years of the fifth century, the years in which Plato was born and grew to manhood. His experiences during that time must have had a permanent influence on his thought, but they would be particularly influential in his earliest speculations. We must always remember that Plato was twenty-eight when the new century began. We must not fall into the error of regarding him as exclusively the product of the fourth century, and of drawing too sharp a dividing line between his period and the period described in the dialogues. None the less the activities by which we know him were carried on in the fourth century, and covered more than the first half of it. So any further developments in his thought must be mainly due to experiences during that period. It is desirable, therefore, to consider any special features that we may find in the political and moral situation of the fourth century. By so doing we shall understand not only the influences which first formed Plato's thought, but the influences under which it grew and developed throughout his lifetime.

We must beware, however, of making too sharp a distinction between this period and that which immediately precedes it. We to-day are apt to think of the close of the fifth century as marking the end of a great age in Greece and the beginning of a period of decline. That is partly because we think so largely in terms of literary history. We know that Sophocles, Euripides and all the best work of Aristophanes come before 400 ; and the next century is known to us mainly by the work of orators and literary journalists like Xenophon. But it was not thus that those who lived through this period regarded it. To them the fourth century, up to the final triumph of the

Macedonians, appears rather as part of a single period which begins with the Peloponnesian War or even before it. When Isocrates or Plato want to find a time to which they can look back with satisfaction, they turn, not as we should do, to the glories of the Periclean age, but to the simpler virtues of the men of the Persian Wars. Whether those virtues would have appeared quite the same when seen more closely as they did in retrospect, one may doubt. But in refusing to put a sharp dividing line at the turn of the century they were clearly, from the point of view of political and social developments, in the right. In general, we get the clearest light on the developments of the fourth century by looking at them as the continuation and intensification of the tendencies which were already showing themselves clearly in the Peloponnesian War. And, if our knowledge was greater, we should probably see many signs of them earlier still. We, who still enjoy so many of the artistic and literary fruits of the Periclean age, can scarcely find it in our hearts to speak hardly of it. But we should not forget that Plato must have had some reason for his harsh judgment of its effect on the moral character of the city. And the attraction that we cannot but feel for the sympathetic personality of Pericles should not blind us to the fact that, as a statesman, he never rose above the level of a mere party leader. Even the policy that he carried out was not originated by him. And we look in vain for signs of a far-sighted care for anything beyond the immediate needs of the moment.

The struggle for power between the cities in the fourth century is really no more selfish or sordid than that which began in the middle of the fifth. Why it attracts us less is largely because it is more futile and has less prospects of permanent success. Partly the thing has been going on too long, and the combatants are becoming exhausted. And partly also the game has by this time begun to attract too many players. We can no longer see it as a straightforward contest between two groups with Athens at the head of one and Sparta of the other. The groups are shifting and changing all the time, Persia reasserts her influence, Thebes appears as a third claimant to the leadership, and affairs in Sicily begin to develop an independent interest which distracts our attention from Greece itself. And there is no one power which has sufficient strength left to carry out its ambitions for more than a moment. That is obvious from the beginning to us who look at it in the light of subsequent events. But Isocrates is evidence that there were some Greeks to whom before long it became apparent too. Sparta had the best chance. But she soon lost her naval power, even after she retained her domination over the Peloponnese and most of continental Greece. Even here, she owed a good deal of her success to the support of Persia. Thebes finally ousted her after about thirty years of a greater or less degree of supremacy. But Thebes never attained quite the same position. And what she had only lasted a few years while her armies were still led by a soldier of genius. Athens showed a wonderful recovery after the disaster of the Peloponnesian War, and at the end of our period her position was equal to that of any state in Greece. But the attempt to restore her naval empire, after a moment's success, had to be abandoned finally. By the end of Plato's life the states of Greece seemed settling into an uneasy condition of unstable equilibrium.

A somewhat similar spectacle is presented by the internal politics of Athens during this period. In political ability the men of the fourth century need fear no comparison with those of the fifth. In military ability they were undoubtedly superior. As generals men like Iphicrates and Chabrias were in an entirely different class from amateurs like Pericles or Nicias and probably were not very much less superior to the more specialized soldiers such as Lamachus and Demosthenes. About the political leaders we would gladly know more. The glimpses that we get of Timotheus and Callistratus are far from unattractive, both as individuals and as politicians. Certainly those responsible for the formation of the second Athenian league were capable of something like real statesmanship. In the earlier years of the century the figure of Thrasybulus, from all that we know, is one that arouses nothing but respect and admiration. But there was no one who seemed able to establish a permanent leadership, and there was consequently no continuity of policy. No doubt this was largely due to the extreme difficulties of the situation : modern historians seem often to make insufficient allowances for these and to be unduly ready with blame for the statesmen who could not produce an ideal solution. But the fact remains, and it gives an air of futility to the activities of the fourth century which makes it easy, perhaps unfairly so, to lose interest in them. It is only in the last seven or eight years of Plato's life that some sort of settled policy seemed to be reached. Athens, under Eubulus, seemed reconciled to the sensible but unromantic task of avoiding foreign adventures and restoring order and prosperity at home.   Yet even before Plato's death this momentary lull was being broken by the events that were developing around her.

Of the general tone of political life in Athens and elsewhere we get some sort of picture from the historians and the orators. In Athens the constitution itself enjoyed a welcome stability during this period.   The slight changes that we do know of are all in the democratic direction.   Thus pay for attendance at the Assembly was first introduced somewhere in the late 'nineties of the fourth century.   The experience of the Thirty had discredited the oligarchical movement too deeply for any attempt to be made at overthrowing the democracy.   But fears and suspicions of such an attempt did not disappear. Isocrates expresses alarm lest in criticizing any act or policy of the people he should lay himself open to suspicion of oligarchic tendencies.   And Lysias shows us again and again how useful the insinuation of such tendencies could be if it was desired to discredit any enemy or political opponent.   Perhaps to some extent the old partisan feeling found vent in affecting the attitude of Athenians towards other States.   The young Demosthenes, speaking a few years before Plato's death, lays it down almost as an axiom that there can never be real and abiding friendship between a democracy and an oligarchy.

How political opinion was divided is obscure.   It is certain that there was a constant tendency for the division to come where it had begun to come in the Peloponnesian War, namely between the richer citizens, supported by the agricultural population, who in general wanted peace, and the poorer population of the town, who had dreams of a revival of the vanished empire which had been a profitable source of income to them.   How far there was anything in the nature of a direct social conflict between rich and poor in Athens it is difficult to say.   There are slight indications of an increase of ill-feeling between the two classes.   On the other hand, there are no hints of a definite revolutionary programme, a cry for redistribution of land or cancellation of debts such as mark the social struggle at other times and in other cities. Perhaps the immediate needs of the proletariat were met sufficiently by the payments for public services and the Theoric Fund.   The chief financial preoccupation of statesmen of all parties seems to have been to raise sufficient funds to retain a large proportion of the population in the service of the State.

And on the whole the social difference seems to have expressed itself rather by differences on foreign policy than by direct conflict. Yet even here there was no clear-cut and continuous division of opinion. Too many other motives were always coming in and obscuring the issues before the city. Fear of any one state attaining too dominant a position was always present. But above all the personal conflicts and jealousies between individual politicians made anything like a stable policy or even a stable division of opinion impossible. Though we are much less well informed about the details, it seems that the people, both in their assemblies and their law courts, were swayed this way and that by the appeals of different orators even more, perhaps, than in the time of Cleon and Nicias and Alcibiades.

The results of this were serious. One thing that strikes any one who studies the period is the extraordinary sense of insecurity which all public men, orators and generals alike, must have felt. Hardly any one of prominence escaped trial at some period of his career, and few avoided condemnation either to payment of a heavy fine, to exile, or even to death. The great liberator, Thrasybulus, for all his services was only saved from trial and probable condemnation by his timely death. Isocrates tells us how he used to warn Timotheus that mere honest and successful service to the State could never make a man safe unless he made friends with those who could control the assemblies and the law courts. And his neglect of this advice led to his ultimate condemnation. It was, thus, mainly in the courts that the political battles were fought out. We can see from the orators the kind of charges that might be brought. If no more specific accusation could be made, there was always the charge of having deceived the people by giving bad advice that might secure a condemnation.

This necessarily had an effect on the type of man that entered public life. We have seen that the attractions of a political career were still sufficient to bring to it some men of ability and character. But they were, perhaps, the exception. We must not, of course, take too seriously the laments of Isocrates over the moral degradation of the men whose advice was taken by the people in preference to his own. But, allowing for that, there seem to have been plenty of opportunities for the rise to power of politicians of a very undesirable type. Agyrrhius, for instance, who raised the fee for attendance at the assembly and his contemporary Cinesias, even

when all allowance is made for the exaggeration of orators
and comedians, can hardly have been anything much better
than political adventurers, whose main object was their own
aggrandisement.

An effect about which there can be no dispute is the prominence that this state of things gave to the orator.  The fourth
century is the age of political oratory.  And it is also the
age in which political oratory is becoming more and more
divorced from executive, particularly military, responsibility.
This tendency was already becoming noticeable in the time
of the Peloponnesian War.  And it never at any time became
an absolute rule.  But it was certainly intensified in the fourth
century.  Isocrates, in 355, can speak of it as specially characteristic of his own age.[1]  Its results on political life are
generally represented as wholly undesirable, and it certainly
had some unfortunate effects.  But in other respects, particularly in the growing separation of military from political
activities, it expressed a tendency which was becoming unavoid-
able and is taken for granted in modern times.

This growing specialization of public functions, particularly
in regard to military matters, is a mark of the century not only
in Athens but all over Greece.  The development of the
mercenary and the professional soldier is one of its most
prominent features, and is a constant subject of reference by
contemporary writers.  Sometimes they mention it to blame
the citizens for allowing their fighting to be done for them by
mercenaries and refusing to face service themselves,—not
altogether a fair reproach, if we consider the demands made
by almost continual warfare and the superior efficiency of the
professional over the amateur.  And in any case the citizen
soldier still played a large part in the fighting in Greece throughout the century.  Sometimes it is held out as an inducement to
some leader to undertake an expedition, that it will be easy to
find all the soldiers that were wanted for any such purpose
from among the unemployed mercenaries.  Sometimes the
dangers of the situation are emphasized, with the continual
presence of a crowd of men whose only trade is war, who have
lost their ties with any particular city, and who form a material
ready to the hand for the conduct of any desperate enterprise.
One of the advantages urged by Isocrates for his policy of a
great pan-Hellenic expedition against Persia is that it would

[1] *De Pace*, 54.

draw off this dangerous element from Greece by giving it employment elsewhere.[1]

This reserve of mercenaries was created partly, of course, by the constant fighting and the fluctuations between war and peace, or rather perhaps between greater and lesser degrees of war. But it was recruited also from a class whose prominence is one of the most distressing features of the time. That was the political exile. Except in a few relatively favoured cities, the intensification of the bitterness of party warfare is a striking characteristic of the fourth century. Party warfare was, of course, no new thing in Greece. But the state of affairs that Thucydides describes with such unsparing realism in his account of the Corcyrean civil war had become almost normal. A particular feature of it, which had also made its appearance earlier, though never to such a degree, was the readiness of the defeated party to call in the aid of a foreign power against their own city. Whenever one city made war against another, it could count on the exiles from its enemy as among its own most reliable troops. And a victory was generally followed by a massacre of the leading politicians in the defeated city. It is counted as a special sign of generosity in Agesilaus when in some cases he refused to allow this, and was content to inflict banishment on them.

There were, of course, exceptions. Sparta was generally too prompt in executing any disaffected elements for such a danger to assume serious proportions in her case. Whatever we may say against Athenian politics, a comparison with most other cities shows Athens in a very favourable light : at her worst she never sunk to this level. We hear, too, good things of the little city of Megara, which, by keeping the peace abroad and at home, had attained a degree of prosperity quite out of proportion to its size and natural advantages. But if there were bright spots on the picture, the picture as a whole, if we can believe the contemporary evidence, was very dark.

It would be interesting to know more of the inner details of this fierce party warfare. It took the form in general of the familiar struggle between oligarchy and democracy. But it is difficult to say exactly what these names stood for. It was certainly not an abstract devotion to rival forms of political organization. At the back of it in many cases no doubt we can see the eternal warfare between the poor and the rich. Aristotle, a little later, puts forward, as an obvious definition of

[1] *Philip.* 120, 121.

8

democracy, the statement that it is a constitution in which the poor rule and use their power to oppress and live off the rich. Variations in the distribution of taxation, and the introduction of pay for public services and, of course, the question of a property qualification for the franchise and for the magistracies, seem to have been the main points of policy on which the struggle turned. There are few, if any, signs of a more systematic policy of social reform or revolution. And at times it seems as if the party names indicated merely rival bands of politicians, and had as little real significance as Guelph and Ghibelline came to have in the later Middle Ages.

By the observers of our own time it has generally been felt that none of these developments compare in importance with the rise of Macedon and its consequences, which have sometimes been described as the end of the free Greek city-state system. It has even been made a reproach to Plato and Aristotle that, with the possibility and, in the case of the latter, the actuality of this before their eyes, they cling to the outworn forms of the old city-state, and say nothing of these new developments. This criticism betrays such a singular lack of understanding both of the actual situation and of the objects of thinkers like Plato and Aristotle, that it calls for a careful investigation.

In the first place it must be pointed out that a hegemony like that exercised by Macedon over the Greek cities was no new thing in Greece. It was a perfectly familiar phenomenon both to Plato and Aristotle. There is a popular impression that Greece before Philip's day consisted in the main of free and independent cities, and that after this time their freedom and independence ceased. The historians, of course, know better. But it must be confessed that they have not always been careful enough to warn us against this error. The error arises mainly perhaps from our inveterate habit of keeping our eyes fixed on Athens, with an occasional glance at Sparta, to the exclusion of the rest of Greece. If we take a wider view, we can see that, at least from the time of Crœsus onwards, absolute autonomy was the exception rather than the rule among the cities of the Greek world as a whole. Their relations to each other and to other great powers, such as Persia, vary from common membership of leagues and confederacies, through hegemonies and suzerainties to absolute subjection. Many instances of all these relations can be found.  What is much harder to find are the cases of complete independence which existed.

Nor is the destruction of independence by Macedon in any way so complete as is sometimes supposed.  To many states in Greece, indeed, Macedon might have been rather regarded as their guarantee of freedom against the imperialism of a state like Sparta.  If we read the neglected history of the third and second centuries we shall be struck by how often the Greek states, particularly in the Peloponnese, conduct their wars and alliances, not to speak of their internal affairs, as if Macedon did not exist at all.  As a matter of fact, in the course of these centuries Macedon was gradually becoming exhausted, and on the whole her power in Greece seems distinctly less at the end of this period than it was at the beginning.  It is a plausible conjecture that, left to themselves, Macedon might have sunk back into the position from which Philip raised her and the cities of continental Greece might have resumed their old life, with such changes as experience had taught them.  As it was, some individual states managed to maintain not only their independence but their power for long after this.  If we could forget Athens and fix our eyes on Rhodes or Cyzicus, we might well think that the great age of the city-state was just beginning.

Of course, it was different in the lands ruled by the Seleucids and the Ptolemies.  But even there many of the cities enjoyed a large degree of internal freedom.  And the unit of Greek civilization was always the city.  This was so not only under these kings but for long after the rule of Rome was established.  The power of Rome was always there.  But for each man the centre of life and interest was his city.  And for long most of the cities enjoyed a greater or lesser degree of freedom in the government of their own affairs.

This is the essential point.  Plato and Aristotle were thinking of the State, not in terms of power, but in terms of spiritual values, as an educational instrument.  And from that point of view the great country-states were simply irrelevant, as their own rulers showed that they realized when they made the foundation of cities their chief instrument in the spread of Hellenism.  The powers which they refused to the cities that they founded or conquered were in the main the powers of making wars on other cities and trying to extend their own dominions.  And those were just the powers that it would have seemed to Plato and Aristotle of least importance to keep. For the purposes that they required of a State they felt that they could think only in terms of a city-state, familiar though they were with other kinds. And in this they were quite right and saw far more clearly than their modern critics. It is indeed impossible for a large country-state ever to be all that Aristotle and Plato wanted the State to be to its individual members. And so events proved. For when, centuries later, the crushing weight of Roman domination at length ground out the last relics of active civic life, the city was not replaced in men's minds by any other political organization. Their devotion and loyalty turned instead to something that was not of this world, a moral ideal, a divine object of worship, a church, or some shadowy 'city of Zeus'.

This tendency was already beginning to show itself in the fourth century. It is, indeed, one of its most significant developments, even though for many generations its influence was confined to a limited circle and did not touch the ordinary man's thought. But it is significant for its future potentialities. And the mention of it may help to remind us that the century which saw such widespread moral decline also saw a widespread interest in moral problems and some of the most serious and interesting contributions to their solution which have ever been made. Plato was not entirely a voice crying in the wilderness of a demoralized world. He was one of a band of many workers who, not always in harmony with each other, were labouring to rediscover some standard of right conduct.

What is of particular interest to trace is the development of that line of thought which expressed itself in terms of the distinction between Nature and Convention. We have seen the form it took in Plato's youth, and its general effect in weakening the claims of moral obligations and restraints, leaving no motive for action but personal pleasure and profit. No doubt this still continued throughout Plato's lifetime. Even Aristotle mentions, as a living belief, the view that all moral judgements are merely matters of convention and not of nature. And, indeed, from one point of view his whole ethical and political theory is an attempt to refute this doctrine. Plato, in his *Laws* written at the end of his life, refers to views almost exactly similar to those expressed by Callicles as being among the most subtle dangers that a lawgiver and teacher has to contend with. The only advance that the unnamed people of whom he speaks seem to have made in these views is in bolstering them up by a materialist metaphysic with which they very naturally connected them.[1]

Plato's reaction against such views consisted in the main in an attempt to re-establish the claims of the organized community, and by reforming and purifying this community to make it possible once more to regard it as the chief moral agent. But there was also the other possible line of development which would lie in establishing the independence of the moral life and its separateness from the claims of society. And it is evident that there were quite serious movements which really began in the fourth century working in this direction.

On the negative side we find criticisms of institutions and ideas which had hitherto been taken for granted. Thus there are traces of an attempt to limit the functions and powers of the State by defining its objects in a narrower sense than would have been possible at any earlier period. Aristotle tells us of a ' sophist ', Lycophron, who seems to have regarded the whole function of the State and its laws as consisting in the protection of the citizens from violence and wrongdoing. He would presumably, like Herbert Spencer, have limited the work of government to keeping the peace between the members of the State and protecting them against external aggression. There is no question of the city and its laws exercising any educative effect on the moral character of the citizens. There are signs also of protest against the ideals of patriotism which still dominated Greek politics. The distinction between one Greek State and another, and even for the more radical minds between Greek and barbarian, was attacked as purely conventional and having no basis in the nature of things. There is a story told of a famous figure of this period being asked the usual question, Of what city are you ?, and replying, I am a citizen of the world (κοσμοπολίτης). Other distinctions also, which must have seemed almost equally profound to the ordinary Greek, were now made the object of criticism. The same Lycophron, according to a fragment of Aristotle, denounced the distinction between well-born and lowly as having no real ground in nature. Other thinkers, to their own great credit, made the same criticism of the universal institution of slavery. ' God made all men free,' says one writer of the period :  ' Nature has made no man a slave.'

[1] Aristotle, *Eth. Nic.* 1094b 16. Plato, *Laws*, 890a, 7-9.

A point of interest is the effect of this development on the position of women, particularly in Athens. There are undoubted signs in this period of a reaction against the condition of comparative inferiority in which they were kept there. Indeed, it goes back beyond this period. Of course, long before this there had been great differences in this respect between different States : the freedom of the Spartan women was well known. There are indications that men's minds were being stirred on the question in Athens before the end of the fifth century. We can guess from the plays of Aristophanes that there was a certain uneasiness on the matter : by the time he wrote the *Ecclesiazusae* it must have expressed itself in far-reaching claims to equality. Socrates, too, seems to have been interested in the movement. At any rate, all his disciples whose works remain represent him as questioning on occasions the conventional assumption of the absolute inequality of the sexes.[1] He is often, in this connection, brought into relation with Aspasia, who seems to have become the literary embodiment of the emancipated woman.

The movement certainly gathered strength during the fourth century. Isocrates in the address that he wrote for Nicocles makes him protest against the double standard of morality for husband and wife. Two comic poets of the period wrote plays on the Regiment of Women ($\Gamma v\nu\alpha\iota\kappa\kappa\rho\dot\alpha\tau\iota\alpha$). It is unfortunate that only the titles survive. And there is certainly plenty of evidence that the position of women at the end of the century was different from what it was at the beginning. This is often represented as being mainly due to the Macedonian influence. No doubt that helped in this direction. But it had certainly begun before this influence could have become very powerful. And we may reasonably claim for Plato and his teaching some share in this result. His own views, as expressed in the *Republic*, on the position of women are familiar. And, if we can believe later writers, he did not hesitate to recognize in practice the position he claimed for them. Dicaearchus, a pupil of Aristotle, who was probably well informed, tells us that there were two women among his pupils in the Academy. He adds the intriguing detail that one of them—why not both, we may wonder—wore men's clothes.

---

[1] See e.g. Xenophon's *Symposium*, ii, 9. For Socrates and Aspasia besides Plato's *Menexenus* see the fragments of Aeschines' *Aspasia*, and Xenophon, *Mem.* II, vi, 36, and *Oeconomicus*, iii, 14

All this criticism of accepted conventions, if it had remained negative, might have resulted merely in the abandonment of all obligations and restraints. As we have seen, that was its first result, and this aspect of it continued to be noticeable throughout the period. But alongside of this there developed a positive side to it, which so far as we know really originated in the fourth century. This was the doctrine that the true end of man was to be found, not in social or political activity, not even in any kind of relation to other men, but in something, some experience or state of mind, which he could attain by himself, independently of his fellow-beings in his own soul alone. Few thinkers of the period are altogether untouched by this idea. Plato himself, though he could never accept it as a statement of the ideal, believed at times that in practice, in the present state of affairs, something of the kind is the best that the true philosopher could aim at. Of course, for him this would never be more than a second best. But Aristotle, who throughout the greater part of his work appears as the typical representative of the orthodox view of the State and political life, is driven at the end of his *Ethics* to put the highest good for man in the life of contemplation and not in social and political activity at all.

But the typical expression of this point of view is to be looked for in the Cynic movement. ' Movement,' not ' school ' ; for, as many ancient writers realized, the Cynics were never a philosophical school. They bore, indeed, somewhat the same relation to the philosophical schools as the Salvation Army bears to the systematic theology of the churches. There were other ways in which they might be compared to this organization, if allowance is made for the differences of period and custom. They had their methods of drawing the attention of the people which must have seemed to the head of a philosophical school as crude and vulgar as the methods of the Salvation Army might seem to an orthodox bishop. And the same phenomenon is to be seen in them of sudden conversion to the gospel which they preached.

Preaching was, indeed, their work. And their gospel was the gospel of absolute self-sufficiency and freedom from dependence on any external conditions or circumstances. They called on their followers to show their contempt for all that the world could give in the way of wealth and comfort, social intercourse or political activity, by taking up the beggar's scrip and staff to embrace a life of poverty. Only so could they attain the life according to nature, the absolute independence of everything outside themselves, which alone could make the soul free. The familiar figure of Diogenes in his tub is the holy picture of Cynicism.[1]

This remarkable man was the real founder of the movement. Later they traced their descent back to Antisthenes, the friend of Socrates. But, though there may have been some connection, he was never a Cynic preacher. It was undoubtedly Diogenes who gave the movement the form it took. The details of his life are very uncertain. But he was probably about twenty or thirty years younger than Plato; at any rate their lives certainly overlapped by a considerable period and Diogenes was already a well-known figure when Aristotle was writing. The life of Diogenes, as it has come down to us, besides a few contradictory historical details, is made up of a series of anecdotes, illustrating his peculiar methods, his contempt for public opinion, his disregard of ordinary conventions of social life, his courage and independence, and above all his mordant and—sometimes—witty raillery against his contemporaries. Many stories are related of his encounters with Plato, in which he does not always shine. If the stories are to be believed, Plato was one of the few men who could stand up to Diogenes in verbal conflict. The stories themselves cannot be relied upon. But one of them, which is certainly *ben trovato*, indicates what would undoubtedly have been Plato's attitude towards the Cynics, his appreciation of the germs of nobility which their gospel contained and the revulsion that his sane and balanced nature must have felt towards their extravagances and exaggerations. It is related that Plato was asked what he thought of Diogenes : ' A Socrates gone mad,' he replied.

The later history of Cynicism does not concern us. One is tempted to linger over the picturesque figure of Crates, the best known of Diogenes' followers. His own sudden conversion and sacrifice of great wealth, his romantic marriage, his unconventional conversion of his brother-in-law, his

---

[1] It is an incidental point of interest that their asceticism, unlike the asceticism of Christianity, does not seem to have included any rule of chastity. From such evidence as we have, their attitude towards sexual experience seems to have been to treat it as a simple natural need to be stripped of any trappings of sentimentality, or any accompaniment of luxury, or any conventional feelings of shame or modesty.

method of giving instruction in the ' facts of life ' to his son,[1] his campaign to purify the street life of Athens,—all these things may be read in the narrative of Diogenes Laertius. For the future of philosophy his importance lies in the fact that he was a teacher of Zeno.    And through him, the essentials of Cynicism, sobered and made respectable, live on in the long and significant history of Stoicism.

[1] This seems to be the meaning of the curious story in Diogenes, VI, 88.

# CHAPTER IX

## PLATO ON CONTEMPORARY POLITICS

THE discussions on political questions in the dialogues generally aim at seeking some philosophical understanding of the underlying principles of all political activity. As such they seek to go beyond the particular circumstances of any one time or place. And in this attempt they attain a large degree of success. Even in our own so very different conditions we find, if we study them rightly, Plato's discussions of political principles extraordinarily helpful and suggestive. But, of course, those discussions assume an incidental background of political conditions peculiar to the time at which they were written. And the question has been raised, with special reference to the Socratic controversy, whether the conditions thus assumed are more naturally to be taken as those existing at the time of writing or those existing at the time at which the conversations described in the dialogues are supposed to have taken place.

If the conclusions of the previous chapter are correct, it would follow that on many points no answer to this question could be given. For there is no such sharp distinction possible between the conditions at the two periods as the question implies. Most writers of the period recognize this. Their strong sense of the continuity of their history is indicated by the fact that, as many indications show us, historical controversies about the figures and conditions of a past generation were regarded as having a direct application to the problems of their own age. Plato makes Socrates appeal to examples taken from a previous generation in order to emphasize conclusions about contemporary conditions just as freely as he appeals to examples from his own time. Isocrates constantly does the same : in one of his speeches he puts the question to the Athenians as expressing the present alternatives before them, whether they want to model themselves on the generation of the Persian War or the generation of the Deceleian War.[1]

[1] *De Pace,* 37.

122

And there is plenty of evidence for the fact that the figure of Alcibiades was the subject of a lively literary controversy for many years after his death. The controversy could hardly have attracted so much attention unless it had been felt to bear in some way on contemporary problems. Indeed, in modern times, too, we can find plenty of instances of what is really political propaganda taking the form of ostensibly historical work. So that the mere fact that Plato places his dialogues in a past period is no indication at all that they were not meant primarily to bear upon the conditions at the time of writing. Let us examine them on that assumption, and we shall find that in no point does it raise any difficulties : the discussions always apply at least as well to the later period as to the earlier. And we shall find a few points, not in themselves of great importance but significant for their bearing on the general purpose of the dialogues, in which they could only with great difficulty be made to apply to the earlier period at all.

Consider the *Gorgias*, the most important of the earlier dialogues in which political conditions are referred to. The general stricture made in that dialogue against contemporary statesmen is that they have no moral aim, indeed no consistent principle of action at all, but are satisfied to deal only with immediate problems ; and they handle even those from the point of view of what will please and attract the people at the moment, not of what will leave the citizens better men than they were before. No one could possibly suggest that Plato would have exempted the statesmen of his own age from such a criticism. The Seventh Letter makes it obvious that he would have applied it to them with particular emphasis.

It is the same if we consider the other features of the state of society assumed in the *Gorgias*. There is the enormous power attributed to the successful orators. ' Do they not ', says Polus, ' put to death any one they want to, and take away his property, and expel from the cities any one they like ? ' That is certainly at least as characteristic of the fourth century as of any earlier period. Isocrates echoes almost the same words in his advice to Timotheus.[1] Equally characteristic of the period is the uncertainty and insecurity of public life which is referred to in the dialogue. It is not only men like Socrates, unversed in oratory, who are in danger, but a politician like Callicles himself is no more certain of safety, for

[1] *Antidosis*, 141–145.

all his oratory, if popular feeling turns against him.   This is spoken of as the common fate of statesmen, and one which they have brought upon themselves.   For they have only used their power to gratify the immediate desires of the mob, and have never done anything to raise their standards of thought and behaviour.

If we recognize that it is only conjecture, and do not commit ourselves too seriously to it, we might use these indications to make a guess at the date of the dialogue.   No reader of this dialogue can fail to be struck by its difference from those which precede it and even, though to a lesser degree, from those which follow it.   Nowhere else do we find quite such a stern note of condemnation for the loose moral thinking and acting that are to be observed on all sides or such a sombre mood of despair of any good coming out of society as it actually is.   It is not that the opinions themselves change in later dialogues ; just the same view is expressed as an intellectual conviction, in the *Republic*.   But we get a very strong impression that emotionally it is felt with a greater intensity in the *Gorgias* than elsewhere.   And it is permissible to conjecture that the realization of the situation had come with a special shock to Plato at the time of writing this dialogue.   Certainly in the *Meno*, which would most naturally be taken to be a little later, the judgements of prominent statesmen are much more charitable.   Even in the *Republic* there seems rather more readiness to explain and understand and less readiness to condemn.

This does suggest that the *Gorgias* might be regarded as in some degree reflecting a mood induced by some special set of circumstances at some particular time.   And if we are to suppose that these circumstances were partly or wholly political, it would be reasonable to look for them in the circumstances which induced a similar mood, though expressed very differently, in Aristophanes when writing the *Ecclesiazusae*.[1]   It is evident that about 393 a wave of depression and disillusionment, natural enough in the circumstances of the time, was passing over the Athenian people.   And they were expressing it in their accustomed fashion by turning round on the orators and politicians who had previously enjoyed their favour.   The man, unknown to us, who had proposed and carried the adhesion of Athens to the anti-Spartan league had had to fly from the city.   The attack on Thrasybulus had begun,

[1] See especially ll. 169–203.

and for the time being he had lost his influence and popularity. Does this not make us think of Socrates' warning to Callicles ? ' And when they have lost not only their recent gains but their former possessions as well, perhaps, if you are not careful, they will turn and attack you, and my friend Alcibiades as well.' Another event which was, we know, of recent occurrence at that time was the rise of Agyrrhius to popularity by his introduction of the three-obol fee for attendance at the Assembly. If the *Gorgias* was written at this time, its readers could not have missed the application of Socrates' remark about Pericles. ' This is what I hear,—that Pericles made the Athenians lazy and cowardly and loquacious and avaricious, by introducing them to the system of payment for public services.'

Such conjectures are no more than a harmless game. But when we turn to the *Republic*—the *Meno* adds little in this connection—there are more definite facts to deal with. And an examination of the allusions in that dialogue seem to make it highly probable that it cannot have been written before, at least, the first visit to Sicily. But before going on to that point, it is interesting to observe how the general historical development of the conditions in Greece helps to throw light on the arguments of the *Republic*. It is much easier to understand the emphasis—what might seem to us the over-emphasis—on unity if we look at the history of Athens from the point of view recommended above. If we watch the city over a long period gradually struggling out of the evils of disunity and divided loyalties, we can understand how the loss of this unity, so painfully attained, might seem the worst of all evils to be guarded against. We understand Plato's proposals better if we think of them as the consistent carrying on of the developments which had occupied the greatest part and the best part of the history of Athens.

In general we gain considerably in understanding of the argument if, without for a moment forgetting the wider application of its fundamental principles, we try to think of the circumstances of the time which might have brought that particular aspect of the truth to special prominence. And it is certainly, in most cases, easier to find such circumstances in the fourth century than during the first half of the Peloponnesian War. Consider, for instance, the qualifications for military service discussed in the Second Book. The realization of two points is brought out very clearly. On the one hand, there is the great increase of efficiency produced by the specialization of the function of fighting.    And, on the other, there is the great danger that such a specialized force, separated from the ordinary body of citizens, should lose all sense of unity and common loyalty with the rest of the city and should become a greater danger to the citizens than to the enemy. It does not seem unreasonable to suppose that the realization of both these points had been intensified by observation of the rapid growth of a class of mercenary soldiers in fourth-century Greece.    At any rate it is hard not to believe that his readers would have had this in mind, whatever Plato himself may have intended.

There is another passage where the application to fourth-century conditions is much more obvious.    That is the passage in the Fifth Book where Plato introduces a denunciation of warfare, particularly warfare of the usual ruthless kind, between Greeks, and a recommendation that this kind of warfare should be applied only to barbarians, that is to all non-Greeks.    Indeed, Greeks should avoid fighting against each other largely in order to save their energies for an attack on the barbarian : for barbarians and Greeks are natural enemies, and war between them is a natural and proper thing. This passage is introduced abruptly, and has no obvious connection with the rest of the argument, which could certainly dispense with it quite well.    The natural explanation of this is that the matter was very strongly in Plato's mind and that he felt impelled to introduce it somewhere, even if it was not particularly relevant.

He could hardly have had it in his mind by reflecting on the situation at the dramatic date of the dialogue.    Nor would Socrates have been particularly concerned to bring it into a discussion at that period.    For at that period the relation between Greeks and barbarians was nowhere a living and urgent problem at all.    It developed some degree of importance in the later years of the Peloponnesian War. But it was not really prominent in men's minds until the fourth century.    It became so to a special degree after the disgraceful peace of Antalcidas, in the year of Plato's return from his first visit to Syracuse, when the Persian king appeared to be dictating terms to the states of Greece as if they were his vassals.    It is clear that the revulsion of feeling after this humiliating incident was of great influence in strengthening the idea of a crusade of united Greece against Persia.

Isocrates, who devoted a large part of his energies to preaching this for the rest of his lifetime, first gave expression to the idea in the *Panegyricus*, published in 380. And Lysias had spoken in similar terms four years earlier.[1] The sudden intrusion of this appeal by Plato into the course of his argument in the *Republic* is most naturally to be understood as an effort to support the movement. His realization of the danger to Greek civilization from barbarian encroachments would probably have been powerfully reinforced by his visit to Syracuse. For there a series of wars with Carthage after seventy years of peace broke out before the end of the fifth century. And Dionysius had brought one such war to a conclusion just before Plato's arrival. Plato may also have been impressed by the constant state of danger in which the Greek cities in Italy lived from the pressure of various Italian tribes. Dionysius himself did not scruple to make common cause with these tribes against his enemies among the Greek cities.

But it is to his criticisms of existing constitutions, particularly in the Eighth and Ninth Books, that we should naturally turn for comment on contemporary conditions. And here we find descriptions so characteristic of the fourth century that we can say once more that, whatever Plato's intentions may have been, his readers must have taken them to apply to their own time. Thus they could hardly help making such an application when they read of the two cities of the rich and poor into which every city was divided. They could probably, too, think of many contemporary incidents which would support Plato's suggestion that a city like his ideal city could always hope to be victorious against an enemy by supporting the opposition party in it against the rulers of the moment. His study of revolutions and the causes of change from one constitution to another must have seemed particularly apposite to the period. Indeed, we can tell from the Seventh Letter that it seemed so to Plato himself. For he speaks of the Italian and Sicilian cities, which are unceasingly changing from one form of government to another, in terms which strongly remind us of his study of revolutions in the Eighth Book.

It is the same with his criticisms of particular constitutions.

[1] The arguments for this date for the Olympian Oration, as against the traditional 388, seem to me decisive. The allusions seem obviously to be to the state of affairs after the Peace of Antalcidas.

Of course a good many of them apply to no special period. His fundamental objection to democracy that it ignores the true principle of differentiation of functions is applicable to all Greek democracies, and indeed to the democratic ideal at any time and in any place. And the same criticism applies, as he points out, to the claims put forward for an oligarchy of wealth. There are other criticisms directed particularly against the evil effects of government by a mass meeting like the popular assembly. Such criticisms apply equally to any ancient Greek democracy at any time : they only apply to modern states so far as an element of mob rule enters into their politics. We may note, among other points, his account of the varying moods and tempers of the mob, of the undesirable arts that are called into play to control these moods and tempers, and of the corruption that this sort of life can bring even to the finest minds. All these are at least as applicable to the fourth century as to any other period.

There are some details which, though doubtless applicable to other periods, are particularly so to the fourth century. The description of the crowd of idle drones, the poor who live off the spoils of the rich and will not come together except to secure their share of the honey, has a special application to the democracy of this period. It suggests at once the payment for attendance at the Assembly which was only introduced in the fourth century : the reference to it becomes particularly obvious when we remember that, according to Aristotle, this measure had to be introduced because it was impossible to secure a proper quorum otherwise.[1] Similarly, when we turn to the oligarchic constitution, the description of the crowd of desperate men, disfranchised and in debt, a material ready to the hand of any leader of revolution, is of special application to the conditions of the fourth century in many Greek states.

There are certain details in the account of the democratic State which we cannot, with our limited knowledge, assign to any particular place or period. Such is the description of the lack of traffic regulations which allows the animals in the street to shoulder the passers-by out of the way. Again there is the mention of condemned criminals who go on living in the city in sublime disregard of the law. This last point, indeed, does not seem characteristic of anything that we know of Athens at any period. And that may warn us against the

[1] *Ath. Pol.*, 41.

mistake of trying to fit the account too exclusively to Athenian conditions. Plato was by now a widely travelled man and had connections with many different cities. He was addressing himself to a wider audience than his own citizens alone, and he would naturally draw on all his different experiences to support his conclusions. We have already seen reason to think that his observation of conditions in Italy and Sicily had particular influence in leading him to these conclusions.

This comes out particularly clearly when we turn to his account of the establishment and maintenance of a tyranny. For this has too close a resemblance to the details of the career of Dionysius I, for it to be possible seriously to doubt that Plato had him in his mind. It is extremely unlikely that Plato would have studied all the details of his career before he had actually visited Sicily. And that is but one more reason for thinking that the *Republic* must have been written after the first journey.

We need not suppose that Plato intended his account of a typical rise to tyranny to apply solely to the career of Dionysius. But it is noticeable how closely the two coincide. Dionysius seems to have begun his career as a popular orator and a champion of the people against the supposed designs of the rich. Then followed the alleged attack and the demand for a bodyguard, which was always the first necessity of a would-be tyrant. And so to the popular dictatorship which, once attained, was held whether the people wished it or no. So far the story is the same for many Greek tyrants. It would be as true of Pisistratus as of Dionysius. But the later developments as described by Plato are specially applicable to the latter, and some of them would not apply at all to Pisistratus. There are, of course, the foreign mercenaries, whom Plato knew from personal experience. There was the device of crushing the spirits of the citizens by the weight of taxation, which Aristotle in the *Politics* mentions as a method characteristic of Dionysius. There is the confiscation of the temple treasures, of which also Dionysius was guilty. And there was the constant stirring up of wars in order to make a strong leader essential, which was a common accusation against Dionysius, even though its justifiability may be doubtful. All these are mentioned by Plato in his account of the tyrant's rise. And all of them are characteristic of Dionysius, and some of them, so far as we know, of him alone. It seems impossible to doubt that the parallelism is intentional.

9

Above all, the conditions in a democracy which give occasion for the rise of a tyrant are described in very similar terms in the *Republic* to those used in the Eighth Letter when Plato is speaking expressly of the rise of Dionysius in Syracuse. It is the excess of liberty, we are told in the *Republic*, which is characteristic of a democracy and which opens the way to a tyranny. And in the Eighth Letter, speaking of the Syracusans, Plato talks of their ' insatiable appetite for liberty' and their ' unmeasured passion ' for it. ' They would obey no master,' he says, ' but would be free absolutely in every way. And it was from this that their tyrannies arose.'

As we are not attempting to investigate the whole of Plato's political theory, we need not linger over the *Politicus* and the *Laws*, partly because there are few, if any, references which imply a situation substantially different from that already considered, partly because no one doubts that such references as there are must be to the conditions of Plato's own time.

It is sometimes maintained that the judgement of democracy becomes much more favourable in these later dialogues. But this is only true to a very limited degree. In the *Politicus* Plato seems more impressed by its futility than by its positive mischievousness. He says that of relatively good constitutions, the good democracy is the least good. But a bad democracy is less capable of doing harm than a bad oligarchy or tyranny. That is hardly very enthusiastic praise. And in the *Laws*, though he advocates a degree of democracy, it is only on condition that none of the citizens should be allowed to engage in crafts or trades, which have to be carried on by non-citizens. On this point the view in the *Laws* differs from that in the *Republic*. But the difference is only on a point of detail. The essential principle that the work of production should be in different hands from the work of controlling the State is preserved in both. And that is the general impression left by a careful study of the relations between the *Republic* and the later dialogues in regard to their political principles. The fundamental principles are the same throughout. The differences are only what we should expect from the different purposes of the dialogues.[1]

---

[1] One alleged difference that has been discovered by some scholars between the *Republic* and the *Politicus* disappears on closer examination. It has been maintained on the strength of the passage beginning at 262D, that in the *Politicus* Plato asserted the distinction between Hellenes and barbarians to be merely conventional and to have no

The general conclusion is that an examination of the political discussions in the dialogues throws no doubts at all on the hypothesis which is adopted in this work, that Plato meant the dialogues to apply to the problems of his own time. On the contrary it strongly confirms it. Even if we could imagine Plato himself being seriously interested in the purely historical reconstruction of a past period, we have seen how unlikely it would be that his readers would be able to look on his work in that light. There would be so many points in which it would be obvious and natural to see some allusion to contemporary conditions. And, if we admit that his readers would have seen these allusions, we can hardly doubt seriously that they must have occurred to Plato himself.

natural basis. But he asserts nothing of the sort. What he is really protesting against is the habit of lumping all non-Greeks, regardless of the great differences between them, into one class which has nothing in common but the mere negative fact of not being Greek. He throws no doubt at all on the importance of the characteristics which distinguished the Greeks from other races. We can see from the letters written about this time how acutely conscious of it he was.

# PART III

# THE LITERARY AND PHILOSOPHICAL BACKGROUND

## CHAPTER X

### THE SOCRATIC LITERATURE

ANY discussion of the literary background of Plato's work must necessarily be disconnected and inadequate. For we know only a fraction of the contemporary literature. There is no question that if the bulk of it had been preserved, Plato's work would stand out far more clearly against the more detailed background. This applies mainly, of course, to the strictly philosophical and scientific writings. But we should learn much also from the recovery of the more general literature. Thus, for instance, if we knew enough of it to detect the main artistic tendencies of the period, we might understand more clearly what seems to us Plato's severe attitude towards art and poetry and literature generally. Here, once more, his main argument has reference to any period in which these things exist at all. But his special emphasis on it would appear, perhaps, less unsympathetic than it usually does if we could see it as a reaction against certain tendencies which were developing particular force at that time.

We are not without certain hints that this may have been so. What is chiefly characteristic of Plato's attitude in the matter is his strong opposition to all the tendencies which in modern times have been summed up in the phrase, Art for Art's sake. He was concerned to make his protest against the idea that any particular artistic activity could claim an autonomy for its own aims and standards, apart from the activities of society and ' the good life ' as a whole. Thus he could never admit the legitimacy of admiring and enjoying literature for the beauty and perfection of the form apart from the truth and rightness of what it said. This comes out both in his criticism of the false teaching of Homer and the poets and in his attack on the oratory which practised the art of persuasion irrespective of the rightness or wrongness of the cause which it served.    It comes out, too, in his attitude to music.    Music has been acclaimed in modern times as the art in which the perfection of pure form, with no reference to anything beyond, was attained.    But this was just its danger in Plato's eyes.    And in the *Laws* we find that music is not allowed except in the form of simple and appropriate accompaniments to the words of songs.

Whatever may have been the situation with regard to music, there is some evidence that literature about this period was showing signs of developing the tendencies to which Plato would have most objected.    There does seem to have been an increasing interest in and admiration for the pure literary form apart from the views expressed and apart, even, from the subject treated.    Of course, in a sense, the great growth in the influence and popularity of oratory was itself a move in that direction.    For the success of oratory depended on its form, not on the merits of the thoughts expressed.    But we see it more clearly in what we hear of some of the rhetorical essays of the time.    For they clearly depended purely on the literary skill of their expression and not at all on the interest and value of their theme.    That would be true even of the studies on some of the well-worn subjects of mythology and legend, Isocrates' Praise of Helen or Polycrates' Defence of Busiris.    In his discussion of these Isocrates conveys the impression that it is not the subjects themselves that matter but what clever writers can find to say about them.    But it would be still more obviously true of some of the trivialities of which he tells us, the essays in praise of salt or bumble-bees.    These are the first symptoms of that purely literary civilization into which the classical world declined at some periods of its later history.

We are, of course, a long way from that yet.    And another feature of the literature of the period is the tendency to use the figures of history and legend as instruments for the inculca-tion of moral truths.    There is, of course, nothing new in the practice of drawing a moral from the behaviour of past ages. But what does seem to be new was the degree of freedom exercised in re-writing the history of these past ages in order to make it point the moral.    When the practice began is uncertain.    In one form it goes back at least to the earlier half of the Peloponnesian War.    The purely fictitious constitution of Draco, which Aristotle accepted as historical fact and included in his history of the Athenian Constitution, is recognized to be the programme of the oligarchic reformers of that period, presented in the guise of history. But another form which the tendency took is of more interest to us in this connection. This was the device of taking some figure of history or legend and working it up into the shape of the ideal expression of some movement or point of view which the writer desired to advance. We have already seen indications that the figure of Aspasia was thus worked up into the ideal of the emancipated woman. How much historical truth there was in this presentation of her we have no material for judging. Later historians like Plutarch took a good deal of their information from literary sources of the type we are now considering and therefore cannot be used for checking them. But if we can judge from the one piece of literature of this kind that is still extant in a complete form, such writers would have felt no hesitation in departing as widely from historical fact as their desire to make their point demanded.

This is the famous *Cyropaedia* of Xenophon. In form a biography of Cyrus, the first king of Persia, it is in fact an attempt to draw a picture of Xenophon's ideal ruler and of the kind of training that might produce him. With an undisguised openness, which cannot have been meant to deceive, Xenophon departs, on occasion, widely from the known historical truth. The work is, indeed, frankly a historical novel, though written for purposes of edification rather than amusement, and it can never have been meant to be taken for anything else. Now Xenophon does not impress us as a man of great originality, so that we can hardly ascribe to him the invention of this form of literary device. It is much more likely that he used it because it was already familiar and recognized. We have considered the possibility that the figure of Aspasia was used in somewhat the same way. And we know that Antisthenes, who has been thought by some scholars to have been the chief influence on Xenophon, used the legendary figure of Heracles and the historical figure of this same Cyrus as the types of the life and the virtues which he was upholding. A kind of deliberate hagiography was growing up, the creation of patron saints for this and that creed.

Some scholars have been so much impressed by the liberties which writers of the period were ready to take with historical figures that they have carried their suspicions to extravagant

lengths.  They have applied it in particular to the portraits
of Socrates that have come down to us.  And they have
presented us with the conclusion that we have practically
no information about the historical Socrates at all, but only a
series of literary figures, each one composed in this way in the
interest of some school or group.  Though the extreme forms
of this point of view have little to recommend them, they
have at least this value, that they force us to face the question
of the nature of that large mass of Socratic literature of which
Plato and Xenophon are almost the sole survivors.

Besides these authors we have fragments of Socratic dialogues by Aeschines, and still smaller fragments of the works
of Antisthenes, some of which were probably not Socratic
dialogues at all.  We have the names of alleged works by
other intimate friends of Socrates, some of which are certainly
spurious and some, at the least, very doubtful.  But these
were evidently only a fraction of the Socratic literature which
existed in the fourth century.  Xenophon, for instance, speaks
of a number of different accounts that had appeared, prior
to the publication of his own *Apology*, of Socrates' defence
at his trial and of his behaviour during the last days of his
life.  We may suppose that his friends started to write about
him immediately after his death.  But the literature was
not all on one side.  The best known of the anti-Socratic
writings was the accusation of Socrates by the sophist Polycrates.  This was cast in the form of the speech for the prose-
cution made by Anytus at the actual trial.  But from allusions
to later events made in it it was evidently actually composed
some time after 392.  It is this pamphlet that Xenophon
was answering in the first book of the *Memorabilia*.  There is
a brief mention of it by Isocrates in his *Busiris*, and—probably
—a much fuller reply to it by Libanius, a rhetorician of the
fourth century A.D.  We can get a fair idea from these sources
of the general line of argument adopted in the pamphlet.
But we have nothing but pure conjecture to help us to solve
the problem of the relation of this work to the actual attack
on Socrates made by his accusers at the trial.  Besides this
Xenophon refers to the written and spoken criticisms of a
less severe kind, which suggested that Socrates might have
been capable of making men desire virtue, but that he gave
little help in the actual attainment of it.

In making conjectures—for we can do little more—about
the purpose of all this Socratic literature we must not fall into

the error of ascribing a precisely similar purpose to all of it. It is a good thing to remember the readiness of some writers of the period to idealize and even distort altogether the historical figures with which they dealt, in the manner suggested above. But we must also remember that there were historians and biographers writing at the time as well as philosophers and moralists. If Xenophon wrote the *Cyropaedia* he also wrote the *Agesilaus*. It is true that the desire to glorify the memory of an admired friend might also lead to idealization and even distortion. But it would be a different form of distortion, and could not depart so openly from historical fact as in the other case. Discussion about the actual condemnation of the real historical Socrates would, for some time, at any rate, have been just as likely to arouse interest as discussion of a moral ideal personified by a literary figure of Socrates. Indeed, the line between the two might not always be easy to draw, particularly for those who regarded themselves as followers of an ideal which they had learned from Socrates. We should therefore naturally expect to find all degrees of historical accuracy in the Socratic writings. A brief consideration of what we know of them, apart from Plato, may help to confirm this expectation.

## XENOPHON

The best known of these writers is, of course, Xenophon. Of Xenophon's life we know a considerable amount, mainly from his own account. But on the point that most concerns us here, the extent of his knowledge of Socrates, our evidence is uncertain. It cannot have been a very long acquaintance. For Xenophon was probably some years younger than Plato : he emphasizes his youth more than once in the *Anabasis*. And he was, of course, absent on this expedition during the last two years of Socrates' life. But he may well have enjoyed several years of acquaintanceship with him, and he evidently knew him well enough to ask his advice about going on the expedition. On the other hand, he nowhere represents himself as among the most intimate circle of Socrates' friends, and he probably owed as much of his knowledge of him to the accounts of others as to his own observation.

As a writer Xenophon must be pronounced a typical journalist, of the better sort. He has an easy and pleasant style, and an eye for the picturesque. He enjoys discovering a fact, but we get the impression that he would not consider it worth the effort of too long and painful research. As a historian he allows himself to be influenced by his political sympathies, and often slurs over or even omits facts which it would be unpleasant to him to record. But it must be said to his credit that modern critics have not succeeded in convicting him of any serious sins of commission or positive misstatements of facts. As a Socratic, Xenophon has had the great misfortune to get mixed up in the modern controversies on this question. He has naturally been an important witness. And, as such, he has been handled by the eminent advocates who have appeared on one side or the other in the case in a way which may seem to have left him not a shred of reputation. But we know by experience that forensic methods of handling a witness are not always the best methods of eliciting the truth. And he deserves a more generous and more impartial treatment than he has received in some modern discussions of the subject.

In considering the Socratic writings of Xenophon it is convenient to begin with the one about which there is least dispute. No modern scholar suggests that the *Oeconomicus* is meant as a representation of the historical Socrates. Indeed, it is only in the first part of this dialogue that Socrates is the principal figure. He is replaced in the latter half by Ischomachus. And Ischomachus, though the name may have been that of an actual person, is here obviously the ideal country gentleman. He represents, if not precisely Xenophon, at least Xenophon as he would have liked to imagine himself. But even in the earlier part Socrates is clearly discussing the subjects that Xenophon was specially interested in and expressing the views that Xenophon would have wished to express about them. He is even represented as displaying knowledge about the battle of Cunaxa which he could hardly have possessed, but which would, of course, be particularly familiar to Xenophon. So that the *Oeconomicus* is undoubtedly a treatise on husbandry or farm and household management, expressing Xenophon's views, but cast in the form of a Socratic dialogue. It probably has but little connection with the historical Socrates.

The *Symposium* also is undoubtedly a fiction, in the sense that the conversations were composed by Xenophon himself, and quite probably the meeting described was itself his own invention. He begins by saying that he was present at it, but, as far as we know, he would have been an infant at the time at which it is set. In any case, he takes no part in any of the conversations. But it is a fiction of a different kind from the *Oeconomicus*. It is not written with any didactic purpose, or to advocate any particular point of view. The traces of special doctrines which some scholars claim to have detected in it are too slight to be taken seriously. It is rather a 'slice of life', a naturalistic representation of a typical convivial gathering at Athens. We can see from other works that Xenophon was fond of picturing this kind of scene. The characters in it are all real people, most of whom were probably, at a later date, known to Xenophon personally. It is probable, therefore, that he attempted to preserve some kind of verisimilitude in his account of their manner of talking and the views that they expressed. There would have been little or no point in distorting these. On the other hand, the speeches are clearly his own composition, though he may have incorporated in them remarks that he had actually heard on different occasions. It is, in short, his general impression of the characters and points of view of the persons represented which is given us. How much reliance we place on it depends upon our view of his abilities firstly for forming a correct impression, and secondly for conveying it to others by his description.

But when we turn to the *Memorabilia*,—with which, for what it is worth, may be associated the *Apology*,—we are at the centre of controversy. For the *Memorabilia* differs in form, not only from the other writings of Xenophon, but from all the other Socratic writings that we know anything about. It introduces itself expressly as an attempt to defend the memory of Socrates, particularly against the attacks of 'the accuser', who is now universally identified, not with the actual prosecutors of Socrates, but with Polycrates, the author of the pamphlet referred to above. It answers with reasoned argument some of the accusations which it quotes from this source, and gives in Xenophon's own words a summary of Socrates' character and mode of life. This is a kind of introduction to the work, and the same method of presentation reappears at intervals throughout, particularly in the last book. There are also a few isolated sayings of Socrates quoted, and a few of the definitions that he gave of various general notions. And the rest of the work consists of a series of conversations on different topics with different people. There are only a few of them which Xenophon claims to have heard himself, and only one in which he actually took part. On one point—the behaviour of Socrates in his last days—

a definite authority, Hermogenes, is quoted, both in the *Memorabilia* and the *Apology*, as having given Xenophon his information.[1] Most of the subjects discussed and views advanced are connected with one or other point in the general defence of Socrates at the beginning and are, sometimes expressly, put forward as illustrations of these points. A few, such as the discussions on military matters, have no very obvious connection with this, but are, of course, connected with the special interests of Xenophon.

Looking at the work as a whole, then, it seems impossible to deny that it makes claims that works such as the dialogues of Plato and Aeschines do not. It is not primarily presented, like these works, as a dramatic composition, but as an attempt to answer a series of charges actually made against a historical personage. As such, it would have no point unless it was true to the facts. It is presented to us as history. And this fact by itself is sufficient to account for our natural tendency in first reading it to exclaim, Or here or nowhere is the historical Socrates. The fact that this impression has been further supported in the past by some very bad arguments ought not to be allowed to obscure the strength that it receives from a mere inspection of the form of the work.

But the bad arguments that have been advanced to support the claims of the *Memorabilia* could not possibly be worse than some of the arguments that have been brought against these claims. Few scholars show at their best in dealing with Xenophon. There seems to be something about him which makes even the wisest of them lose all sense of evidence. And there can be few cases in which so many arguments have been brought forward with confidence which have in reality no weight at all. Thus, sentiments ascribed to Socrates sometimes resemble those expressed by Xenophon himself elsewhere in his writings. And it is at once assumed that Xenophon must have invented them. But it ought to be obvious that the facts are just as naturally explained by supposing that on some points he held the same opinions as Socrates, very likely owing to the effects of his influence.

[1] Perhaps statistics may be of interest. There are about forty conversations recorded, allowing for occasional possibilities of dispute about what constitutes a conversation. Five are introduced by a positive assertion, ἤκουσα or παρεγενόμην. Five more are introduced by οἶδα : how much that implies I am uncertain. One suggests a personal impression : ἐδόκει ἐμοὶ λέγων. One quotes Hermogenes. The rest—about thirty—make no claim.

Again, there are points on which Xenophon's picture of Socrates resembles closely that given by Plato. Why is it necessary to suppose, as some scholars do, that Xenophon must have been dependent on Plato for the information? There is nothing very strange in the fact that two writers might give a similar picture of the same person, even if they were independent of each other.

This question of Xenophon's debt to Plato has produced some of the most eccentric arguments. Thus in Xenophon's *Apology* Socrates is represented as stroking Apollodorus' head while making some remark. Because Plato in the *Phaedo* represents Socrates as stroking Phaedo's head, while making an entirely different remark in an entirely different connection, it has been said, and by a very great scholar, that Xenophon must have copied the incident from Plato. Again, Xenophon puts a criticism of Anaxagoras into the mouth of Socrates which has no single point in common with the well-known criticism ascribed to Socrates in the *Phaedo* and indeed suggests an entirely different attitude towards Anaxagoras. And yet it has been argued, on the sole ground, apparently, that Anaxagoras is mentioned in both passages, that here again Xenophon must have copied from Plato. Such arguments are hardly to be taken seriously. Of course we need not doubt that Xenophon read Plato. In fact, there are some unmistakable references to Plato's *Symposium* in the *Symposium* of Xenophon. But in the *Memorabilia*, although the general picture is often similar, the close verbal resemblances to anything in Plato are extraordinarily small. In general there is not the slightest real evidence that Plato was a principal or even an important source for Xenophon's picture of Socrates.

Of the more serious arguments against the historical character of the *Memorabilia*, we may distinguish two main kinds —those directed to prove that Xenophon did not himself intend his account to be taken as history, and those which argue that, while it was put forward as history, it is to be regarded as bad and unreliable history.

The first point is very difficult to maintain in view of the form of the work. It is true that some of the conversations in it are prefaced by an assertion that Xenophon heard them expressed in exactly the same phrase as that which opens the obviously fictitious *Oeconomicus*.[1] But the significance of the phrase cannot legitimately be judged apart from its context.

---

[1] ἤκουσα δέ ποτε αὐτοῦ καὶ περὶ . . . διαλεγομένου.

It is not the use of the phrase by itself that makes us believe that Xenophon intended his account to be historically accurate, but the general setting of the account, which is expressly presented as a defence of Socrates against an actual accusation. Nor is there any real justification for doing what is often done and separating up the different sections of the work, taking the general description of Socrates as meant historically and the conversations as avowedly fictions. The two are mixed up in a way that would make it hard to separate them. And in any case Xenophon presumably meant something by putting them together in the same book, unless, indeed, we suppose, without the slightest evidence, that it was done after his death by some later editor.

On the other hand, it is obviously not to be supposed that the conversations are verbatim reports taken down at the time. Xenophon only claims to have heard a few of them. And some of them obviously—as, for instance, when Socrates reproves his son for ingratitude towards his mother—would not have been held in the presence of a third party at all. Nor can we suppose that Xenophon knew before he left Athens in 401 that he was going to write anything about Socrates, and therefore took notes at the time. His work was begun some ten years or more after Socrates' death.

But this does not mean that Xenophon invented the whole thing from beginning to end. The simple and natural supposition—much too simple and natural for some of our more ingenious scholars—is that he collected his material in the same manner as he would collect material for his history. The *Hellenica* and *Agesilaus* give us the true standard by which to judge of the *Memorabilia*, not the *Oeconomicus* nor yet the *Cyropaedia*. He would use his own memory as far as it went. He would use other written sources, with some of which he was evidently familiar. And there is no reason at all to doubt that he would be able to collect, at first or second hand, verbal reports from some of those who remembered Socrates. But there is another thing that the comparison with the *Hellenica* might suggest. That is, that, when it came to reports of speeches or conversations, Greek historians allowed themselves a considerable degree of latitude in working up their material in their own way. Even Thucydides feels free, as he tells us, ' to put into the mouth of each speaker the sentiments appropriate to the occasion, expressed as I thought he would be likely to express them '. He adds, of course, that as far as possible he tries to give what they actually said.  But he admittedly does not confine himself to this.  And Thucydides was far more careful and accurate than Xenophon would ever think it necessary to be.  So while we may believe that in every case some conversation of the kind recorded took place, the actual words employed are probably very largely Xenophon's own, though he would try to make Socrates speak as would seem to him appropriate to his habit of speaking, and there may well be at times reminiscences of phrases actually used.[1]

As to Xenophon's qualifications as a biographer, there is little that can be said with confidence.  Of course, there must have been a good deal of selection, and he would be largely guided in his selection by what appealed particularly to his own tastes and interests.  It is to that, perhaps, that we owe the emphasis on the common sense and sound judgement shown by Socrates in practical affairs.  Of course to some modern scholars this quality has seemed unworthy of what they think Socrates must have been, and the emphasis on it has been held to cast suspicion on Xenophon's account.  But this mode of arguing is very dangerous.  We have really no right to set up our own standards and insist that there must be something wrong with a writer who does not conform to them.  A good deal of the greatest Greek literature might be disposed of in that way.  And it is therefore wise not to be too ready to doubt the accuracy of Xenophon's picture because his Socrates sometimes seems a little commonplace and obvious by our present-day standards, or because his morality sometimes seems rather pedestrian and utilitarian.

On the other hand, Xenophon was obviously not a very profound or original thinker, though he was quick-witted enough.  And he was therefore very likely not greatly interested in profound or original speculations.  It is true, also, that he wrote as an apologist of Socrates, to defend him against certain charges, and that his material would be selected

[1] The kind of thing that I imagine taking place might be illustrated from the scene described in *Mem.*, III, x, when Socrates visits the painter, the sculptor and the armourer.  We may imagine Xenophon's informant saying, ' I remember once going with Socrates into Pistias' shop, and he seemed as interested in his work, asking questions and so on, as if he had been an armourer himself.  And he seemed to grasp as well as Pistias himself what made a good fit in a breastplate.'  This would be quite sufficient basis for the passage in which Xenophon— not very successfully in this case—tries to throw his information into the form of an actual conversation.

and arranged with that end in view. But the bearing of this fact has been sometimes misunderstood. It would mean, no doubt, that if Xenophon knew of anything about Socrates which would have seemed to him—Xenophon—unworthy or discreditable, he would have been very likely to suppress it. But it does not mean that he would have had any motive at all to suppress anything that might possibly excite prejudice against Socrates among sections of the Athenian public. He was not writing to appeal to the Athenian public in particular, but for the whole of the educated public of Greece, and in particular for those who would be interested to hear about Socrates.

These conclusions, then, seem reasonable : (1) The *Memorabilia* is on a different footing from the *Oeconomicus* and the *Symposium*, and must be judged by different standards. (2) It is intended to be a defence of the actual Socrates, and must therefore have been intended to be taken as historically correct. (3) There are not likely to be any intentional misstatements in it, and the general picture conveyed by it is probably correct, as far as it goes. (4) There may be misunderstandings on particular points, but if they are suspected it ought to be possible to give a reasonable explanation of how they might have arisen and what facts they were based on. (5) There are very probably some omissions, but it is not safe to assume any particular ones, unless there is strong and definite evidence from other sources. Above all, we must never assume an omission in order to justify us in putting in something which would make Socrates resemble more closely what we personally should like him to have been.

## NOTE TO CHAPTER X
### RECENT LITERATURE ON XENOPHON

As Xenophon is handled somewhat cursorily in the text, it may be of interest to those who wish to pursue the subject further to give a brief survey of some of the recent work that has been done on the subject. There is a vast Xenophontic literature, of which I do not pretend to have read more than a small fraction. Of course, as many of these writings discuss or answer each other, it is possible to derive from the study of a selection of them a good deal of second-hand knowledge of the arguments brought forward in others. I mention here only works (1) that I have read myself, (2) that are of a comparatively recent date, i.e. with the partial exception of one of them, they all fall within the present century, and (3) that deal directly with Xenophon as a biographer of Socrates. There are, of course, many incidental comments of interest to be found in works primarily concerned with some other subject. I omit also standard histories of Greek literature or philosophy. Of these, perhaps, Gomperz is of most interest in this particular connection.

(1) K. Joel, *Der echte und der xenophontische Sokrates*, 3 vols., 1893–1901. This is one of the works that began the attack on Xenophon which marks so much of the modern literature. Its main thesis is that Xenophon's Socrates is simply a literary figure, drawn in the interests of Antisthenes and his school. Almost everything reported by Xenophon of Socrates is represented here as Antisthenean. It is a work of great erudition, and there are undeniably arguments of importance to be found in it for those who take the trouble to look for them. But I think most readers of the work agree that the writer is obsessed by the Antisthenes theory, and in advocating it shows too often little sense of the difference between a precarious hypothesis and an established fact. The logical connection of the argument is often extremely tenuous. And the book as a whole is very diffuse and prolix, and far from easy reading.

(2) L. Robin, *Les Mémorables de Xénophon et notre connaissance de la philosophie de Socrate* (Année philosophique, 1910), with which may be associated (3) Burnet, *Plato's Phaedo*, particularly pp. xii–xxiii, and (4) A. E. Taylor, *Varia Socratica*, particularly ch. i. I group these together as being typical of the anti-Xenophon polemics. The fact that three of the greatest Platonic scholars of the age take such an unfavourable view of Xenophon is no doubt in itself impressive. But personally I find that the impressiveness is considerably diminished when I study their arguments. For with the best will in the world I cannot regard them as anything but forensic advocacy, of a very clever kind, but in general unconvincing. So many of the arguments seem to rest on mere hypotheses, on purely personal impressions, and on the magnification of quite trivial details, which cannot really bear all the sinister significance which is found in them. Robin, in particular, who makes a sweeping attack on the whole of Xenophon's personality, moral and intellectual alike, gives the impression throughout of arguing to a brief.

On the other side, we have (5) H. v. Arnim, *Xenophon's Memorabilien und Apologie des Sokrates*, published in the Proceedings of the Danish Academy for 1923. This is a very careful and ingenious defence of Xenophon's credibility, and certainly deals successfully with some of the criticisms that have been made against him. But it has two weaknesses. It deals almost exclusively with the hostile arguments of one man, H. Maier. And it confines its attention in the main to points of detail, and is much less satisfactory on questions of general probability.

(6) A. Diès, *Autour de Platon*, Book II, chs. i and iv. Admirable in its fairness and impartiality, like all the work of this writer ; but it confines itself mainly to an account of the current literature on the subject.

(7) E. C. Marchant's introduction to his translation of the *Memorabilia* and the *Oeconomicus* in the Loeb series. This seems to me the most sensible thing that I have seen written on Xenophon, though I would not commit myself to agreement with it on all points. But it is far too short to deal with the subject as fully as we should like this author to deal with it.

Perhaps I might also mention (as 8) the chapter on Xenophon in T. R. Glover, *From Pericles to Philip*. Critical questions are not discussed there in detail, but it is instructive as showing that a historian quite as competent to judge as any of those quoted can form a very much more favourable impression of Xenophon both as a man and a writer.

10

# CHAPTER XI

## THE SOCRATIC LITERATURE (*continued*)

### AESCHINES [1]

THE only other Socratic writings which we possess now are the few fragments that remain of the dialogues of Aeschines of Sphettus. About Aeschines himself we know but little. We have no information about his age : he was probably approximately a contemporary of Plato. He is mentioned together with him in the *Apology*, as one of the young men who associated with Socrates, and his father is spoken of as still alive at the time and present in court. Aeschines is also mentioned in the *Phaedo* as present at the death of Socrates. So we are justified in regarding him as one of the more intimate circle of Socrates' closest friends. Later stories speak of his poverty, and he is said to have become eventually a courtier dependent on the bounty of Dionysius at Syracuse. According to one version he was introduced there by Plato. We know from the fragments of a speech of Lysias that at some period he tried to keep himself by starting a business in the manufacture and sale of perfumes, and that he borrowed money for the purpose. The speech, which is written for his opponent, accuses him of habitually failing to pay his debts, and also of scandalous misconduct with the elderly wife of a trade competitor. But we need not accept as gospel all the statements that were made in the law courts.

His writings were greatly admired in antiquity. All who mention them praise their literary qualities. Aristides, the rhetor of the second century A.D., to whom we owe the preser-

---

[1] In my treatment of Aeschines I am largely indebted to two German scholars, H. Krauss, who edits the fragments with introduction and commentary in the Teubner series, and H. Dittmar, who gives a study of Aeschines and also a collection of the fragments in the *Philologische Untersuchungen*, edited by Wilamowitz under the title *Aeschines von Sphettus*. This last work is a very complete study of the literary connections of Aeschines, and contains interesting suggestions and valuable material. But it shows rather a fondness for unproved hypotheses, and in general I have relied more on the soberer judgement of Krauss.

vation of most of the fragments, makes a point of their historical accuracy, for which he compares them favourably
with the work of Plato. But there are slight indications that
his contemporaries regarded them more as moral treatises than
as biographical sketches. The speech of Lysias speaks of him
as ' the author of many noble discourses on justice and virtue ',
which would not be a very natural mode of speaking of works
whose intention was mainly historical. On the other hand,
there are no suggestions, either in the fragments or in the
remarks of later writers, that Aeschines belonged to any
philosophical school or ever developed any original theories
of his own. We may, therefore, reasonably conjecture that,
while not intended to give an account of conversations which
actually took place, the dialogues were intended to represent
the kind of thing that Socrates thought and said. And they
probably did represent this, as far as Aeschines' impression of
it was reliable. It is very difficult to judge how far this was
so. The fragments do not give us a very exciting picture of
Socrates. But at least we can suppose that Aeschines was
free from the temptation which would beset a really original
thinker of developing the implications of Socrates' arguments
on his own lines.

The only works of Aeschines of which we have record are
seven dialogues, all of them, so far as we know, introducing
Socrates as the principal figure. The titles of them are
*Alcibiades, Axiochus, Aspasia, Callias, Miltiades, Rhinon,
Telauges.* We have far fuller remains of the first named than
of any other, preserved partly by Aristides and partly in a
papyrus from Oxyrhynchus.[1] As the work of Aeschines is
not very familiar to English readers, it may be of interest to
give here a complete translation of the extant fragments of
this dialogue. From this it should be possible to judge something of the picture of Socrates that he gives.

The conversation appears to be narrated by Socrates. The
first part of it is between him and Alcibiades, but there are
some remarks at the end about Alcibiades and Socrates' feeling
towards him evidently addressed to another person. One
would naturally suppose that this is the person to whom
Socrates relates the story of the main conversation. This
main conversation is begun, as far as we can gather, by the
young Alcibiades vaunting himself on his natural gifts, claiming, perhaps, that these are enough to qualify him to play

[1] *Oxyrhynchus Papyri,* Part xiii.

a great part in the city without any further knowledge and training. In the course of this some reference is made to Themistocles. And the first fragment that we possess begins. according to the most convincing restoration, thus :

' " Would you care to behave to your parents as Themistocles is said to have behaved to his ? " " Hush, Socrates," he said.'

The argument probably is that Themistocles showed undesirable traits in his youth, and that, therefore, his later greatness could not have been attained by the natural gifts, which Alcibiades thinks of as sufficient, but demanded the acquirement of knowledge and training. It goes on in a manner familiar to readers of Plato :

' Do you consider that men have to begin by being ignorant of music before they become musicians ? Or ignorant of horsemanship before they become good riders ? ' ' I think they have to begin by first being ignorant of music and horsemanship.'

In a later fragment Alcibiades expresses doubts whether Themistocles can really have been so stupid, even in youth, as to have quarrelled so violently with his father that the latter disinherited him. There is evidently some further discussion about Themistocles, in the course of which Alcibiades lets fall some slighting remarks about him. And then in the next and longest fragment Socrates takes up the tale again.

' Knowing that he is inclined to feel jealous of Themistocles, I said, " Since you have ventured to attack the life of Themistocles, consider what sort of man it is that you have thought fit to criticize. Think where the sun rises and where it sets." " Well, there is no difficulty about knowing that sort of thing, Socrates," he said. " Then has it ever occurred to you that all that tract of land called Asia, which is as great in extent as the sun's journey, is ruled by one man ? " " Of course," he said, " the King of Persia." '

Then Socrates gives an account of the Persian attack on Greece, and tells how the whole hope of the Athenians rested on Themistocles.

' And he did not let himself be dismayed by the great superiority of the king's resources in wealth and ships and men over the Greeks. He knew that unless the king showed himself wiser in counsel than his opponent, all his great superiority in every other respect would avail him nothing. . . . And on the day on which the king met a worthier man than himself, on that day he had to recognize that his was the weaker side.'

Socrates goes on to emphasize the extraordinary astuteness of Themistocles in making personal connections with the king, even while he was engaged in fighting against him, so that later, when he was banished, he was able to take refuge at his court and attain there a position of wealth and power.

' " Bear in mind, then, Alcibiades," I said, " that even for such a man as that his knowledge was not sufficient, great though it was, to protect him from disgrace and banishment at the hands of his city : it fell short of what was needed.  What do you think it must be like, then, with inferior men who take no such pains with themselves ?  Is it not surprising if they achieve even the smallest success ?  Do not, then, Alcibiades," I said, " accuse me of taking up a shocking atheistical attitude towards the gifts of fortune and the work of the gods, if I ascribe to Themistocles full knowledge of all he achieved, and deny that such achievements could be the work of mere good luck.  I could show you much rather that those who take the opposite view are the real atheists. For they suppose that good fortune comes alike to the evil and the good, and that the gods show no special favour to noble and pious men." '

Here the fragment ends.  But we have descriptions of what follows.  Socrates ends by bringing fully home to Alcibiades his inferiority to Themistocles and his lack of proper training and education.  He humbles him so successfully, that at last Alcibiades is reduced to tears, ' resting his head on his knees '. Finally he turns to Socrates to find out how to educate himself in the right way.

Socrates ends up by saying to another friend, either in recounting the conversation or after Alcibiades has gone :

' If I thought I knew some art by which I could do good to men, I should have charged myself with great folly : but, as it is, I thought that these things came to me as a divine gift for the sake of Alcibiades.  And there is nothing that calls for surprise in that. . . .  Through the love which I felt for Alcibiades I had had the same experience as the Bacchae.  For the Bacchae, when they are inspired, draw up milk and honey from the wells from which other people cannot even get water.  And so I too, though I have no science with which I could help a man by instructing him in it, nevertheless felt that by being with him I could make him better through my love for him.'

It is possible to conjecture the purpose of this dialogue. It is partly no doubt an exposition of how an ambitious youth could be brought to self-examination and self-criticism, by

Socratic methods, and so led on to self-improvement. But there can be little doubt that in this particular dialogue there was also a definitely apologetic purpose. For there is evidence that Socrates' relation to Alcibiades was a subject that excited great interest in the Socratic controversies of the time. It was an important element in the accusation of Polycrates that Socrates was responsible for Alcibiades' later development and all the evil he did. And it is quite likely that a similar accusation was also brought at the actual trial.[1] At any rate, it is evident that it excited much attention, and all the Socratic writers found it necessary to give some account of the relations of the two. The general lines of their defence seem to have been the same in all cases. They represented Socrates as anxious above all things for the conversion of Alcibiades to a proper frame of mind, and they try to show that the evil in the career of Alcibiades was due to his own natural tendencies, which proved too much for Socrates' efforts. Some of them seem to have dwelt with much emphasis on the evil tendencies of Alcibiades. We are told that Antisthenes charged him with every possible vice. And there is another dialogue of Aeschines, the *Axiochus*, about which we have practically no information except that in it there is a bitter attack on the dissolute life of Alcibiades.

Another dialogue of Aeschines of which we know something is the *Aspasia*. From fragments and allusions to it in later literature it is possible to make a plausible reconstruction of the plot. Socrates discusses the education of children with Callias and advises him to let his son learn from Aspasia. Callias expresses astonishment that Socrates should suggest that a man could be educated by a woman. In reply Socrates gives an account of the great achievements of some of the famous women in history. In particular, he emphasizes the achievements of Aspasia herself, her influence on the great Pericles, and her success in raising Lysicles, with whom she lived after Pericles's death, from comparative obscurity to a leading position in Athens. He further relates, as an illustration of her capacity for teaching right behaviour to men and to other women also, the story of her interview with Xenophon and his wife,—whether it is our well-known Xenophon or another, we cannot tell,—in which she reconciles

---

[1] Joel, *op. cit.*, argues that Polycrates must have been the first person to make this accusation. But the words which he quotes from Isocrates (*Busiris*, 222c) do not seem to imply as much as that.

them after a dispute and points out the proper attitude to adopt towards each other. A fragment of the conversation is preserved in a Latin translation by Cicero, and, though we do not know how faithful and literal the translation is, it certainly shows the main lines of the argument. As such it seems worth reproducing as the only connected fragment that we have from the dialogue.

' " Tell me, I beg, wife of Xenophon, if your neighbour should have a better piece of jewellery than you have, would you rather have that one or your own ? " " That one," she says. " And if a woman has a more valuable dress or other ornament than yours, would you rather have yours or hers ? " She replies, " Hers, of course." " Well, then," says Aspasia, " if she has a better husband than you have, would you rather have yours or hers ? " The lady blushed. And Aspasia took up the conversation with Xenophon himself. " Now, Xenophon," she says, " if your neighbour has a better horse than yours, would you prefer your horse or his ? " " His," he says. " And if he has a better farm than you have, which farm would you rather have ? " " The better one, I suppose," he says. " And if he has a better wife than you have, would you rather have your own or his ? " At this Xenophon also was silent. Then Aspasia went on : " Since neither of you will tell me the only thing I want to know, I will tell you what you have in mind. You, madam, want to have the best husband, and you, Xenophon, want above all things to have the most excellent wife. So, unless you succeed in making yourselves better than any other husband and wife in the world, you will never attain what you regard as the best thing of all." ' [1]

The *Aspasia* appears, then, to deal partly with the question of education in ' virtue ', but mainly with the advocacy of the claims of women. Of the other dialogues we know even less. From such indications as we have, we may conclude that they deal with allied subjects. They appear to treat of questions of moral education, the relation of parents and children,

---

[1] I have paraphrased this last sentence in order to bring out what I take to be the point of the argument, i.e. an exhortation to a joint effort in self-improvement : Xenophon gives his wife what she wants by making himself the best possible husband, and vice versa. The original runs : ' Quare nisi hoc perfeceritis, ut neque vir melior neque femina lectior in terris sit, profecto semper id, quod optimum putabitis esse, multo maxime requiretis, ut et tu maritus sis quam optimae et haec quam optimo viro nupta sit.' Victorinus paraphrases : ' Quare nisi et tu vir optimus fueris et tu femina lectissima, id est in gratiam regressi fueritis, semper et tibi uxor lectissima et tibi vir optimus deerit,' which seems to confirm the interpretation I have given.

wealth and poverty and their significance for the good life. It appears likely that in most of them Socrates is represented as using one or other of the famous figures of history as a model lesson, in the way in which he uses the example of Themistocles in the *Alcibiades*.

We must, of course, be very reserved in drawing conclusions from such scanty information. We should, for instance, probably get a much more favourable impression of Aeschines' power of description and character-drawing if we could read his dialogues as a whole. The fragments, it must be admitted, are rather dull and uninspiring. They give us no instances of the ironical humour of Socrates which the later writers of antiquity found in Aeschines as much as in Plato. So that we should probably find them more amusing if we had the dialogues complete. Whether we should find the arguments more profound than the rather commonplace specimens we have is more doubtful. But it does seem probable, taking all the evidence into account, that we should look in vain in them for any philosophical discussions. As far as we can judge, the Socrates of Aeschines even more than the Socrates of Xenophon is entirely occupied with problems of practical morality.

### PLATO AND THE SOCRATIC LITERATURE

An examination of the Socratic literature suggests that in the different examples of it we may find different motives at work on the part of the author : motives which, naturally enough, are sometimes combined in varying proportions. There is the biographical and apologetic interest : the two seem naturally combined, and the controversies about Socrates seem to have afforded the most potent motive for a historical treatment of him. There is the literary or dramatic interest, exemplified most obviously in Xenophon's *Symposium*, which is clearly aimed at drawing a lively picture of a scene. This interest is probably nearly always present in some degree, but here it seems to stand by itself. And there is the interest in the argument, in the subject discussed and the views expressed : the *Oeconomicus* is the most striking example of that interest at work. We do not know enough to say with certainty which interest predominated in the work of Aeschines. But, as there always seems to have been a definite problem discussed and views advanced, we must suppose that the last named generally at least played a prominent part. Sometimes, as in the *Alcibiades*, there seems to have been a reference to the controversies about Socrates. But, in general, Aeschines seems to have been one of those who acted on the view that the best defence and memorial of the master was to help in carrying on the discussions and investigations that he had been interested in. If in doing this, Aeschines, as later writers of antiquity supposed, never went very far beyond the historical Socrates, that would have been, as these same writers hint, because he had not got the originality of mind to make contributions of his own. The example of the *Oeconomicus* proves that a writer would not have felt any scruples about departing as far from the original as his purposes required.

The parallel of the other Socratic writers, therefore, shows no grounds for doubting the view of the Platonic writings advocated in this work. On the contrary, it provides instances of the most varying purposes for which a Socratic dialogue could be used. Which purpose we ascribe to any particular dialogue must be decided for us in the main by a study of the dialogue itself. And surely most people must feel in reading Plato that, with all his brilliant literary powers, his chief interest in the great majority of the dialogues lies in the arguments put forward and the subjects investigated. Can any one doubt in reading the *Gorgias*, for instance, that it was written with a real intensity of personal conviction in the truth of the views advocated there and in the importance of urging these views on the world ? But there are one or two exceptions to this general impression which suggest that at times Plato may have written with a different purpose in the forefront of his mind.

The *Apology*, for instance, is obviously on a different footing from the other dialogues, and is naturally to be taken as Plato's contribution to the controversies which centred round the real Socrates. What its exact place is in this literature is impossible to determine with any certainty. It has been maintained that it is Plato's report, as far as he remembered it, of the actual speech delivered by Socrates. And it has also been maintained that it is Plato's own composition written to defend Socrates against charges which were made, not at the actual trial, but in the course of subsequent controversies. It does not seem to have much reference to what we know of the pamphlet of Polycrates, the principal literary contribution on the anti-Socratic side. And there is one other point which suggests that it claimed, at any rate, to be a historical document. In none of the dialogues is Plato himself represented as present, and in many of them his presence would have been historically impossible. In the *Apology* alone is he described as present : indeed, his presence is definitely called attention to in a way which can hardly be merely accidental. These considerations suggest that the work is Plato's version of the actual speech. It need not, however, have been composed and published immediately after the trial. That is possible. But it is equally likely that Plato was led to publish it by the appearance of other inferior accounts of what happened, of which we know that there were several. There is really no way of deciding between these possibilities.[1]

There is one other dialogue of importance in which other interests seem to occupy a place at least as important as that occupied by the philosophical interest. And that is the *Symposium*. This also, though to a lesser degree, differs in form from the other dialogues. The serious argument occupies a relatively small place, there is a much greater amount of narrative, and in particular there is the intervention of Alcibiades which appears to have no philosophical bearing at all. It seems natural to suppose that in this dialogue, though he could not keep off philosophical discussion altogether, Plato was to a greater extent than usual yielding himself to the pure dramatic impulse and the mere pleasure in drawing a picture of a scene. But it can hardly be doubted that there was also present a serious apologetic intention, and that the Alcibiades passages were intended to put the relations of Socrates and Alcibiades in a light which would refute the accusations that had been made against Socrates in that connection.

One question still remains about which a word must be said, though it does not strictly fall within the scope of this work. That is the question of the relations of these other Socratic writers with Plato, from the point of view of our knowledge of Socrates. Does their picture differ substantially from the picture given by Plato ? And if it does, should it be used to correct it or check it ? It has been suggested in the preceding argument that a comparison of detailed points

---

[1] Von Arnim, *op. cit.*, gives arguments which certainly make it plausible to believe that Plato's *Apology* was published after Xenophon's *Apology* and before the *Memorabilia*.

in the different pictures is much less likely to throw light on the nature of Plato's dialogues than the general comparison with the objects pursued, as far as we can judge them, in the other Socratic writings as a whole. There seems a curious logical weakness in the arguments of those who seek to discredit the *Memorabilia* as intentional fiction in order to establish the reliability of Plato. In reality if Xenophon, in a work which definitely claims a historical character, felt justified in making up a purely fictitious account of Socrates, it would enormously increase the likelihood that Plato, in writings which make no such claim, should have done the same.[1] Even if we do not throw the *Memorabilia* overboard in this fashion, the existence of the obviously fictitious *Oeconomicus* is a far stronger argument against the historical character of Plato's account than any discrepancies of detail with the account of the *Memorabilia*.

It would take a detailed comparison which cannot be attempted here to establish fully the relation between the different pictures given of Socrates by these different writers. But if we do not look too closely at the details of individual arguments, but consider the general impression that Xenophon seems to be trying to convey by his account of various conversations, we shall find that it agrees very closely with the general impression that we get from most of Plato's dialogues. The general method of arguing, for instance, ascribed to Socrates by Xenophon (*Mem.* IV, vi, 13), is precisely the same as that illustrated by Plato in so many of his dialogues. The main difference is in the range of subjects touched on by the Socrates of the two portraits. Plato's Socrates does not appear as a practical counsellor in the everyday affairs of life. Xenophon's Socrates shows few signs of being interested in philosophical problems other than those concerned with human conduct. It is perhaps connected with this that Xenophon's Socrates does not regard advanced mathematics as a necessary part of the education of a ruler.

---

[1] I have heard it argued that while Xenophon might have felt justified in doing this it does not follow that Plato would. But such an argument misses the point. It is not a question of individual standards about what is justifiable. For no moral question is involved. No one suggests that either Plato in his dialogues or Xenophon in the *Oeconomicus* deliberately intended to deceive. It is a question of what the accepted literary conventions of the time were, which would have influenced both men. And for these Xenophon's practice is quite good evidence.

On such points as these, as far as we can judge, the Socrates of Aeschines agrees more closely with Xenophon than with Plato. There are no signs of any interest in philosophy other than ethical, and no signs of any demand for scientific or mathematical education. On another point, too, the Socrates of Aeschines seems to disagree at any rate with the Socrates of the *Gorgias* and the *Republic*. And that is in his estimate of the merits of the great Athenian statesmen of past times. Indeed, in general, the Socrates of both Xenophon and Aeschines seems much more at home in an ordinary Greek city than the true philosopher of the *Republic* sheltering behind a wall from the great storm of dust and hail. Aeschines in his manner of presentation, no doubt, follows Plato rather than Xenophon.[1] But in what he presents his connections seem all the other way.

If we ask how much weight to attach to these differences, it would be hard to find an answer, except for one consideration. Taken by themselves, the greater part of these discrepancies could be explained by the limitations of knowledge and even more perhaps by the limitations of interest of these writers. It is indeed extremely likely that Socrates's active and inquiring mind did touch on problems and discussions of contemporary philosophy, even metaphysics. And it is quite as likely that Xenophon, and perhaps Aeschines, too, would quickly have drifted away from the company if the talk turned in that direction while they happened to be there. What does strengthen our faith in the correctness of their evidence on such points as these is that it seems in very close accord with the picture given in some other Platonic dialogues, particularly the earliest ones. Plato himself does not always represent Socrates as so critical of contemporary and earlier statesmen as he is, for instance, in the *Gorgias*. He does not represent him as putting forward the necessity of mathematical studies in education when he is discussing problems of education in some of the earlier dialogues. Above all, he represents him in most of the dialogues as purely critical in his attitude, and not having any positive philosophical doctrine to teach. And this is not easily reconcilable with the ascription to him in the *Phaedo* of a definite philosophical theory which he is

---

[1] This seems the only grounds for Burnet's remark (*Year's Work in Classical Studies*, 1919) that ' the Socrates of Aeschines is much liker the Socrates of Plato than that of Xenophon '. I cannot see any other point on which this could be maintained.

said to be constantly putting forward, nor with the elaborate constructive political proposals of the *Republic*. Those who cannot believe that the biographical or historical interest is very important in Plato's writings may find incidental support for their belief from comparisons with the writings of Xenophon or other Socratics. But they certainly would not base their case on these. Their conviction, which would be just as firm if no word of Xenophon had survived, owes its chief strength to a study of the writings of Plato himself.

# CHAPTER XII

## THE SOCRATIC PHILOSOPHERS

TO give a complete account of the philosophical background of Plato's thought it would be necessary to describe, not only the contemporary movements of thought, but also the principal doctrines of his predecessors from the earliest philosophers of Miletus down to and including Socrates. But this tale has been too often told to need repeating here. And it would in any case involve too great an extension of the plan of this work to be attempted. What will be attempted is a brief account of what we know of the schools of thought strictly contemporary with Plato. A brief account, indeed, is all that is possible. For what we know of them with any certainty is very little. It is a curious fact that, while we know more about Plato than about any of his predecessors, since he is the earliest philosopher whose writings have come down to us in their entirety, we are considerably less well informed about his contemporaries than we are about the principal figures of the earlier period. And this fact is apt to intensify the mistaken impression of Plato as a solitary figure with no philosophical affiliations to men of his own time.

If we are looking for the thinkers with whom Plato would most probably have been in close contact, we naturally turn to those who shared with him the intimate friendship of Socrates. As we have seen, there is every reason to suppose that some of those who enjoyed this friendship sought from it something that would help them in the pursuit of their philosophical interests. And we know with certainty that several of these, besides Plato, were known to later ages as thinkers of importance in their time. Another fact that we know is that they differed in their views among themselves, and that on some points—though the precise extent of these is uncertain —they were in active opposition to each other. There was, therefore, no one Socratic school. And this is but one more piece of evidence which makes it very difficult to believe that

Socrates maintained such positive and systematic doctrines as are ascribed to him in some of Plato's dialogues. The facts about his successors make it much more natural to think of him as a critical and stimulating influence whose suggestions were capable of being developed in various different directions. We know practically nothing of the subsequent career of some of those friends of Socrates in whom the philosophical interest predominated. We are told that Phaedo, the narrator of the dialogue, who was hardly more than a boy at the time of Socrates' death, started a school at Elis. But this is only mentioned by late writers and may not be true at all. In any case we know nothing about his teaching. The mention of Phaedo naturally reminds us of Simmias and Cebes, who take the lead in the discussion with Socrates on his last day, and who are evidently meant by Plato to be represented as men of real philosophical ability. But we know little more of them than what we are told there. They had been before they came to Athens in the habit of associating with Philolaus the Pythagorean at Thebes. This is of interest as an illustration of the fact that few, if any, of the companions of Socrates appear to have owed their first introduction to philosophical thought to him. Even Plato began as a pupil of Cratylus the Heraclitean. But we cannot infer too much from this. To speak of Simmias and Cebes as Pythagoreans, and still more to use the opinions ascribed to them in the *Phaedo* as evidence of Pythagorean doctrine, as some scholars do, is going very much further than the evidence warrants. We have no trace of any subsequent contributions by them to philosophical thought. Simmias, if we can believe Plutarch, returned later to Thebes, and his house was the meeting-place of those who overthrew the Spartan occupation of the city in 378. Cebes is mentioned by Plato in the Thirteenth Letter, and from the way in which he is spoken of we get the impression that he had settled in Athens. But except that he is ' in the closest sympathy and intimacy with us all ', Plato tells us nothing of him.

There is one of the companions of Socrates who still makes his appearance in some of the histories of philosophy as the founder of a school, though the tendency of modern criticism is to deny him this title altogether. This is Aristippus of Cyrene. That he was a genuine intimate of Socrates we can tell from the *Phaedo*, where Plato finds it necessary to explain why he was not present on the last day. He is

probably the same Aristippus who is mentioned by Xenophon as being reproved by Socrates for the luxury of his life.
Such slight references to him as we have in contemporary or
nearly contemporary literature present him to us as a professional sophist or teacher of rhetoric. But later writers ascribe
to him the foundation of the Cyrenaic school, whose chief
tenet was that pleasure was the sole good, a doctrine which
they seem to have combined not unnaturally with some form
of sensationist psychology. It is almost certain, however,
that the school is of later origin. Aristotle, who mentions the
doctrine that pleasure is the chief good, nowhere associates it
with Aristippus. This by itself is not decisive, for he seems to
have been thinking chiefly of the dispute on the question of
pleasure which arose within the walls of the Academy. That
is no doubt why he mentions only Eudoxus and Speusippus
as the two protagonists. But if we read the confused account
of the origins of the Cyrenaic school in Diogenes or Aristocles,
we shall see that there was obviously no record of any positive
doctrine that could be traced back certainly to our Aristippus.
It is an extremely plausible conjecture that a confusion may
have arisen with his grandson, also an Aristippus, who probably
really was one of the originators of the Cyrenaic school.

## ANTISTHENES

The Socratic philosopher about whom we know most is
probably Antisthenes. But when we say that we know most
about him, that must not be taken as meaning that we know
very much. Our knowledge of him is slight and fragmentary.
But such as it is, it has served to stimulate an immense amount
of conjecture and hypothesis about him, particularly about
his relations with Plato and about supposed references to him
in the Platonic dialogues. It is therefore of the first importance
to distinguish clearly what we know about him with reasonable
certainty from the great erections of theory that have been
built up on a very scanty foundation.

We know very little of his life. He passed as an Athenian,[1]
but according to later stories he cannot have been an Athenian
citizen, being born of a Thracian mother. Such stories, of
course, may not be true : there is no contemporary confirmation of them. Tradition also stated what is likely enough,

---

[1] He is mentioned by Plato in the *Phaedo* as one of the ἐπιχώριοι
present at the death of Socrates : there is no indication that he is on
any different footing from Crito, Aeschines and the rest.

that he studied rhetoric under Gorgias before attaching himself to Socrates. If we can trust the chronology of Xenophon, he must have been a generation older than Plato and Xenophon himself. But we have no reliable information either of the date of his birth or of the date of his death. His intimacy with Socrates is attested not only by Xenophon but also by Plato, who includes him among those present on the last day. He certainly had some kind of philosophical school at Athens after the death of Socrates, though it cannot have been an organized society like the Academy. The most probable—though very uncertain—conjecture for the date of his death is about 365.

Of his writings we know the titles, as given us in the list preserved by Diogenes, but only very few and very brief fragments remain. From such quotations as we have, we know that some of them, at any rate, were Socratic dialogues. And we know also that, like other Socratics, he thought it necessary to say something about Alcibiades. It seems likely from certain references that, while emphasizing his physical attractions, he gave a very unfavourable picture of his moral character. He also seems to have dealt with Aspasia. From very slight indications it has been conjectured that he took a less favourable view of her than seems to have been fashionable among the Socratics. We are also told that in some of his writings—perhaps in the *Aspasia* itself when dealing with Pericles—he made a violent attack on the famous Athenian statesmen of the past.

But the bulk of the indications that we have of his writings refer to his views on moral questions. Many of these are epigrammatic moral maxims, for the construction of which he seems to have had an undoubted gift. Such was the saying from the *Cyrus*, quoted with approval both by Epictetus and Marcus Aurelius : ' It is a king's part, Cyrus, to do well and to be evilly spoken of '. Some of the sayings attributed to him by later authors may not be quotations from his writings at all : we find, indeed, that some of them are told of more than one person. But confining ourselves to undoubted quotations or summaries of his writings, we find that the outlines of a clearly defined moral point of view emerge. That a life according to virtue is the end, that virtue can be taught and when once acquired cannot be lost, that virtue is sufficient in itself without external goods or the gifts of fortune, that hard work is the essence of a good life, that pleasure is

11

only worth having when it follows hard work,—all these are well-attested features of the teaching contained in his writings. And they are confirmed by the only contemporary account that we have which mentions Antisthenes by name, the *Symposium* of Xenophon. Antisthenes is there represented as maintaining that true wealth and poverty are to be looked for not in the purses but in the souls of men, and as congratulating himself on the independence and freedom from care that his own material poverty gives him.

In his writings, so far as we can judge, this point of view was maintained by direct preaching and exhortation, and perhaps still more by the telling use of examples from the great figures of myth and history. He preached his gospel of hard work by telling the stories of Heracles and Cyrus, and his idea of education in virtue is presented through the account of the education of Heracles by Cheiron the centaur. The teaching of virtue, therefore, seems to have consisted for him in the main in direct precept and example, not in any scientific or philosophic examination of its theoretical basis. He would have approved of the earlier stages of the training of Plato's guardians in music and gymnastics. But we may doubt whether he would have thought the later developments in science, mathematics, and philosophy at all necessary. At any rate, there is no trace in what we know of him that he contributed anything to a systematic theory of ethics, nor that he connected his moral teaching with his other, more strictly philosophical investigations. The evidence is, of course, practically entirely negative. But in the present state of our knowledge that is the conclusion that seems to follow most naturally from it.

When we consider what we know of his general moral point of view, it is easy to see how it could have found its first inspiration in the life of Socrates. It is also easy to see its connection with the subsequent development of the Cynic order of preachers. But, as has already been hinted, it would probably be a mistake to accept uncritically what was till recently the orthodox view of Antisthenes as the first founder of a Cynic school of philosophy. There was no Cynic school of philosophy, and the ' way of life ' which the true Cynic preached went further than anything we can safely attribute to Antisthenes. At any rate, in practice it is clear that he never gave himself up to this kind of life, and that he never confined his activities, as the true Cynic did, to moral preaching. On the contrary, we know both from the list of his writings and from the traditions of his work that have come down that a large part, certainly, and perhaps the main part of his life's work was devoted to other interests. He was probably a teacher of rhetoric or the art of discussion, in some form. He was certainly a prolific commentator upon Homer. He was interested in the study of words and names, and may therefore have been something of a philologist. Above all, he was known to Aristotle, who probably arrived in Athens before his death, first and foremost as a logician, and his followers are mentioned only as the adherents of a particular logical theory.

Even the name ' Cynic ' is only connected with Antisthenes by later writers. Aristotle, who knows of the nickname ὁ κύων as applied to Diogenes, speaks of the followers of Antisthenes simply as 'Ἀντισθενέιοι. And even among late writers there was not absolute unanimity in the attribution of the foundation of the school to Antisthenes. There were some who traced it back beyond him to Socrates, or further back still to Heracles. But what is more to the point is that there was one tradit:on which definitely attributed it not to Antisthenes but to Diogenes. And this is almost certainly the truth. Diogenes probably owed some ideas to Antisthenes. He may have been in personal contact with him for a time. There are many stories of this, but none very well attested. And it is just as likely that what he learnt from him only came through his books. Perhaps the picture he found in them of Socrates was the decisive influence on him, as it was later to Zeno. But at any rate it is clear that nothing like the Cynic order existed before Diogenes, and that all its most distinctive features were due to him.

Of Antisthenes' opinions on other subjects we find a trace in a fragment preserved by Philodemus, to the effect that in his book on Nature he said that there was but one god according to nature but many according to convention. With this is perhaps to be connected another quotation which says that the divine being has no resemblance to anything else, and therefore cannot be represented by any image. How he developed these views we do not know. Incidentally the quotations are of interest as indicating the kind of subject treated in the book on Nature. There is no warrant in the title of the book for regarding Antisthenes as interested in natural science.

But the most important contribution of Antisthenes to the discussions of his day undoubtedly lies in his logical theory. Yet even of this we know no more than an outline, which can only be filled in by conjecture. Our outline is given us by Aristotle, who mentions Antisthenes more than once, and it will be convenient to begin by giving the most important statements of Aristotle. The doctrine which he particularly associates with the name of Antisthenes is that it is impossible to contradict. And in our first passage he expands this as follows :

' So Antisthenes showed his simplicity by his contention that nothing should be spoken of except by its proper verbal expression (or " phrase " or " formula " : λόγος), one expression for one thing : from which it followed that it was impossible to contradict, and it almost followed that it was impossible to make a false statement.' [1]

The second and longer passage presents certain difficulties in interpretation. In the first place, it speaks not of Antisthenes but of the Antistheneans. But it is doubtful whether too much importance should be attached to that. There is no suggestion that Antisthenes and his followers are distinguished here. And, while we may conclude from the language that the view in question was the doctrine of a whole school of thought, not of a single man only, there is no warrant for supposing that it represents a further development by his followers which went beyond what Antisthenes himself taught. A further difficulty arises from the fact that, in part of the passage at any rate, Aristotle is clearly re-stating the doctrine in his own words, and we cannot therefore be sure how far he may not have developed it beyond anything that its original defenders formulated. The passage itself runs as follows. After discussing certain difficulties that arise about the true analysis of material objects, Aristotle goes on :

' So there is some point in the difficulty raised by the Antistheneans and similarly uneducated people, that it is not possible to define what a thing is,—for they call the definition a roundabout formula,—while it is possible to explain what sort of thing it is. For instance, we cannot say what silver is, but we can say that it is like (or " the same sort of thing as ") tin. So that

---

[1] *Metaphysics*, 1024b 32. The second passage quoted is 1043b 24. The doctrine of the impossibility of contradiction, referred to as being held by Antisthenes, is mentioned in passing elsewhere, e.g. *Topics*, 104b 21.

there is a kind of substance of which it is possible to give a definition and an account in words, namely the composite substances, whether sensible or intelligible. But it is not possible in the case of the primary elements out of which these are composed, since the defining phrase has to indicate something by asserting something else of it, and so it has to treat one of these " somethings " as the matter and the other as the form.'

What is the significance of this ? We know from Plato's *Euthydemus* that some arguments of this kind were used as part of the stock in trade of the cheap-jack sophist, whose sole aim was to puzzle and confuse his audience. But there is no reason to ascribe anything of this kind to Antisthenes. On the contrary, it is clear that such arguments in his hands were part of a very serious attempt to deal with the problem of what is implied in predication. It is natural that Socrates' insistence on the importance of definition for clear thinking should start those who were influenced by him on investigations about the true nature of definition, and, more widely, of predication or asserting one thing of another in any form. It is evident from the different results that they reached that Socrates' influence merely extended to setting the problem and gave no distinct answer to it. But most of his friends whose interest lay in philosophic thought at all, seem to have attempted some answer to it, and one of them—Plato—gave in substance an answer which would be generally accepted at the present day.

Antisthenes' theory, so far as we can reconstruct it from these scanty indications, would hardly appear plausible to us now. But none the less in the state of thought at this period it might perfectly reasonably be maintained, and indeed it called attention to difficulties which are not completely disposed of even now. To understand it, we should begin perhaps from the denial of the possibility of contradiction, the doctrine which is especially associated with his name. We are not to suppose that he raised any silly difficulties about the physical possibility of pronouncing sentences which in form appeared to contradict each other. His teaching would rather be that they could not both be significant propositions, and that no one could logically attach any meaning to both at the same time. The argument for this is simple. The words used, if they are significant at all, indicate a particular thing. If different or contradictory words are used, they cannot be indicating the same thing. This argument, which is a mere trick in the hands of a Euthydemus, is made the basis of a considered theory by Antisthenes. And it will help us to take it seriously if we consider certain instances in which, even nowadays, we should recognize its correctness.

When we say, for instance, that a triangle has three sides, we recognize, if we reflect, that we cannot attach any meaning to the contradictory assertion. If any one says that a triangle has not three sides, we know that, if they mean anything at all, they must be talking about something else and using the word to mean something quite different. This example might make us suppose that Antisthenes regarded the definition as the type of the true statement. And we shall see that there is a certain amount of truth in this supposition. Antisthenes certainly paid careful attention to the nature of definition. But Aristotle, at any rate, found his views on definition curious and thought that he allowed very little virtue to it. For in the second quotation given above he tells us that, according to Antisthenes and his followers, there is no such thing as a definition which really tells us what a thing is. All we can have is a roundabout formula which indicates a thing by comparing it to something else. We might illustrate this point by an example which, we may venture to think, would illustrate the argument of Antisthenes better than the instance chosen by Aristotle. No definition or explanation could tell us what purple is. We must know it directly, and indicate it by the single word. But we can say something about it by giving its relation to other colours, i.e. that it comes between red and blue on the scale. So far we get the impression of Antisthenes' doctrine as a belief in a world made up of simple reals which have to be cognized directly and indicated each by a single word or name. These simple reals have certain—probably equally simple and un-analysable—relations among themselves, in particular the relation of resemblance.

If, however, we are justified in taking the second part of the quotation from Aristotle as referring to Antisthenes, we can carry our account further than this.[1] And it seems an

---

[1] I follow Mr. Ross in taking the passage thus, in spite of the authority of Campbell and Burnet on the other side, because I cannot read it in any other sense. The incidental arguments against this view, e.g. that Aristotle would not have called a view with which he agreed the view of uneducated people, or that the view itself does not deserve such an epithet, do not seem to me very convincing. We cannot always account for Aristotle's choice of epithets.

additional justification for so taking the passage when we find that the further development seems to follow naturally and logically from what we already have. For, according to this, he recognized not only the simple substances, which were the ultimate constituents of reality, but also composite objects made up of combinations of these simple substances. To these compound objects, presumably, single names might also be applied. But they could be further, and perhaps more correctly explained, by stating their simple constituents. In this sense one could legitimately define, by giving a collection of words or a phrase expressing the elements of the composite object as the equivalent in meaning to a single word, the name of the composite object. And that would appear to be the only kind of predication that was legitimate. So that the definition does appear as the type of a valid judgement, in the sense that the only significant and true propositions were propositions expressing the analysis of such a compound whole into its elements. Here, too, of course, the impossibility of contradiction would apply. The compound object was constituted by its simple elements, and if any person made a different assertion about the elements, he obviously could not be talking of the same object.

What these ultimate simple elements were it is difficult to say with certainty. But it seems probable that they included, and perhaps were confined to, the simple, sensible qualities, such as colours and shapes, of which Antisthenes regarded material objects as being composed. At any rate it is very unlikely that his ultimate reals were the concrete particular material objects, which are certainly not simple. And this has to be borne in mind in considering his relation to certain other lines of thought. It makes it, for instance, quite wrong to describe him, as he is sometimes described, as a Nominalist. For one thing he could never have asserted that a name could ever be merely a name and stand for nothing in reality. It was an essential part of his doctrine that there was a real fact for every word and a word for every real fact. But, beyond this, he does not seem to have been concerned with the opposition between particulars and universals in the form implied by the use of terms like Nominalism and Realism. We have no indication that he ever denied that the word ' white ' stood for one and the same fact which was present in all the particular white objects. It is very likely that he never raised the problem in that form at all.

The same considerations have to be borne in mind in discussing the attitude of Antisthenes towards the theory of Forms of Plato.   There is a story told by Simplicius that Antisthenes, in criticizing the theory, said to Plato, ' Plato, I see a horse, but I do not see horse-ness (or " equinity " ; ἱπποτήτα).'. This is often quoted as evidence for the views of Antisthenes. But, as a matter of fact, the anecdote is not well attested. It does not claim to be a quotation from any work of Antisthenes, and a very similar remark is ascribed by other authors to Diogenes.   It seems, indeed, much more characteristic of the crude common-sense point of view of the latter, and it is quite likely that a story quoted first of the one should get referred back to that other, who was regarded in the popular tradition as his teacher.   At any rate, even if there is anything in the story, it must be interpreted in the light of the rest of our evidence about Antisthenes.   And that would suggest that it was not, as Simplicius suggests, the question of the reality of universals which was at issue between him and Plato, but rather of the nature of those which existed.   Antisthenes would not deny the reality of qualities, though he might or might not have agreed with Aristotle in denying their independence and separability from the particulars.   But the only qualities that he recognized were the sensible qualities, whereas Plato would give even these only a derivative existence, and would have allowed ultimate reality only to the nonsensible Forms or numbers which could be known by pure reason alone.

There is little more that we can say with safety about Antisthenes.   We can see easily enough how important in his view the careful study of language would be, and the saying attributed to him by Epictetus that ' the beginning of education is the examination of names ' may well be an actual quotation from his works.   But we cannot conjecture from this anything about the view that he would have taken on the problems discussed for instance in Plato's *Cratylus*.   His general doctrine would be equally compatible with the view that each name was assigned to its appropriate object by the agreement of the people who used that language and with the view that the name was connected with its object by nature.   There is no real evidence for associating him with either view.

What does need to be insisted on is the general character of the attitude which Antisthenes took up towards the problems that he discussed. Nothing could be wider of the mark than to speak of him, as is sometimes done, as a subjectivist, a relativist and a sceptic. He was a good enough Socratic to entertain no doubts of the reality of knowledge and the possibility of true thinking. Indeed, his view asserts this so strongly that it finally, as Aristotle saw, seems to leave little room for the possibility of wrong thinking or error. Nor does he show the slightest leaning towards the Protagorean doubts about the principle of contradiction. Rather he applies it so rigidly that he ends by maintaining, not merely that two contradictory propositions cannot both be true, but that they cannot both exist at all. There is least foundation of all for the accusation of subjectivism. His view is much more truly described as an uncompromising realism, which presents us simply with the knower and the known object face to face with one another. Indeed, most of his difficulties arise from his failure to make allowance for the subjective element in thinking, which makes error and differences of opinion possible.[1]

## THE MEGARIANS

Euclides of Megara is one of the great mystery-figures in the history of philosophy. We hear of him more than once from Plato. He was present at the death of Socrates, and he is the chief figure in the brief introduction to the *Theaetetus*. In fact, he is represented as recounting the conversation there recorded. What we can infer from the choice of Euclides for this part it is very difficult to say. It has been described as dedicating the dialogue to Euclides. But there is really no warrant for assuming that it was equivalent to what is implied by the dedication of a book in modern times. Even if it were, it would be very uncertain how much to infer from that, except perhaps that Euclides had some general interest in the subjects discussed. Further we know, from the passage already quoted, that Plato and other Socratics went to stay with Euclides at Megara immediately after the death of Socrates. From all this we can gather that he was in the

[1] I am much indebted to Professor Gillespie's article on the Logic of Antisthenes in the *Archiv für Geschichte der Philosophie*, 1913, 1914. But I cannot accept all his conclusions. In particular he seems to me much too ready to identify particular characters in Plato's dialogues with Antisthenes and to assign without qualification all the views ascribed to them to him.

inner circle of Socratics, and was on terms of intimate friendship with other members of that circle. But when we want
to carry the inquiry further and ask about his philosophical
relations to these other members and about his views and
teaching in general, we find only the slightest guidance from
our available evidence.

Of Euclides' own writings not the smallest quotation remains.
And the extant summaries of his teaching are bald and jejune
in the extreme. We know that he and his school were regarded
as carrying on the tradition of the Eleatics. Cicero numbers
him in the succession which, beginning from Xenophanes,
went down through Parmenides and Zeno to Euclides. And
Aristocles, writing in the second century A.D., after summariz-
ing the Eleatic doctrines, adds that these doctrines were also
held by the Megarians. There are very few specific doctrines
ascribed to Euclides by name. We are told that he held that
the Good was one, though called by many names, and that
the opposite of the Good did not exist. One would have
thought it superfluous for a thinker who held that everything
was one to argue this in the special case of the Good. We
hear, also, something about his contribution to the logical
discussion of methods of argument. We are told that he
always attacked the conclusion not the premises of his
opponent's argument. And we are told also that he denied
the validity of argument from analogy. His school, particularly under his successor, Eubulides, the opponent of
Aristotle, acquired a great reputation for sophistical dialectic :
some of the verbal tricks of Eubulides, such as the famous
fallacy of the Sorites, are still familiar in contemporary logic.
Timon of Phlius ascribes to Euclides the original responsibility
for giving this ' eristic ' character to the discussions of his
school. And this may well be true.

What part, then, are we to regard Euclides as filling in the
philosophical world of the time ? The Eleatic teaching, which
he represented, is probably best known to modern readers
through its advocacy of the doctrine that reality is one,
without change and without difference. And we find it
difficult to take the assertion very seriously as the central
point of a systematic philosophy. It seems impossible to
make any use of it : indeed, strictly speaking, it leaves no
room for any further thought or assertion about reality at
all. But, when we regard it not so much as a final statement
of the truth, but as an ideal of explanation and a point of

view from which to examine and criticize ordinary experience and popular beliefs, our judgement of it will be very different. And we cannot fail to see that as a regulative principle of thought its importance and influence have been profound. For it represented the complete and logical formulation of the principles which underlay, implicitly or explicitly, the development of the greater part of Greek philosophy and indirectly of the greater part of modern science. It only arrived at its apparently extravagant results by a long and systematic examination of these principles.

The principle from which this examination started is of much greater significance for the development of thought than the final results to which it led. This was the principle that the real was that which could be most completely and consistently thought out by our reason. ' It is the same thing which can be thought and can be,' Parmenides says. The real is the intelligible and the intelligible is the real. It is his complete faith in that principle which does much to explain the admiration and respect that Parmenides aroused in the minds of thinkers like Plato, who could not accept his final conclusions. When he came to apply this principle he found, as earlier thinkers had, without fully realizing it, implied, that identity was more intelligible than difference, that change and motion and coming into being and going out of existence could not be clearly grasped by the reason. It has been shown by modern writers that it was by an application of those principles, as demands of reason or ideals of explanation, that the most important developments of modern science took their rise. The idea that the apparent diversities of the physical world are really only appearances of an underlying homogeneous material, the idea that ' nothing comes from nothing ', that absolute creation and destruction are inconceivable, that, as a living scientist puts it, ' what is real is conserved,' and the expression of these views in the doctrine of the Conservation of Energy,—all these notions form the very foundation of most modern scientific thought.[1]

Parmenides formulated these demands as a positive system of philosophy. But this left little for his followers to do on the positive side except to repeat the formula that reality

[5] See particularly E. Meyerson, *Identité et Realité*. For a short account of this point of view, with special reference to Greek thought, see my paper on *Ancient Philosophy and Modern Science*, in the Proceedings of the Aristotelian Society, 1925–26.

was one. They found the best scope for their activity, therefore, in taking this as a standpoint from which to criticize
ordinary experience and other philosophical views. The para-
doxes of Zeno with reference to the possibility of motion are
well known. Later the disciples of Euclides developed a
criticism of Aristotle's theory of potentiality, which has a
recognizable kinship with certain developments in modern
scientific thought. Euclides himself seems to have devoted
some of his energies, at any rate, to a criticism of current
ethical notions from this point of view, attempting to show
the unity of the good under the diversity of the things we call
good. It is possible that this interest in ethical matters may
have been the result of Socrates' influence. Otherwise we
can see little definite trace of the working of this influence.
And there are no further indications of any influence exercised
by the Megarians on the ethical thought of the time.

It is clear that their real influence lay in the developments
of logic and the methodology of thought and argument.
No doubt, Euclides with a taste in this direction would have
found great interest and stimulus in observing the methods
of argument adopted by Socrates. But, if he was a true
Eleatic, it is clear that his interest in this direction was not
originally roused by Socrates. For dialectical argument was
almost the invention of that school, particularly of Zeno.
Plato, with one of his characteristic flashes of insight, traces
back almost the whole development of the sophistic argu-
mentation which was current at the time to the influence of
the Eleatic philosophy, particularly to their denial of not-
being or negation. And it is easy to see how their general
line of thought would lead in this direction. We must look
for the influence of their fourth-century representatives,
therefore, mainly in the direction of criticism of current ideas,
popular and philosophical. And it is clear that their influence
may have made itself felt beyond the limits of those who
accepted the strict Eleatic doctrine of the One. We should
probably, if we knew enough, find the effects of Megarian
methods of argument showing themselves in many directions
outside the boundaries of the school itself.

Among those who were subject in a greater or lesser degree
to this influence, we should probably be safe in including
the names of Bryson and Polyxenus. In our authorities,
we get nothing but occasional fleeting glimpses of these
enigmatic figures, who move like transient phantoms across

the stage of Greek philosophy.  But that they were people of importance in their time there can be no doubt.  And many conjectures have been made about the degree of their importance, and in particular about their relations with Plato. We hear of them both from Plato himself, though he tells us little about them.  In the Thirteenth Letter he introduces Helicon to Dionysius as one who has studied, not only with Eudoxus, but also with a pupil of Isocrates, and ' with Polyxenus, one of the associates of Bryson '.  And he adds ' what is not common on the top of all this ', that he is not at all ungracious or difficult to get on with.  How far this is meant as a definite hit at the unpleasant disputatiousness that association with pupils of Bryson and Isocrates would produce, and which of the two would be regarded as having the greater share of responsibility for this tendency, it is hard to say.  What is clear is that a mere mention of Bryson's name is given as a sufficient account of any one connected with him, while the name of Polyxenus is not yet so familiar, at any rate in Sicily.  In a later letter, the Second, a Polyxenus, who is undoubtedly the same man, is described as having come to the court of Dionysius with Plato's recommendation, which argues a certain degree of intimacy.  But he seems to have been ready to make mischief, at any rate for Plato's friends, while he was there.

Aristotle mentions Bryson more than once in connection with an attempt at squaring the circle.  He also quotes him as the author of a sophism about the impossibility of using bad language, which reminds us of some of the efforts of the successors of Euclides.  Bryson's name also occurs in a fragment of a comic poet, contemporary with Plato's later years. Unfortunately the reading is disputed, and the change of a single letter makes the difference between representing Bryson as a colleague of Plato, in the Academy and as a mercenary sophist of the type of Thrasymachus.  The latter version is that usually accepted.[1]  Finally, to complete the remaining contemporary evidence, the historian Theopompus is quoted as making the spiteful accusation against Plato of having plagiarized the works of Bryson in his own writings.  Such

---

[1] The one reading makes the author speak of a young man educated at the Academy ὑπὸ Πλατῶνα καὶ Βρυσῶνα.  The other joins up the last word with the following into a compound word of the kind beloved of comic writers and makes him Βρυσωνοθρασυμαχειολημψικερμάτων πληγετς ἀνάγκη.

charges, of course, are worthless. But they suggest some kind of relation between the two.

The later notices are obscure and sometimes hopelessly confused, so much so that the existence of several Brysons has been conjectured as an explanation of some of the contradictions. The account in Suidas gives the clearest information about our Bryson. He tells us that he was a Heracleote and a companion of Socrates, and that, together with Euclides, ' he introduced the eristic dialectic.' The association with Socrates is not supported by any other evidence. And Suidas also quotes a rival account, according to which he was a disciple not of Socrates, but of Euclides, and himself the teacher of Pyrrho, the great sceptic. This last suggestion seems to put him rather too late, but the association with Euclides emerges clearly. And it is clear also that this association was particularly marked in their logical work.

Of Polyxenus the one important later piece of information is the statement quoted from Phanias by Alexander in his commentary on the *Metaphysics* that he was responsible for one form of the famous ' third man ' argument which was brought against the Platonic Theory of Ideas. The argument is described by Alexander in terms so hopelessly obscure that it is impossible to say with any certainty what its precise meaning was.[1] But at any rate it reveals the existence of a lively polemic, in which those associated with Polyxenus took part, against Plato's great theory. And it is natural and reasonable to look for traces of these controversies in the later Platonic dialogues. But for confirmation of any conjectures on the point we have only the scanty evidence just outlined to turn to.

[1] For one explanation see Burnet, *Greek Philosophy*, pp. 259, 260. For another see Professor A. E. Taylor's paper in the Proceedings of the Aristotelian Society, N.S., Vol. XVI, on *Parmenides, Zeno and Socrates*. Professor Taylor certainly seems successful in throwing serious doubts on other explanations of the passage. But I can feel no certainty that his own explanation is correct.

# CHAPTER XIII

## THE PYTHAGOREANS [1]

NO study of the philosophy of Plato's time would be complete without some treatment of the Pythagoreans. And yet there would be a good excuse for omitting it on the plea that so complicated a subject should either be treated much more fully than is possible here or left out altogether. The complications here do not arise so much from an absence of information : for we have a great deal of information, of one kind or another, about the Pythagoreans. But our difficulty is that so much of this information is certainly false. And though modern scholarship has made great progress in separating the false from the true and, sometimes, in detecting the substratum of truth underlying the falsehood, it cannot be said that anything like complete agreement has been obtained. Every one, however, recognizes that a great deal of our material must be rejected. Attachment to Pythagoreanism, at any rate in later times, does not seem to have inculcated a very high standard of historical truth. And there is probably no philosophical school which has produced so many forged documents and misstatements of fact.

The names of Philolaus, whose much-discussed fragments are now generally admitted to be probably entirely, and certainly in large part spurious, Ocellus and Timaeus Locrus are sufficient instances of supposititious authors of treatises now known to be later forgeries. Again, some of the more absurd falsehoods about Plato that were circulated in later generations seem to have been conceived under the influence

---

[1] In this chapter I am indebted, even more than elsewhere, to Burnet. Though I have hesitated to adopt a good many of his conjectures, I have followed his general presentation, and there is comparatively little that I have said which is not based on his authority. Among modern works on the question which differ to a greater or lesser degree in their point of view, I would mention specially E. Frank, *Plato und die sogenannten Pythagoreer* and the writings of A. Delatte, particularly his *Etudes sur la litterature Pythagoricienne* and his edition of Diogenes' life of Pythagoras.

and in the interests of Pythagoreanism.   One of the most
ridiculous of these is the story, originated, like so many of these
stories, by Aristoxenus, that Plato wished to burn the works
of Democritus, but was dissuaded from this unreasonable
action by two Pythagoreans.   From the same source, probably,
comes the story, so widely disseminated later, of Plato buying
Pythagorean books and composing the *Timaeus* from them.
This is one instance of the general accusation which, according
to Porphyry, was brought in later times against Plato and other
thinkers, of appropriating as their own without acknowledgement what was really the teaching of Pythagoras.   Perhaps
it is to the same source that we must trace the attempt ascribed
by Diogenes to one Alcimus, to make Epicharmus the originator
of many of Plato's doctrines.   Epicharmus was certainly
claimed as a Pythagorean by later writers.

There is thus evidence of a vigorous and not very scrupulous
propaganda going on for many generations after Plato with
the object of claiming all the credit possible for philosophical
and scientific developments for Pythagoras and the Pythagoreans.   And there is evidence, too, that this propaganda had
some effect on the standard histories of philosophy.   It is
difficult not to suspect its influence in the stories told of so
many famous thinkers of having been taught by a Pythagorean
at some period of their lives.   Some modern scholars seem
inclined to accept this point of view, and to see Pythagoreanism
everywhere.   But, just because the propaganda was evidently
so vigorous, it would seem more reasonable to regard all such
stories with the greatest scepticism, and not to ascribe more
to Pythagorean influences than we are absolutely obliged by
certain evidence.   No doubt, of course, the different philosophic
schools of all periods were in contact with each other and
influenced each other.   But such influence would be mutual,
and it is wise to distrust any suggestion of a special position
for the Pythagoreans in this respect.

Another difficulty, perhaps the greatest with which we are
faced, is that of dating even approximately the various philosophical and scientific developments in the school of Pythagoras.
This is of special importance when we are trying to get some
idea of what was going on in that school in the lifetime of
Plato.   The difficulty arises, in part at any rate, from the very
common Greek tendency of pushing back the origin of beliefs
and discoveries to the earliest possible date.   Even the philosophers themselves sometimes seem anxious to disclaim the credit

of discoveries which really belongs to them, and to try to assign it to some earlier authority.    And the historians of philosophy outdo even the most zealous of modern researchers in their anxiety to discover earlier sources for doctrines which had been generally attributed to some later thinker.    It is to this tendency, no doubt, that we owe the appearance of satirists and poets like Xenophanes, and even Homer and Hesiod, as founders of a philosophical school or originators of some philosophical doctrine.    And this tendency shows itself to a special degree among the Pythagoreans.    For the religious flavour about their movement tends to give a special position to the founder of it, and to make it of special importance for his successors to attempt to claim his authority for any doctrine that they wished to inculcate.    Some modern scholars, indeed, have been so impressed by this tendency that they have relegated Pythagoras altogether to the ranks of poets and religious preachers.    They would maintain that he was no more of a philosopher or scientist than Homer or Hesiod, and that the philosophical and mathematical developments associated with Pythagoreanism were entirely the product of a later age, in particular of the age of Plato.    This seems to be carrying scepticism to unnecessary lengths, and it is difficult to maintain in the face of all the evidence.    But that some degree of this kind of thing went on is undoubted, and adds considerably to the difficulty of any estimate of the importance of Pythagoreanism in Plato's time.

Very few of the personalities of these later Pythagoreans stand out at all clearly.    Philolaus belongs rather to the generation of Socrates, but probably outlived him.    The mention of him in the *Phaedo* speaks of him as having left Thebes, but implies that he was still alive.    Lysis is also mentioned by later writers as the teacher of Epaminondas, who must have been younger than Plato.    We hear a little of Echecrates in the introduction to the *Phaedo*, and we are told of him, though not by Plato, that he represented the Pythagorean school at Phlius.    Eurytus, of whom Aristotle tells us one instructive anecdote, must have been living at about the same time.    And there are others, such as Xenophilus, said to have been the teacher of Aristoxenus, who are little more than names.    The only one who stands out at all as a living person is Archytas, the friend of Plato, of whom we have already had occasion to speak.    Aristotle, who says a good deal about the Pythagorean doctrines, hardly ever mentions any of them by

12

name.   He speaks generally of the Pythagoreans or of ' those
who are called Pythagoreans ' (οἱ καλούμενοι Π.), a curious
phrase which some scholars, translating it ' the so-called
Pythagoreans ', have taken as distinguishing these men from
the real Pythagoreans.   But for this conclusion there does not
seem to be sufficient warrant.   In any case this school is
represented as having established the general lines of its philosophy before the time of Plato.   Aristotle speaks of them
as both contemporary with and earlier than Leucippus and
Democritus, and expressly speaks of Plato as having developed
his philosophy after theirs.   On the other hand, he makes no
suggestion that the Pythagoreans contemporary with Plato
had in any way modified the main lines of these doctrines.   And
he himself must have begun his philosophical career in the
lifetime of the last of these men.   He is thus to be regarded as a
contemporary authority.   And for most of our knowledge of
the Pythagoreans he is our only contemporary authority.

Our other contemporary references to them amount to very
little.   The fragments of fourth-century comedy which have
been preserved give little or no indication of a Pythagorean
school of mathematics and scientific research.   A Pythagorean
for them means a kind of fakir, noted for his eccentric asceticism
and the poverty and squalor of his life.   This picture of them
suggests the Cynics, though without their missionary fervour,
and, perhaps, with even less of a reasoned justification for their
way of life.   Such men could have had little in common with
Archytas and his friends.   And later tradition represents the
Pythagoreanism of this period as sharply divided into two
opposing tendencies, the school of scientific research and the
devotees of a religious cult, in sharp hostility to each other
and both claiming to be the legitimate heirs of the
Pythagorean tradition.   There seems no real reason to doubt
that both these tendencies did go back to Pythagoras himself,
though there are scholars who represent the scientific side of
Pythagoreanism as being entirely the product of the end of
the fifth and the fourth centuries.   We know other cases in
which these two tendencies were combined.   But it is not a
natural combination, and it is not to be wondered at that at
the time of which we are speaking the two lines of development
had in general fallen apart.   At any rate it is with the scientific
side that we have to deal now.

Plato himself hardly ever speaks of the Pythagoreans by
name, which is a curious fact on any theory.   The only express

mention of them is in the *Republic*, where they are quoted as authorities on mathematics and particularly on harmonics. The criticism is made on them in this passage that they confine themselves to the observation and measurement of observable phenomena, audible sounds and the like, and do not carry their investigations beyond this to discover some deeper and more philosophical explanation. Such a criticism is extremely significant. Even if we hold that it was intended to refer exclusively to the Pythagoreans of the dramatic date of the dialogue, there is no suggestion at all in any evidence we have that any substantial alteration in the attitude of the school in this or any other respect took place between that date and the date of composition of the *Republic*. And according to our canons of criticism it is not to be supposed that Plato would have made a point of this unless it applied at the time he wrote. The only other mention of the Pythagoreans is in the same dialogue, where he speaks of them as people who have adopted from their original teacher a certain attitude and way of life which still marks them off as in some way different from other people.

Individual members of the school are occasionally mentioned in the dialogues, but we can learn little about them. Philolaus appears only as a moral and religious teacher, who preaches the unlawfulness of suicide. It may be he, as has been generally supposed, who is referred to in the *Gorgias*, as the author of the saying that the body is the tomb of the soul. Echecrates, who was certainly a Pythagorean, is represented in the *Phaedo* as declaring that he had become convinced of the doctrine that the soul is a harmony, on which Simmias bases one of his suggested objections to Socrates' proof of immortality. There would not have been any particular point in ascribing such a view to Echecrates without historical warrant. But it does not necessarily follow that it was specially characteristic of the Pythagoreans of the period. It would be absurd to argue that any view that any Pythagorean held must have originated in the school. And such contemporary evidence as there is does not suggest a special connection of this doctrine with the Pythagoreans. Simmias, who puts it forward in the *Phaedo*, speaks of it as a widespread opinion,[1] resting on no very

---

[1] *Phaedo*, 92d, ὅθεν καὶ τοῖς πολλοῖς δοκεῖ ἀνθρώποις. Burnet in his note interprets this as meaning the majority of people who hold the view, and denies that it indicates that the view in question was widespread. But as far as the Greek goes the interpretation I have

thorough examination of the subject.    This manner of speaking
does not suggest that he had learnt it from Philolaus.    There
seems no reason why he should not have mentioned Philolaus'
name in connection with the doctrine, as he does in connection
with other doctrines, if it had come from him.    Philolaus is the
only link of which we know connecting Simmias with Pythagoreanism.

Aristotle's treatment of the theory leaves us with a similar
impression.    He discusses it at some length in the *De Anima*,
and apparently discussed it more fully still in his lost dialogue,
the *Eudemus*.    He, too, speaks of it as a widespread popular
belief.    But what is perhaps more significant is that he says
no word to connect it with the Pythagoreans, though in an
earlier part of the *De Anima* he mentions the Pythagoreans
in connection with an entirely different doctrine.    There is,
indeed, no explicit attribution of the view to Pythagorean
sources earlier than Macrobius, not a very weighty authority.
And the general impression is that it was a popular view
originating from some other source, at which we can only
conjecture,[1] and appealing to individual Pythagoreans, but
having no special connection with the school.

This introduces us to the testimony of Aristotle, from whom
the greater part of our knowledge of the Pythagoreans is
necessarily derived.    And the first and most important point
in his testimony with which we have to deal is his account of
the fundamental philosophical position of the school.    The
central point of this is expressed in the well-known statement
that things (i.e. the things which make up the material physical
world) are numbers.    Much confusion has been introduced into
his account from the fact that in one passage he also describes
them as holding that things imitate or are like numbers.    The
two statements are not easy to reconcile.    And there are hints
in the obscure tradition of later times that there was a dispute
on the subject in the school itself.    But the former is Aristotle's
normal account of their doctrine.    And in any case it is easy
to see how either view might arise from the considerations
which led them in this direction.    Their interest in mathe-

given is at least equally possible, and in view of the similar way of
speaking adopted by Aristotle (*De Anima*, 407$^b$ 27, πιθανὴ μὲν πολλοῖς
οὐδεμιᾶς ἧττον τῶν λεγομένων) it seems the most natural.

[1] Very likely, as Burnet suggests, from medical writings.    But it
by no means follows that the medical writings must have been Pythagorean.

matics, he tells us, led them to look for the explanation of everything in mathematical terms. And they discovered that physical objects (musical tones, for instance) did possess mathematical relations to each other. Because, therefore, physical objects were found to have the same qualities and relations as numbers, it was quite natural to say simply that they were numbers. On the same grounds, it would be equally open for the more cautious to say that they were like numbers in so far as they had the same qualities and relations. Indeed, it is not impossible that for a time both ways of speaking might be used indiscriminately to express the facts from which they started. At a later stage there are slight indications that the difference implied became clearly realized, and that it was asserted in some quarters that things had the qualities of numbers without themselves being numbers. But the facts about this controversy are very obscure.

The original genesis of this point of view is, however, fairly clear, and it takes its place in that process of developing the ideals of rational explanation and the presuppositions of scientific thought in which early Greek philosophy consists. The first Ionian physicists saw that to make the physical world intelligible we must look for some one homogeneous reality underlying all the apparent differences and changes. The actual accounts they gave of this were naturally not such as would be taken very seriously now. But the fact that they put the question in that form is of immense significance, and this has been the ideal of scientific explanation ever since. But the work in this respect was still only partly done. For even if a correct answer to such a question was given it would only give a general account of the whole physical world and would not make any particular facts or events more intelligible. The next step was taken when it was realized that particular events must be regarded as determinations of this homogeneous reality, and that the only kind of determination that really met the demand for rational explanation was numerical determination, expressible in mathematical terms. This step we owe to the Pythagoreans, very probably to Pythagoras himself, and it is a step of the first importance, which had a profound influence on later scientific developments.

The doctrine does not, however, seem to exclude every element from reality except the numbers. It holds on to the idea of a formless or indeterminate something, τὸ ἄπειρον, the Infinite or Boundless, which had come into Greek thought from the speculations of Anaximander and other Ionian physicists.    It was this which was determined by the numbers, and from the determination of the Infinite by the numbers the physical world arose.   By the Pythagoreans that Aristotle knew this was represented as a definite physical process taking place in time. There seem to have been differences among different Pythagoreans in the way in which they thought of the Infinite.[1] At any rate, the accounts we have of their views on the subject are obscure.   But the general idea of an Infinite or Boundless was, of course, neither originated by them nor in any special degree characteristic of their school.   It might almost be described as a commonplace of early Greek philosophy.   What was peculiar and original to the Pythagoreans was their notion of the determination of the Infinite by numbers.   And this was their great service to philosophy.

All this, of course, is long prior to the time of Plato.   What the Pythagoreans of his period or immediately before it were doing it is difficult to say with any certainty.   In part, no doubt, they must have been occupied in developing the details of their philosophy and applying it to particular problems. But their work in this respect, so far as we know anything of it, does not impress us very favourably.   We can find no speculation which suggests a philosophical ability comparable to that which conceived the great original inspiration of the school.   Their applications of the doctrine in detail can, in general, merely be dismissed as fanciful.   The numbers and the places in the heavens assigned to marriage and justice and opportunity, of which Aristotle tells us, are mere fantasy. Little more can be said of the attempt ascribed to Eurytus to decide what actual numbers were to be assigned to different

---

[1] Sometimes it appears to be a boundless substance, the air or ' infinite breath ' which Aristotle speaks of in the *Physics*.   According to some Pythagoreans this was inhaled by the physical world.   Sometimes, perhaps for the later Pythagoreans, it seems to be merely space. The quite sensible argument ascribed to Archytas in a fragment of Eudemus for the infinity of space appears to take it in this sense : it seems here to have little metaphysical significance, but the general view may have some connection with the idea of the formation of solid bodies out of points.   In other passages (e.g. *Metaphysics*, 986a) it appears, not as that which is determined by number, but as itself an element of number, being identified for some reason with the even while the odd was identified with limit or determination.   And again the infinite and finite appear merely as one among the pairs of opposites. See the notes in W. D. Ross's edition of the *Metaphysics* and the valuable appendix on τὸ ἄπειρον in R. G. Bury's edition of the *Philebus*.

living creatures. Aristotle tells us that he would mark out the figure of a horse or man in pebbles and then see how many pebbles were used in the process. This procedure was not, perhaps, quite as absurd as it sounds. It was an extravagant extension of the method of representing numbers by dots arranged in a geometrical pattern, a method which is best illustrated, as Burnet suggests, by the numbers marked on dice or dominoes. But in any case this does not give us a very exalted idea of the intellectual ability of some of the leaders of Pythagoreanism at the beginning of the fourth century.

Of other philosophical doctrines that arose in the school we only have slight indications. Thus, Aristotle mentions a view held by some Pythagoreans, and later accepted by Speusippus, which made the good, not itself an ultimate cause or first principle, but something which arose at a definite period in time in the evolution of the physical world. He also tells us of a doctrine of some of them which connected the soul with the motes or specks of dust that we see floating in the air in a strong light. This is the only certain indication that we have of a specific doctrine about the soul held by later Pythagoreans. It has been held, on the strength of late testimony, that the doctrine of the tripartite division of the soul, familiar to readers of the *Republic* and *Timaeus*, was the product of the Pythagorean school and taken over by Plato from them. The earliest authority who can be definitely traced for this view is Posidonius, and we do not know on what he based his assertion. He appears to ascribe its origin to Pythagoras himself, and says that Plato developed it and made it more complete. The doxographers make the same assertion, but we cannot argue with certainty that on this point they go back to Theophrastus. If one can judge from the *Magna Moralia*, the established Peripatetic tradition ascribed the origin of the theory to Plato himself.

There is a small piece of evidence on the subject which is worth quoting, though it is of no very great weight in itself. For it suggests a possible solution of the problem which, if correct, would throw some light on the relations of Plato and the contemporary Pythagoreans. A fragment of Iamblichus refers the theory to ' the followers of Plato and Archytas and the rest of the Pythagoreans '. This would suggest that the theory came to the Pythagoreans from Plato rather than to Plato from the Pythagoreans. Or at any rate it was developed in the fourth century jointly by Plato and his Pythagorean friends, particularly Archytas. And this may very well be the truth. It is quite possible, of course, that the hint which started them on such a line of thought was given by the division of the three kinds of life, the life of enjoyment, the life of action, and the life of contemplation, which tradition assigned to Pythagoras himself. But the developed psychological theory of the *Republic*, of course, is something very different from this. And it would be absurd to describe this division of the three lives as an early form of the Platonic doctrine. What is of importance is the suggestion that Plato was working with and influencing the later Pythagoreans. It should serve to keep us on our guard against ascribing a Pythagorean origin to doctrines that we meet with in Plato's writings, until we are quite sure that they did not come into Pythagoreanism at a late period in its history from Plato himself.

It is interesting to try to connect this with the hint that we have already found in Cicero that Plato's interest in the proof of the immortality of the soul began with his visit to the Pythagoreans in Italy or elsewhere. It is well known, of course, that Pythagoras and his earlier followers taught the doctrine of transmigration, and some memory of this must certainly have survived among Plato's contemporaries. But so far as we can judge it did not take an important place in their thought. Echecrates, indeed, if Plato's representation is true, held the quite incompatible doctrine of the soul as the harmony of the body. But he does not seem to have realized the absolute incompatibility of this belief with a belief in immortality. It seems going too far to say that the Pythagoreans of the period had entirely dropped the original belief. And it seems likely from what we have seen that there were plenty of discussions about the soul going on in the school. Plato may well have felt stimulated by these to attempt to work out his own position. It is not suggested by the passage in Cicero that he borrowed his doctrine directly from the Pythagoreans.

To return to our main argument, then, it does not seem likely that after the great initial revelation the Pythagoreans, particularly during the period under consideration, added very much of value to strictly philosophical speculation. On the contrary, the tendency seems, in general, to have been one of degradation, in that this initial revelation was subjected to purely fanciful explanations and applications, which are apt to-day to obscure its real significance. But, alongside of this, there seems to have gone a great deal of activity in investigating the subject-matter of various special sciences. We have a good many allusions to Pythagorean views on these matters, views which, on some points, differed widely among themselves. There does not seem, so far as we can judge, to have been one single Pythagorean school of scientific research. Each individual, or at any rate each group, went its own way, and what they had in common was only the original inspiration to pursue this kind of investigation. At any rate, it is significant how often we are told of different views on particular points being held by different Pythagoreans.

Most of the special sciences of the time seem to have received attention from some group of Pythagoreans. Philolaus wrote on medical theory, though, as far as we can judge, his contributions were not of great interest or originality. There were some contributions, also, to the zoology of the period. Aristotle tells us in the *Parva Naturalia*, for instance, that some Pythagoreans held that there were animals which received all their nourishment from odours alone. But these are isolated cases, and their contributions to the biological sciences do not, in general, seem to have been very considerable or important. Their interest was, as we should expect, far greater in the mathematical sciences, particularly astronomy. Their most important contribution in this direction, the notion that the earth was not fixed and stationary but revolved round a central fire, may well have been, as the best authorities suppose, the work of contemporaries of Plato. Of their other theories in this line, some were no doubt earlier but some must certainly have belonged to his lifetime. There was a continual tradition of astronomical investigation throughout the history of the school. We have many statements of their beliefs on questions such as the nature of the Milky Way, the nature of comets, the cause of eclipses, the phases of the moon, and other similar problems. But we have few accounts of the methods by which they arrived at their conclusions. Such as we have do not increase our respect for their scientific abilities. There is far too much of the appeal to that kind of mathematical superstition to which they were undoubtedly prone, such as the idea that the right position was somehow superior to the left and that, as ten was the perfect number, there must be ten planets. Of course, this sort of thing can exist side by side with real scientific reasoning. And even in the cases in which such arguments as these are quoted there may have also been some serious reasoning which was what really led to the adoption of the belief in question.   Modern scholars have in several cases made conjectures of what this reasoning might be.   But they remain conjectures.[1]

Alongside of this must have gone a continuous devotion to mathematical studies.   The only parts of this that we can date with certainty in Plato's lifetime are the mathematical researches of Archytas.   But these are sufficiently remarkable. We have extant his solution of the problem of the duplication of the cube, a remarkable construction which excites the admiration of modern historians of mathematics.   He also made important contributions to the science of harmonics, and discovered the correct numerical formulae for certain musical intervals which had so far remained unknown.   He seems, also, to have laid the foundations for the development of a science of mechanics.   We are even told that he used his knowledge in the construction of ingenious mechanical toys, such as a mechanical pigeon that would really fly.   Altogether, he was certainly a mathematician of the first rank.   But it is very doubtful if his interests extended very much beyond the limits of his special science.   At any rate, we hear of no original contributions to philosophical thought ascribed to him, and the genuine extant fragments are purely on mathematical subjects. We may probably conjecture that his philosophical views were those that he took over from the tradition of his school, possibly modified by the influence of Plato, while his real interest lay in mathematical investigation.

From these scanty indications we can form some notion of the impression that the Pythagoreans of his time would have made on a man like Plato.   They were the inheritors of one main idea of fundamental importance.   And this idea certainly made a strong appeal to Plato.   But they do not seem to have added much beyond this to philosophical theory, and even their applications and explanations of their main idea were full of mythology and fanciful symbolism.   There was probably,

---

[1] Thus, Aristotle tells us that they introduced the counter-earth to make up the number of the moving heavenly bodies to ten, because ten was the perfect number.   Elsewhere we read that some Pythagoreans used the counter-earth as an explanation of lunar eclipses. So Heath and Burnet have argued that this must have been the real reason for the introduction of the counter-earth.   But this is only conjecture : it is just as likely that the counter-earth was originally introduced for the reasons Aristotle stated, and then used later to explain eclipses.   At any rate, it is hard to believe that Aristotle's statement is pure invention.

indeed, a considerable element of this from the beginning. And this must be borne in mind when we are considering the question of Plato's debt to the Pythagoreans. His supposed borrowing from them may often mean no more than that a mere poetical fancy of theirs suggests to him a direction in which he could work out a serious philosophical theory. We must remember this when a resemblance of phraseology is put forward as evidence for a Pythagorean origin for some of Plato's ideas. On the other hand, there can be little doubt of the seriousness and importance of the work of at least some Pythagoreans in the special sciences, particularly in mathematics. And there can be equally little doubt that this must have both interested and impressed Plato, and so far influenced his thought. Beyond this it is impossible to go without a detailed examination of Plato's philosophy. But enough has been said to indicate the possibilities of exaggerating the importance of the Pythagoreans in this connection. And we must always remember that, as far as Pythagoreanism of the fourth century went, Plato's influence on it may well have been at least as great as its influence on him.

# CHAPTER XIV

## PLATO ON HIS CONTEMPORARIES

THERE is little more that we can say with confidence about contemporaries of Plato with whom we know that he must have been brought into contact, and about whom we have knowledge from independent sources. For further information we must look, if anywhere, to the Platonic dialogues themselves. It would be the task of the commentator on the dialogues to discuss in detail the information that we can derive from them about particular schools of thought. Our task here is to consider rather the general critical principles which would have to be followed in such a discussion.

For reasons already given we have to suppose that the arguments in the dialogues have some reference to contemporary thought. We have already discussed at length how far we can get at Plato's own views from the words that he puts into the mouth of Socrates. What we have to consider now is the question how far we can get at the views of Plato's contemporaries from the words he puts into the mouths of other characters in the dialogues and also from what is said about other thinkers by these characters or by Socrates himself. And we may begin by a threefold distinction between the different kinds of evidence that we have of this sort. We have, in the first place, the opinions expressed by the other characters in the dialogues. Next we have the opinions ascribed in the course of the discussion to some one who is mentioned by name. This is generally a prominent figure of the past, immediate or more remote, such as Protagoras and Heraclitus, whose views are discussed in the *Theaetetus*. And finally we have, particularly in the later dialogues, opinions ascribed to some unnamed person or persons. It is clear that each category must be considered separately.

In the first category there are very few cases in which any real difficulty arises. In most of the earliest dialogues, for instance, it is clear that the other characters represent the

ordinary difficulties or confusions of thought that were likely
to arise in the minds of ' plain men ' in the questions under
discussion.   They are put into the mouths of particular individuals, and these individuals take on a real personality as
the dialogue develops.   How far this corresponds to the personality ·of the historical person of the name, we cannot tell :
obviously in some cases where Plato can hardly have known
the man concerned there must be a good deal of imaginative
reconstruction.   But there is no question of the kind of view expressed being peculiar to these or to any particular individuals.
No one would suggest, for instance, that Laches was the only
person who might have defined courage as holding one's
station and not running away in battle.   The same applies,
very often, when it is a question of a more systematic view.
The theories put forward by Callicles in the *Gorgias* were, as
we have seen, widespread and popular.   They had no special
connection with Callicles, whoever he may have been, though
doubtless a politician of that type would have found them
particularly attractive.   In other cases, again, as in the *Phaedo*
and the *Theaetetus*, the views put forward by the other speakers
are not in any way claimed as original.   They are put forward
as views which have come to them from other sources, and
which they would like to hear Socrates discuss.

The general impression that we cannot but receive from
Plato's writings is that he was mainly interested in the statement and discussion of general views on their merits, and very
little with the details of the formulation of such views by any
one particular person.   What he makes Socrates say to Charmides surely expresses his own general point of view :  ' It is
not who said it that we are concerned to investigate, but
whether it is true or not.'   Any one who has attended philosophical discussions, and noted how easily they may become
diverted into an interminable argument about the precise meaning of a particular phrase used by a particular author, will
sympathize with this.   And from this point of view there were
undoubted advantages to Plato in working with figures from
the past, about whom it was no longer possible to raise the
question whether that was exactly what they meant or not,
particularly as he does not in general choose people who had
put their views on the subject in writing.   No doubt that was
not the main consideration which led him to choose these
characters.   He chose them, in the first place, because for
reasons already suggested he had made Socrates his principal

figure, and the other figures had to be his contemporaries.    It was partly for this reason that he did not make them purely imaginary figures, as a modern author would have done.    But it was perhaps even more because such a procedure would probably never have occurred to him.    The purely fictitious figure was still something of a novelty in Greek literature.    It was already familiar, of course, in comedy.    But for serious discussions, as we can see, for instance, from the *Cyropaedia*, it would still seem more natural to write fiction about a real person than to invent an imaginary one.

In any case, this ought to make us very unwilling to believe that Plato would ever have wished to throw away the advantages of this method by using his characters as a mere mask for some particular contemporary of his own.    The idea that any character in the dialogues represents in detail a contemporary person, so that we can ascribe every statement and argument put into his mouth to the living person whom he represents, is entirely unacceptable.    In this respect, we can find an analogy in the fictitious characters in modern dialogues.    Berkeley's Hylas, though he does begin to come alive in the course of the dialogues, is obviously not intended to represent any particular person living at the time.    He represents only a current point of view.    It is the same with, say, Plato's Cratylus, who has been identified by some scholars with Antisthenes.    Even if it were proved, which it is not, that Antisthenes held the view that names belonged to things by nature, the identification would still be faulty, and it would be entirely unwarranted to ascribe any of the details of the presentation to Antisthenes.    The actual formulation in every case is Plato's, and his chief object would be to bring out the essential features of the theory as clearly as possible for the purpose of examining its truth.    In formulating it he would naturally draw information from every source available.    And he would naturally, also, select as its mouthpiece, whenever possible, some one who actually had affiliations with the view in question.    Thus from the discussion in the *Cratylus* we could infer that Cratylus probably held views which had some connection with the general view ascribed to him there, and that this general view was still current at the time of writing.    But little more could be inferred with safety.

The same would apply to other dialogues.    From the *Euthydemus* we could infer that Euthydemus and Dionysodorus had been in their time trick sophists of the kind satirized, and that such people and such practices still survived at the time of writing. Both these conclusions, incidentally, could be confirmed by independent sources.

On the other hand, we cannot doubt that, if there was any particular reason for doing so, Plato would not have hesitated to depart just as far from the actual opinions of his original as was convenient for the purposes of the particular argument. Consider the *Parmenides*, for instance. It is difficult or impossible to believe that Parmenides himself ever took up such an attitude as is ascribed to him here. And there is no reason, in this case, to dispute the almost universally accepted view that his arguments represent the kind of arguments that were used by the contemporary inheritors of his tradition, the Megarians. ' The kind of arguments,' be it noted. For no more here than anywhere else need we suppose that a particular individual, Euclides or any one else, is represented by Parmenides, or that the arguments, as actually formulated, are simply copied from some written work by such an individual.

There is comparatively little difficulty about our second category, the discussion by name of some great thinker of the past. There is no reason to doubt that, when Plato expressly declares that he is discussing the views of Protagoras or Heraclitus or Parmenides, he really is discussing them. And there is equally little reason to doubt that such discussions would be regarded as bearing on the controversies of his own time. This should hardly need arguing. After all, even in our own day there are works written fifty, sixty or even a hundred years ago or more, which are still treated as the subject-matter of actual controversy. And our age is far more impatient of antiquity than Plato's was. If we needed evidence we could find it from Plato himself and from Aristotle. According to the *Theaetetus*, the Heracliteans and the followers of Protagoras were flourishing sects in 399 B.C., and the former are even described as growing in numbers and importance. And there is absolutely no reason to suppose that they died out in the course of the next thirty years. Aristotle, at any rate, thought it necessary to devote a whole chapter of his *Metaphysics* to the refutation of Protagoras, and he certainly does not suggest that his doctrine had become purely a thing of the past. Relativism, indeed, has a perennial attraction for certain types of mind. And refutations of it even to-day would not be altogether out of place.

It is much more important to note how Plato treats the

theories of these thinkers in the dialogues.    There is no detailed
exegesis of their own words.    Indeed, hardly more than a
phrase or two is quoted direct.    He goes straight to the central
point in the teaching of each of them, and argues it on its own
merits, irrespective of the particular way in which it was
actually presented.    Indeed, he does not, apparently, hesitate
to restate it in his own words and even to construct a defence
of it of his own if he cannot find the points he is raising treated
adequately by the original author.[1]    Such facts do much to
confirm our original impression that his interest lies in the
consideration of the truth and significance of certain general
views, not in a detailed examination of their particular present-
ment by the individuals most closely associated with them.

We have, finally, our third category, the views that are
ascribed to some particular individuals or groups, who are
described in a way which would probably enable those who
knew them to identify them without difficulty, but not named.
Such allusions occur most frequently in the latest dialogues.
But as early as the *Euthydemus* we have the well-known
reference to the unnamed individual who is described as a
writer of speeches, on the border line between philosophers and
politicians.    The identification of most of these allusions has
afforded matter for lively controversy.    Among those which
have been most discussed we may mention the author of the
interesting theory of knowledge which Socrates at the end of
the *Theaetetus* says that he had heard in a dream, the ' Friends
of the Forms ' in the *Sophist*, the materialists discussed in the
*Sophist* and mentioned also in the *Theaetetus* and the *Laws*, and
the two groups mentioned in the *Philebus*, the clever students
of nature who deny that there is such a thing as pleasure at all,
and the smart fellows who try to prove that pleasure is a process
of becoming, not a state of being.

The general principles of interpretation in these cases should
not be very difficult to establish.    We must suppose, even more
clearly here than in the previous cases, that the views expressed
were current at the time of writing.    But there must also be
a special significance in the fact that they are not associated
with any one of Socrates' contemporaries or predecessors by
name.    The natural and reasonable explanation of this, in
view of the fact that Plato mentions names freely in connection

---

[1] See particularly the presentation of the case for Protagoras in the
*Theaetetus*.    Phrases like those at 168c 3 and 169e 3 make it clear that
this is Plato's own construction.

with other views, is that these views were to a special degree the product of the period after Socrates' death. There were no contemporaries or predecessors of Socrates with which they could be plausibly associated. And Plato, therefore, avoids the formal anachronism by not mentioning any name in connection with them. This explanation is entirely in accord with the general account of Plato's intentions given above. It can only be rejected if we adopt as an absolute dogma the view that Plato's intention in the dialogues was purely historical, and that every allusion must refer exclusively to the age of Socrates.

Nobody, probably, does adopt this dogma in its entirety. And it is universally admitted that some of these allusions do refer to Plato's contemporaries. But others would still be contested. Thus the very common identification of the writer of speeches who is half-philosopher half-politician of the *Euthydemus* with Isocrates is challenged by Professor Taylor in his *Plato*, mainly on the ground that 'we have no right' to attribute such an anachronism to Plato without absolute proof, and that there were or might have been people in the fifth century whom the description would fit equally well. But the argument rests on the assumption of what is just the point at issue, namely that Plato would have been at all concerned to avoid anachronisms of this kind. We may ask the same question here as we asked about the allusions to fourth-century political conditions. Would not any one who read the *Euthydemus* when it was published have thought of Isocrates when he read the passage? If Plato realized, as he must have done, what his portrait would suggest to his readers, and yet took no steps to guard against it, we can hardly deny that the allusion was intentional.

There are further questions that might be raised. Are, for instance, the views discussed those of a single individual or a particular school of thought, or are they widespread current views not confined to any one particular school? Such a question could only be answered by a consideration of the way in which each particular view is presented. Thus the account of the materialists in the *Sophist* and elsewhere suggests rather a general and widespread tendency of thought than the doctrines of any particular school. On the other hand, the theory of knowledge quoted in the *Theaetetus* is much too specific in its details to be anything but the theory of one particular man or at any rate of one particular school. Similarly

13

the ' friends of the Forms ' in the *Sophist* are obviously a definite group of persons.   What does seem most improbable in this last case is the suggestion, that used to find favour with some scholars, that Plato had taken this roundabout and unnatural way of indicating his own earlier views, which he now wished to criticize.   Apart from the general improbability of this, it does not seem consonant with any plausible conjecture that we can form about Plato's objects in writing the dialogues.

The identification of the holders of these views obviously depends upon a comparison of the indications in the dialogues with what we know from external sources.   And the scanty amount of these last must make us reconcile ourselves to the fact that in many cases identification must be impossible, except as a mere guess.   The identification of the passage in the *Theaetetus* really turns on the interpretation of the statement by Aristotle, quoted above.[1]   If the second part of that really refers to Antisthenes it would be difficult to resist the conclusion that he is indicated in the *Theaetetus*.   For the identification of the ' friends of the Forms ' we have one definite piece of external evidence in the explicit statement by Proclus that they were Pythagoreans.   But opinions may differ on the question how far Proclus had access to any authentic tradition of interpretation [2] and how far he may have been influenced by Pythagorean propaganda of some intervening period.   On the other side, there is the remark of the Eleatic stranger about his own intimacy with these men which may be taken to suggest a connection with the contemporary representatives of Eleaticism, the Megarians.   They could hardly be identified without qualification with the regular members of this school. But the suggestion of Megarian connections might be regarded as confirmed by a consideration of some of the arguments in the *Parmenides*, supposed to come from Megarian sources.   On one interpretation, at any rate, of these they might be regarded as leading up to the adoption of a position similar to that ascribed to the ' friends of the Forms '.   But any identification is a hazardous matter.

Perhaps it would be well in these questions to adopt a form of Plato's own principle for ourselves and to say that it is more important to understand what views were being maintained at this time than to know the names of the people who maintained them.   And if we look at what Plato says himself we get a clear impression of the contemporary movements of

[1] See page 165.          [2] For this point see Appendix III.

thought which he, at any rate, regarded as of the greatest significance.

If we look at the earliest dialogues we get the impression that he was chiefly concerned with the confusions and inadequacies of ordinary moral and political assumptions. But that is, of course, not specially characteristic of any particular age. Popular assumptions are always and necessarily confused and inadequate. And we soon pass on to the subversive theories to which these confusions and inadequacies made ordinary thought such an easy prey. Enough has been said of these in an earlier chapter. And it has been shown there that, so far as we can judge from Plato's evidence, they must have been still current up to the end of his life. But in his later work he seems less interested in a direct consideration of them than in the metaphysical view which he believes to underlie them. This he finds in the doctrines of materialism. And the first point, then, that we can gather from his dialogues is the prevalence of some kind of materialist view, either in the extreme form that nothing at all exists except what can be touched and handled, or in the more subtle form that anything else that there may be has only a derivative and dependent existence, and that the only permanent and fundamental reality is matter. In either form, he regards it as a dangerous falsehood which he is prepared to devote his best energies to combating. And he leaves us in no doubt that he regards it as a very widespread falsehood.

The other danger with which he seems particularly impressed is the danger of the spread of theories of scepticism, which throw doubts on the possibility of scientific or indeed of any knowledge. And, once more, he shows us that he regards the tendencies leading to scepticism as widely spread and dangerous. He finds them implicit in the tricks of oratory and the sophistic juggles of men like Euthydemus. He finds them in the relativism of Protagoras, which still finds favour in his day in many quarters. With this last he associates theories which make sensation the one form of knowledge, and with both of them he associates the metaphysical views of Heraclitus and his doctrine of perpetual change. This association, it is clear, is his own idea, and it is a very subtle piece of philosophical criticism. All these are prevalent views, which need discussion and receive it in dialogues like the *Theaetetus*. We do not, however, find evidence of a developed and systematic philosophy of scepticism such as arose later. Even the relativism

of Protagoras does not amount to that.    But the tendencies
leading in this direction are manifold.    And it is clear that
Plato thought that they could best be countered by the development of a logic and theory of knowledge, which would remove
the difficulties that provided a favourable ground for their
development.

On the other hand, Plato makes it clear that he did not
regard himself as alone in his task.    There are many indications
of other thinkers working on the same problems.    And even if
he criticizes their views, he makes it clear that in the fundamental division of opinion he regards them as on the same side
as himself.    Both the ' friends of the Forms ' and the author
of the theory of knowledge in the *Theaetetus* are treated with
respect and sympathy as making serious contributions to the
discussion in which Plato was interested.    So are some of those
whose suggestions for a theory of pleasure are quoted in the
*Philebus*.    Further there are clear indications that his own
special theories had become the centre of a considerable degree
of discussion, and that criticisms of them were being put
forward not only by fundamental opponents of his own point
of view, but by those who shared a good many of his views and
may even have collaborated with him up to a point in the
development of them.    But with this we approach the discussion of Plato's own philosophy, and the preliminary task
attempted in this volume must end.

# APPENDIX I

## THE PLATONIC LETTERS

IT seems desirable to develop in somewhat greater detail the view adopted in the text on the question of the Platonic Epistles. I find it very difficult to attach any weight, one way or the other, to a great many of the detailed arguments that have been employed on this question. Thus reminiscences of phrases used in the dialogues, which have sometimes been regarded as favourable and sometimes as unfavourable to the claims of the Letter concerned, seem in reality to be equally compatible with either view. Nor are supposed incompatibilities of particular passages with some preconceived idea of Plato's character of any real weight, considering that the letters are almost the only material we have for the formation of an idea of his character. As a matter of fact the impression they give ought to be favourable enough to satisfy most people's requirements. Various incidental remarks which have appeared to some critics to be not the sort of thing that they would have expected Plato to say are even more worthless. Even apparent contradictions on matters of historical fact with evidence from other sources would not be fatal to the claims of a letter unless we could prove both of two things : firstly that the other evidence is undoubtedly to be preferred to the evidence of Plato, and secondly that Plato could not possibly have made a mistake about the fact.

The real grounds for suspicion of the collection as a whole are the grounds for suspicion of all Greek letters, namely that the forgery of letters for the purpose of selling them to the great libraries was a common practice of the Alexandrian period. And this was undoubtedly the first consideration that inclined scholars to reject them. It ought to be clear that unless there are grounds for suspecting them of being a forgery of that period for that purpose there are really no grounds for suspecting the collection as a whole at all. It is a psychological curiosity that some scholars have not felt themselves able to maintain this, and yet have continued to cling to their faith in the spuriousness of the letters, when they have themselves abandoned the original grounds for that faith. And so we get the curious theories that, for instance, the letters were essays on subjects set by Plato to the students in the Academy, and other equally baseless speculations.

If we recognize that mathematical certainty is unattainable in these matters, certain general considerations seem fairly decisive. It is generally admitted by all scholars who have examined the letters from this point of view, that the language in which they are written is definitely the language of the fourth century, and what is more, that it is as like the language of Plato's later dialogues as one could expect the language of a letter to be to that of a dialogue. We cannot say for certain that no forger would have been capable of this. But most of the forged compositions of later periods generally betray themselves at some point. Further—though this is only valuable as confirmatory evidence—there are several small instances of casual phrases which strike us at first as not what we should expect (and therefore not what a later forger would expect) of Plato, but which on reflection we realize to be quite correct and natural.[1] Finally, as we have seen, there is good reason to suppose that Plato's written works were preserved in the Academy from an early date.

The conclusion seems necessarily to follow that the letters as we have them are part of the collection of Plato's works made by his immediate successors, and that there is just as much reason for believing in their genuineness as there is for believing in the genuineness of the dialogues.

We cannot, however, regard this earliest canon as infallible. It includes one letter at least which is certainly not genuine. And it includes also several smaller dialogues which every one would agree in rejecting. It would be of great interest if we had any information about the conditions under which the collection was made and which enabled a few works to be mistakenly included in it. Unfortunately we can only guess. It was suggested above that there was no reason to suppose that these non-Platonic dialogues were deliberately forged and intended to pass as Plato's work. Further, it is very difficult to imagine any motive that the earliest authorities of the Academy could have had for knowingly including in the collection of Plato's work, dialogues which were not by him. One might, indeed, conceive it as possible that an individual member might try to pass off his own work on them as Plato's, if he cared for the work so much that he was prepared to gain immortality for it at the sacrifice of the reputation that he might have gained for himself as its author. But, on the whole, it seems a good deal more likely that the false dialogues got into the collection by mistake, very likely at a date a generation or so

---

[1] For instance, the phrase used in the Seventh Letter of Socrates, φίλον ἄνδρα ἐμοὶ πρεσβύτερον Σωκράτη. Also the detailed accuracy in the same letter about the numbers of those concerned in the rule of the Thirty. This last point—such is the perversity of which even great scholars are capable—was actually given by the late Mr. H. P. Richards as a reason for doubting the letter!

later than its first compilation. That is, they were preserved in the Academy, and then a little later mistaken by some one who found them there for Plato's work.

But this will not quite do for the bulk of the letters. For there can be no question of their not being intended to pass as Plato's work. If they are not genuine, they must be, with one exception, deliberate forgeries. And, as such, they must have deceived those who first made the collection. They could not, like the dialogues on the above hypothesis, have got into the collection in the Academy under one heading and then by mistake have got under another heading later. The only exception to that is the First Letter which, except for the superscription, which might be the work of any copyist or cataloguer, bears no sign that it was ever intended to pass as Plato's at all.

The natural conclusions seem to be these. (1) The collection of letters as a whole is in all probability genuine. (2) If any particular letter is suspected or doubted, it could only be for reasons that arise from a comparison of this with the other letters. The collection as a whole is the only standard by which any individual member can be judged. (3) Before any letter is finally rejected, a plausible suggestion must be produced of (a) why it was forged, (b) how it came to deceive those responsible for the first collection.

Tried by these tests, the First Letter, as every one admits, must be rejected. The situation of the writer is entirely unlike that held by Plato at any time, and it is the one letter which might have got included by a genuine mistake. On the other hand, the Third, Seventh, and Eighth Letters, which have the appearance rather of public pronouncements than of private correspondence, are certainly genuine. They bear all the marks of it, they are perfectly consistent with themselves and each other, and if, as seems certain, they were written for publication in Plato's lifetime, there would be no question of any one being deceived by a forgery. The Fourth, Tenth and Thirteenth all fit perfectly into the picture. The Sixth and Eleventh have absolutely no suspicious circumstances about them, and there seems no possible motive for forging them. One might say the same of the Ninth, which would seem too short to have been worth the trouble of forging. The Twelfth does not look particularly suspicious, but as it was already suspected in antiquity it is better to let it go. Hackforth and Post have found objections to the Fifth, based on very subjective impressions of what Plato would probably have said or thought, which carry no conviction to me at all. Post does try to meet one of the requirements I have laid down by suggesting that the motive of the forgery was to discredit Plato by dwelling on his connection with Macedon. But if that was the forger's object he would not have shown great skill by associating him with Euphraeus, who, as we can see from Demosthenes, became one of the heroes of the anti-Macedonian party.  And, in any case, there is no explanation of how such a forgery could have been accepted by the Academy.

I have left the Second Letter till last because here there really do seem difficulties and discrepancies which throw a certain degree of doubt on it.  It has been a matter of vigorous dispute even among those who believed in its genuineness whether it should be dated after the second visit to Syracuse or after the third.[1]  To me it seems that the advocates on both sides have succeeded in producing almost conclusive arguments against their opponents, but have been much less successful in explaining away the difficulties in their own view.  Against the first date is what seems the decisive consideration that it is clearly implied in the letter that Dionysius had been receiving instruction in philosophy from Plato, and there is reference to a conversation obviously on philosophical subjects ' in the garden under the laurels'.  I cannot see what other occasion this can be identified with than the preliminary talk on philosophy that Plato says, in the Seventh Letter, he had with Dionysius early in his *third* visit.  It cannot be identified with any occasion in the second visit, because Plato says definitely that he had no discussion of philosophical subjects at all during this visit.  It was only after he left that Dionysius became seriously interested in philosophy.

The objections to the later date are equally serious.  According to the Seventh Letter there was a decisive breach between Plato and Dionysius after this last visit, and it is certainly represented there as going far too deep for such a comparatively friendly letter as this to be exchanged afterwards.  The Third Letter is more typical of the tone of the correspondence at this period.  Further, Plato heard at Olympia immediately on his return that Dion was planning an expedition against Syracuse.  It is hardly conceivable that, knowing this, he would have written to Dionysius about the conversation of his friends at Olympia in the language that he uses at the beginning of the Second Letter.  Finally he speaks (312a) of the reasons for his visit to Syracuse, with no suggestion that there had been two visits.  Whichever date we choose, therefore, the situation assumed in this letter seems incompatible with the information we derive from the Seventh.

Having now raised suspicions against the letter on definite grounds of fact, I may permit myself an excursion into more subjective impressions.  Personally, I cannot swallow the philosophical excursus (312d–313a) in the letter, which seems quite unnecessarily incoherent and vague.  No doubt, with sufficient determination an interpretation of it could be given in the light of what Plato says elsewhere.  But when we remember that it is supposed to be an explanation to Dionysius of a point that he found hard to understand, it is difficult to regard it as a rational piece of work.  Further,

[1] See, for instance, the recent controversy between Messrs. Harward and Post in the *Classical Review* for December, 1926, and May, 1927.

though this is still more subjective, the reason given for making the explanations obscure—namely, that it should not be understood by any one else into whose hands it fell—seems to me very unlike Plato. It is certainly not in accordance with what he says elsewhere about the relation of the general public to philosophical questions. He says, in the Seventh Letter for instance, that he does not approve of trying to expound the profoundest philosophical truths to the general public because they could not understand them and might come to despise the practice of philosophy or to form other wrong ideas about it. He never suggests that he does not wish them to understand, and that he is deliberately going to make his explanations obscure in order to prevent their doing so.

What motive, then, would any one have for a forgery of this kind ? We cannot, of course, do more than conjecture. But it is within the bounds of possibility that the forger might have been Dionysius himself or some friend of his acting for him. It is quite possible that the Academy may have received copies of some of Plato's letters after his death from Dionysius : that might be responsible for the presence of a purely private letter like the Thirteenth. And he might have fallen into the temptation of compiling a letter which represented his philosophical relations with Plato in a more favourable light than the facts warranted, either from motives of mere vanity or to make a favourable impression on the Academy, which was probably still an influence in Syracusan affairs. It is true that certain other passages in the letter make us feel that he might have done it a little more thoroughly while he was about it. But that suggests the further possibility that there may have been a genuine letter (probably written after the second visit) as basis, and that Dionysius interpolated certain passages. What those passages are I should hardly venture to say. At least they would include 312d–313c and possibly down to 314c. I believe that this passage has certain stylistic differences from the rest.[1] But on that point I do not feel competent to pass an opinion.

[1] See Hackforth, *The Authorship of the Platonic Epistles,* pp. 50, 51.

# APPENDIX II

## ARISTOTLE'S ACCOUNT OF THE HISTORICAL ORIGIN OF THE THEORY OF IDEAS

*[Reprinted with some alterations from ' The Classical Quarterly,' July and October, 1923.]*

WHAT the influences were which led to the development and formulation of the so-called Theory of Ideas, usually associated with the name of Plato, is a question of perennial interest. And the interest has been increased by the vigorous controversy that, during the last ten years, has been conducted round the question of the exact part played by Socrates in the development of this theory. All the available evidence on the question is accessible and familiar to students of Greek thought, and has been worked over many times. But as there is still no unanimity among scholars as to its true interpretation, it may be worth while to go over the ground once more, even if the only result is to confirm some view which has already been put forward and disputed.

The evidence of Aristotle in this connexion stands in a special position, because, whatever we may think of his value as a witness, he is the only writer of any importance who gives us what sets out to be a definite and continuous historical account of the development of thought on this and similar questions. No one has suggested or could suggest of Aristotle what could be and has been suggested, for instance, of Plato, that his account was not even intended to be historically accurate. There is, also, very little dispute about the main sources of Aristotle's information. No doubt he had access to any philosophical writings that were published and accessible at Athens. But it is agreed that the main body of his information on the subject under discussion must have come to him from Plato, who undoubtedly held a ' Theory of Ideas ', whether he originated it or no. It must be insisted, on the other hand, that information derived from Plato is not the same thing as information derived from the Platonic dialogues. This is, of course, recognized when Aristotle ascribes statements to Plato which cannot be found in any of the dialogues. But when he is speaking of the influence of earlier thinkers on Plato, and particularly when it is a question of the influence of Socrates, it seems to be assumed by some writers, notably Professor Burnet and Professor Taylor, that his statements must be either pure conjecture or derived from the Platonic dialogues (see e.g. Taylor, *Varia Socratica*, p. 54 ; Burnet, edition of the *Phaedo*, p. xxiv, *Greek Philosophy*, p. 313 and elsewhere). There seems, however, to be no ground for this assumption. Indeed it is very unlikely to be true. In his twenty years' association with Plato Aristotle must have had constant personal intercourse with him and with others who knew him. It is really impossible to suppose that Aristotle would be reduced to mere conjecture or to a reading of Plato's published works when he wanted to know anything about him. At least for twenty years of his life he had far more direct and certain sources of information than that.[1]

On the other hand, Aristotle's defects as a witness are generally recognized. With all his ability he had curious ' blind spots ' in his mind, particularly when it was a question of any mathematical theory. His historical sketches are never undertaken for their own sake, but as a preliminary to the development of some positive view of his own, and in consequence he only treats those sides of other theories which have some bearing on what he is going to discuss. He is always, of course, anxious to show that his own philosophy is the final consummation of previous lines of thought ; and this object does not help him either to understand or to explain the full meaning of these earlier theories. So that it is generally agreed that care must be taken to distinguish between his definite historical statements and his often very doubtful conjectures and interpretations. Unfortunately there is by no means the same agreement about which of his statements belong to one class and which to the other.

With these preliminary considerations, let us consider the passages in the *Metaphysics* which may throw some light on our problem. There is little or nothing of value in this connexion in the other works of Aristotle.

Indeed, in the *Metaphysics* itself the directly relevant passages are fewer than we might have hoped. The criticisms of the Ideas with which the book abounds are directed towards the theory in its developed form as Aristotle knew it, and have little or nothing to say about its origins. Further, it is clear from many passages that these criticisms are directed against more than one person, and that the theory had been developed in different directions. We hear of (990b 22) ' certain people ' who followed the theories about Ideas and came into conflict with their original principles.

[1] Professor Taylor in his review of Mr. Ross's edition of the *Metaphysics* (*Mind*, N.S., No. 135) doubts whether Plato ' was in the habit of entertaining the young recruits of the Academy with personal recollections of his youth '. We are not obliged to suppose that, though there is really nothing very improbable about it. But he certainly still taught the Theory of Ideas while Aristotle was a student. And it is surely extremely probable that he gave some account of its historical origin.

We hear further of definite differences of opinion on certain points among ' those who say there are Ideas ' (e.g. 1036b 14). And the curious use of the first person plural in certain passages seems to admit of no explanation except that usually given, that Aristotle is for the moment identifying himself with the Platonic school, so that the criticism in these passages must be taken to be directed against the disciples of Plato as much as against Plato himself. It would not, then, be safe to take any of the statements made about the Theory of Ideas as certain evidence of what Plato himself said, except when he is expressly mentioned by name.

The first passage in which the Ideas are mentioned is also the first passage in which Plato is mentioned by name. That is, of course, in the well-known historical account, beginning at 987a 29. The passage is too long and too familiar to quote *in extenso*. But we may note the chief points of interest in it. And, first of all, the fact that the first and only mention of the Forms in the definitely historical account associates them with the name of Plato. We may also note that Plato's theory of the relations between the εἴδη and the αἰσθητά is expressed in words at least reminiscent of those put in the mouth of Socrates in the dialogues, particularly in the use of the word μέθεξις in this connexion, which Aristotle expressly declares to be a novelty introduced by Plato. Further, a special feature of Plato's view is declared to be ἡ τῶν εἰδῶν εἰσαγωγή. Burnet (*Greek Philosophy*, p. 316) declares that this phrase does not necessarily imply that Plato first invented the theory. This seems very doubtful. In any sense of the word εἰσαγωγή it would seem to imply bringing something in that was not there before.[1] But even if that were not so, in its context it clearly has that implication. It is mentioned in the same sentence with the ἴδια[2] of Plato's philosophy as contrasted with that of the Pythagoreans, and in the description of how Plato came to ' bring in ' the εἴδη he is expressly contrasted with οἱ πρότεροι.

We come now to the direct statements about the relations of this theory of Plato to earlier thinkers. The first statement is fairly definite. The πραγματεία of Plato followed in most respects the Pythagorean philosophy, but with certain ἴδια. It is difficult to say how far ἀκολουθοῦσα implies that it was definitely learnt by Plato from the Pythagoreans, but it no doubt implies a little more than mere independent agreement. On the other hand, it clearly does not mean that Plato began as a follower of the Pythagoreans,

---

[1] Thus in the passage in the *Ethics* (*Eth. Nic.* 1096a 13) τὸ φίλους ἄνδρας εἰσαγαγεῖν τὰ εἴδη, the verb would imply here not that they invented the εἴδη, but that they were the first to bring them into the consideration of the good. It is worth noticing that Aristotle could hardly have spoken of Socrates or the Pythagoreans as φίλους ἄνδρας.

[2] Note Alexander's gloss in the first sentence of this chapter : ὧν ἰδίων ἐν ἦν αὐτοῦ καὶ τὸ περὶ τῶν ἰδεῶν.

and subsequently diverged from them through the influence of other thinkers. The first influence to which he was subjected in his youth was that of the Heracliteans through Cratylus. He adopted their view of the nature of αἰσθητά. and as a consequence of this (ἐκ νέου τε γ ά ϱ κ.τ.λ.) the philosophy he subsequently developed differed in important respects from that of the Pythagoreans. Burnet speaks of this account of the influence of Cratylus as a mere conjecture of Aristotle.[1] I cannot see why. It reads like a definite statement of established historical fact, and, if Plato ὕστεϱον οὕτως ὑπέλαβεν, one which must have been within Aristotle's own experience. In any case, he could have learnt of it from Plato.

We come then to the well-known statement about the influence of Socrates. It is not clear what Burnet means (Greek Philosophy, p. 315) by saying that here Aristotle ' means ' the Socrates of the Phaedo.[2] If taken literally this would make nonsense of the passage, which can only be read as an attempt to sum up the general influence of Socrates, the historical personage, on Plato. Anyhow, the important point is that Socrates was the first person to think seriously about definitions, though only in the realm of τὰ ἠθικά. Plato took him as a teacher (presumably, as Alexander interprets, in the matter of the importance of definitions), but thought that definition was only possible of non-sensible objects because of the ever-changing character of sensible objects. The passage certainly suggests that this was an addition of Plato's, and that Socrates did apply his definitions to sensible objects, or, at any rate, did not take explicitly the view that they could not be so applied. These non-sensible objects of definition were called ἰδέαι by Plato, πϱοσηγόϱευσε implying, if anything, that it was Plato who applied this name to them first.[3]

The next passage adds considerably both to information about the theory and to the difficulty of interpretation. The εἴδη themselves appear as something composite made up of στοιχεῖα. Taking

[1] There is a most curious suggestion of Professor Burnet's (Greek Philosophy, p. 242, n. 1) that this is Aristotle's inference from the Cratylus and the Theaetetus. But it is surely obvious that if, as Professor Burnet supposes, Aristotle believed in the historical character of Plato's portrait of Socrates, he could not infer anything about Plato from his representation of Socrates.

[2] I suppose if the meaning of τὰ ἠθικά and τῆς ὅλης φύσεως is interpreted in a sufficiently ' Pickwickian ' sense the statements in the passage could just be made to fit in with the picture of Socrates in the Phaedo. But it is interesting to note that the reference to τὴν ἐν τοῖς λόγοις σκέψιν, on which Burnet relies for his identification, is made by Aristotle when speaking of Plato, not of Socrates.

[3] This sense of the word seems to be implied even more definitely in 1078b 31, where he says of those who first said there were Ideas, οἱ δ' ἐχώϱισαν, καὶ τὰ τοιαῦτα τῶν ὄντων ἰδέας πϱοσηγόϱευσαν.

this passage in combination with 988a 10–13, we are presented with
a relation between the elements of the εἴδη exactly analogous to
the relation between the εἴδη and the matter of which the particulars are made. We need not yet discuss exactly what is meant
by the One and the Indefinite Dyad. But what is of immediate
importance is the statement of the chief points which distinguished
Plato's theory from that of the Pythagoreans. These are firstly
the substitution of a dyad for the indefinite general concept of τὸ
ἄπειρον. The next point refers to the position of the numbers.
Plato agreed very closely with the Pythagoreans τὸ τοὺς ἀριθμοὺς
αἰτίους εἶναι τοῖς ἄλλοις τῆς οὐσίας. This is the first passage
(excepting the doubtful reading of τοὺς ἀριθμούς two lines above)
in which Aristotle speaks of the numbers in exactly the same terms
as the εἴδη, and we shall have to consider the significance of this
directly. But, he goes on, Plato disagreed with the Pythagoreans
in making the numbers παρὰ τὰ αἰσθητά, whereas ' they say that
the things themselves are numbers, and do not put τὰ μαθηματικά
between them '. μεταξὺ τούτων could only with difficulty be interpreted to mean anything but ' between the things themselves and
the numbers '. Otherwise the introduction of this last clause as
part of the contrast of the Pythagorean view with Plato's putting
of the numbers beyond τὰ αἰσθητά would make it tempting to
interpret τοὺς ἀριθμούς in the first part of the sentence as referring
to the mathematical numbers. Aristotle certainly is not always
careful to make it clear when he is referring to the mathematical
and when to the ideal numbers, as witness the difficult passage in
*Eth. Nic.* 1096a 19.

The next sentence is perhaps more immediately germane to our
purpose, for it professes to give an explanation of these special
features in Plato's philosophy. The chief point here is the reference
to his investigations ἐν τοῖς λόγοις, which led to his making the
One and the numbers παρὰ τὰ πράγματα, and to his introduction of
the εἴδη. These are definitely spoken of as two separate contributions of Plato's.

There is no further passage where Plato is mentioned by name
which will help us much in this investigation. But there is a
passage, 1078b 7–32, of great importance, which has given rise to
considerable discussion, where he speaks of οἱ πρῶτοι τὰς ἰδέας
φήσαντες εἶναι. I will summarize it, quoting in full the crucial
passages. After he has finished a discussion of the nature of τὰ
μαθηματικά, Aristotle goes on : περὶ δὲ τῶν ἰδεῶν πρῶτον αὐτὴν τὴν κατὰ
τὴν ἰδέαν δόξαν ἐπισκεπτέον, μηδὲν συνάπτοντας πρὸς τὴν τῶν ἀριθμῶν
φύσιν, ἀλλ' ὡς ὑπέλαβον ἐξ ἀρχῆς οἱ πρῶτοι τὰς ἰδέας φήσαντες εἶναι.
He then goes on to speak of the philosophical antecedents of
these persons in almost exactly the same terms as he speaks of
Plato's in the previous passage. That is, they were led to this
conclusion by (1) a consideration of the Heraclitean doctrine

of the flux and the consequent impossibility of true knowledge of material things, and (2) the influence of Socrates, who was the first person to try to get definitions which he looked for in the ethical matters in which he was interested. There is a little more detail than we found in the earlier passage about the exact contribution of Socrates, which is described as twofold : τούς τ' ἐπακτικοὺς λόγους καὶ τὸ ὁρίζεσθαι καθόλου. And it ends up : ἀλλ' ὁ μὲν Σωκράτης τὰ καθόλου οὐ χωριστὰ ἐποίει οὐδὲ τοὺς ὁρισμούς · οἱ δ' ἐχώρισαν, καὶ τὰ τοιαῦτα τῶν ὄντων ἰδέας προσηγόρευσαν.

We proceed then to consider the difficulties which have been raised with regard to the interpretation of this passage. Some writers (e.g. Taylor, *Varia Socratica*, pp. 69, 70) take the words μηδὲν συνάπτοντας πρὸς τὴν τῶν ἀριθμῶν φύσιν to mean that those who first said that there were Ideas are definitely distinguished from those who said that the Ideas are numbers. And, as a result of this, both Taylor and Burnet deny that this passage can refer to Plato. This, however, seems to read more into the statement than it will bear. It is just possible, in view of the context of this passage, especially the plan of the discussion as laid down in 1076a 17–29, that the ἀριθμοί here are the mathematical numbers which have just been discussed, and that the contrast, so far as there is one, is with those referred to at the beginning of this book who identified the Ideas with the objects of mathematics. Even, however, if this is not so, the passage still falls far short of the interpretation under discussion. It implies no more than that the originators of the theory of Ideas did not at first (ἐξ ἀρχῆς) connect up this theory with the question of the nature of numbers. And if we take the following sentences to be a further explanation of this point, as is natural, we see that what it means is that the original considerations which led to the genesis of the theory did not necessitate an identification of the Ideas with the numbers. We may note that this is true of Plato and the Academy. Both here and in Book A Aristotle gives some account of the ways καθ' οὓς δείκνυμεν ὅτι ἔστι τὰ εἴδη. Certainly none of these arguments necessitates the identification of the Ideas with numbers nor connects them in any way. And the same is true of many of the arguments that he brings against the theory. The most that we can say is asserted in the present passage is that the question of the existence of the εἴδη is distinct from the question of their relation with numbers. There is no distinction drawn between the persons who raised these questions.

This interpretation is that of the ancient commentators. The Pseudo-Alexander in the commentary on Book M, identifies οἱ πρῶτοι in 1078b 11 with Plato, and οἱ δέ in 1078b 31 with οἱ περὶ Πλάτωνα. He also incidentally remarks that ὁ δὲ Σωκράτης ἰδέας εἶναι οὐκ ἔλεγεν. But the paraphrase of the first passage, 1078b 9–12, is worth quoting in full, because it confirms so definitely all the points made above. καὶ ἐπεὶ ὁ Πλάτων ἀριθμοὺς εἰδητικοὺς ἐκάλει τὰς ἰδέας ἑπόμενος τοῖς Πυθαγορείοις, πρότερον, φησίν, ὡς ἰδέας αὐτὰς ἐξετάσωμεν μή συνάπτοντες μηδὲ μεμνημένοι μήδ᾽ ὅλως ἀναλογιζόμενοι εἴτε εἰσὶν ἀριθμοὶ τὰ εἴδη εἴτε καὶ μή, ἀλλ᾽ εἰς αὐτὴν τὴν ἔννοιαν ἀνελθόντες καθ᾽ ἥν ἰδέας εἶναι ὑ π έ λ α β ε ν [note the singular], ἐπισκεπτέον εἰ δυνατὸν εἶναι ἰδέας. He thus makes it clear that, in his view, Plato first was led by certain arguments to believe in the existence of the Ideas, and then by the influence of the Pythagoreans to identify them with the numbers. Aristotle wishes to treat of the first arguments, without bringing in the question of the identification of the Ideas with the numbers, which is a point for separate consideration.[1]

If this is correct it is clear that the chief, if not the only, difficulty in the way of identifying οἱ πρῶτοι κ.τ.λ. with Plato disappears. But even without that the difficulty in the way of identifying them with anyone else would be insuperable to any but the most determined controversialists. Professor Burnet admits ' that things are said of them which are said of Plato in A 6 ', but thinks that ' in both cases Aristotle is thinking primarily of the εἰδῶν φίλοι in the *Phaedo* (? *Sophist*).' Why, when Aristotle talks of Plato in the earlier passage, he should be thinking ' primarily ' of someone else, must remain a mystery. And surely to say that ' things are said ' about both is rather an understatement of the fact that precisely the same intellectual history is asserted in the two cases. οἱ πρῶτοι κ.τ.λ. are certainly later than Socrates, because we are told that no one before Socrates considered seriously the question of definition. So that we should have to suppose that besides Plato there were other unnamed people who accepted the Heraclitean doctrine of sensible things, were influenced by Socrates' interest in definitions in the realm of morals, and by exactly the same processes of thought arrived independently at the conclusion that there must be ἑτέρας φύσεις παρὰ τὰς αἰσθητὰς μενούσας, and independently gave these the name of Ideas. The supposition is really incredible. Of course there may have been fellow-workers of Plato with whom he co-operated in the original production of the theory. But there is no evidence of this ; the use of the plural (οἱ πρῶτοι) proves nothing in Aristotle. And the resemblance of this passage to that in the First Book is much too close to admit of doubt that it is Plato with whom the whole of the development of this theory is primarily identified.

This conclusion is strengthened by the fact that Aristotle himself or his editors attached as a criticism of the people mentioned here

[1] Syrianus does not help us much. He is chiefly occupied with a polemic against Aristotle for casting doubts upon the historical character of Plato's representation of Socrates. It is a question which need not be discussed here whether his own views on the subject are of any value. But he makes it quite clear that in his opinion Aristotle's account here is absolutely incompatible with the picture of Socrates given in the Platonic dialogues.

a passage which is verbally the same as that in which he criticizes the theories of the Academy in the First Book. If this is intentional and justified,[1] it incidentally entirely destroys the possibility of the identification of οἱ πρῶτοι κ.τ.λ. with the εἰδῶν φίλοι of the *Sophist*, first suggested by Professor Taylor (*Varia Socratica*, p. 81 et seq.). This identification rests on the argument that οἱ δ' ἐχώρισαν in 1078b 31 means that they denied any μέθεξις or any connexion whatever between the εἴδη and the particulars, which of course is asserted of the εἰδῶν φίλοι. But in the criticism repeated here from the First Book there are constant allusions to the μέθεξις of the particulars in the εἴδη.

The identification rests further on the idea that there is some difficulty and obscurity in Aristotle's use of χωρίζειν or χωριστός. But a glance at the last passage which we have to consider will show that there is not really any very great difficulty on this point at all. In 1086a 31 Aristotle glances at the τρόπος and the ἀπορία of those who say that there are Ideas. Here again we have the familiar statements about the influence of the Heraclitean theory of the nature of sensible objects, and of Socrates through his definitions, by which he set the theory going (ἐκίνησε). But the people under discussion are distinguished from Socrates because they made the Ideas χωριστάς, while Socrates οὐκ ἐχώρισεν. And this process of making the Ideas separate is described more in detail as τοῖς αἰσθητοῖς οὐ τὰς αὐτὰς οὐσίας ἐποίουν, and again as thinking that τὸ καθόλου παρὰ ταῦτα εἶναί τε καὶ ἕτερόν τι εἶναι. It is thus clear that by ' separating ' the Ideas from the sensible particulars Aristotle means simply any view that gives them any independent existence, that he describes and criticizes this view when contrasting it with that of Socrates in exactly the same way as he describes it when talking of Plato, and when talking of ' those who first said that there are Ideas,' and finally that he describes it with a phrase almost identical with one put into the mouth of the Platonic Socrates (cf. *Phaedo* 74a 11, παρὰ ταῦτα πάντα [various sensible objects previously enumerated] ἕτερόν τι, αὐτὸ τὸ ἴσον').

We are now in a position to summarize our results. It seems to me clear that a candid reading of Aristotle's statements can leave not a shadow of doubt that he knew nothing of any Theory of Ideas which originated independently of Plato, and that he regarded Plato as probably entirely, certainly mainly, responsible for the invention or discovery of the theory.

If so much is granted we have next to ask what Aristotle thought

---

[1] The joining on certainly looks as if it were done intentionally. I see nothing improbable in the supposition that it is done by Aristotle himself. The *Metaphysics*, as we have it, may well include more than one course of lectures ; and Aristotle, as other lecturers have been known to do since, may have used over again a passage out of an earlier course.

14

about the influences which led Plato to the formation of this theory. On the face of it his account reads fairly simply. But a great many difficulties have been discovered in it by the ingenuity of modern scholars, some of which, however, appear to arise rather from a wish to prove or disprove a particular theory than from an examination of the text.

The part ascribed to Cratylus and the Heracliteans is fairly clear. The words of Aristotle would rather suggest that the teaching of Cratylus was the first philosophic influence to which Plato was subjected. Later biographers (e.g. Diog. Laert. III, i, 6) say that he studied with Cratylus after the death of Socrates. As, however, they also assert that he left Athens for Megara immediately after the death of Socrates, this seems unlikely. In any case the point is a trivial one. It is probable that he was in contact with them both at the same period. At any rate, it is clear that Aristotle considered the acceptance of the Heraclitean doctrine of the perpetual flux as applied to sensible objects to be one of the first steps in the development of Plato's philosophy.

When we come to the influence of Socrates, however, the meaning of Aristotle's account has been the occasion of much dispute. The statements themselves are fairly definite. Socrates was mainly interested in questions of conduct, and he was the first person, in this connection at any rate, to think seriously about definitions. But he did not separate the universal definition from the particulars. There is the further passage where he asserts that the two things that could be fairly ascribed to Socrates are οἱ ἐπακτικοὶ λόγοι καὶ τὸ ὁρίζεσθαι καθόλου. There are difficulties in the interpretation of the ἐπακτικοὶ λόγοι, not so much in the meaning of the words themselves as in the suggestion which the use of the word ἀποδοίη seems to make, that Socrates was the first person who invented them or brought them into use. But I do not think it necessary to discuss these difficulties here, because it seems to me that this passage is clearly a parenthesis and has little or no bearing on the main line of argument. He never again mentions the use of ἐπακτικοὶ λόγοι as having any particular importance as a factor influencing Plato in the formation of the Theory of Ideas, whereas τὸ ὁρίζεσθαι καθόλου is constantly brought in in this connexion. A careful reading of Aristotle's words seems, then, to confirm the conclusion of Professor Taylor (*Varia Socratica*, p. 81) that there are no grounds for connecting the mention of ἐπακτικοὶ λόγοι with the statement that Socrates did not separate the universals from the particulars.

The other statements, however, admit of a much simpler explanation than either Professor Taylor or some of those whom he criticizes gives to them. Socrates appears as the apostle of clear thinking. When people talked vaguely about justice or piety or courage, and discussed whether this or that action was just or brave, he brought them down to the point by asking, What do you mean by these terms ?  He refused to accept a particular instance or an enumeration of particular instances as an answer to his question ; but an inadequate definition was at once brought to the test by the production of a particular instance to which it clearly would not apply. He did not, however, separate the universal property which he was trying to define from the particulars.  There is no reason and no justification for taking this to mean that Socrates considered the question whether the universals had an independent existence apart from and beyond the particulars, and decided that they had not. Nor is there the slightest ground for ascribing a conceptualist theory of universals to Socrates.  That would indeed be, as Professor Burnet (*Greek Philosophy*, p. 317) points out, an anachronism.  The natural interpretation of the statement is that Socrates did not raise the question at all.  Plato did raise it, thus taking the question a step further forward.  But Aristotle states almost in so many words that Plato was led to raise the question and to answer it in the way he did owing to the difficulty that he found in squaring his Heraclitean view with the possibility of universal definition. It was Cratylus rather than Socrates who drove him to ascribe an independent existence to his εἴδη.

This interpretation in no wise depreciates the services of Socrates to thought.  To have started people on this line of thinking would be sufficient service in itself, even if the problem had never been taken further.  As a matter of fact, it simply ascribes to him the procedure that we most of us follow when we are trying to think clearly in moral or political questions.  When Mill discusses the meaning of Liberty or Justice he does not raise any question about the kind of existence that the metaphysician would ascribe to these universal terms.  But the fact that he does not do this in no wise detracts from the value of his discussion.  And the same would apply to many writers on ethical and political questions.  It would apply, indeed, to the Platonic Socrates himself as he is represented in the dialogues usually considered to be specially Socratic.  They show, at least, that Plato thought it perfectly possible to raise and discuss those questions without necessarily considering the further philosophical problems which they suggested to him.

We come now to the question of the relation of Plato's philosophy to that of the Pythagoreans.  Aristotle says that for the most part Plato's theories followed theirs.  It would be a mistake, however, to exaggerate the extent of the identity of view that this implies. The historical account in which this statement occurs is primarily concerned with the question how far earlier thinkers had anticipated Aristotle in his doctrine of the Four Causes.  And it is from this point of view that he finds such close resemblance between Plato and the Pythagoreans.  In 987b 22–35 he summarizes the resemblances and differences between the two, and the differences are certainly as important as the resemblances.  Further, he never (except on one incidental point in 1036b 18) associates the Pythagoreans with the believers in the εἴδη in the criticisms which he brings against the latter. He tends rather to distinguish them expressly (e.g. 990a 33, 1083b 8), and in general he treats the two as maintaining different and separate theories.

But the more important point for our particular investigation is the influence that he supposed the Pythagoreans to have had on the original formation of the theory. It was suggested above that the words τὰ μὲν πολλὰ τούτοις ἀκολουθοῦσα [1] did not necessarily mean that Plato's theory originated as a form of Pythagoreanism and subsequently diverged from it on certain points. But in view of the whole account we can say more than this, for Aristotle expressly states more than once that the influences which led to the original formation of the theory were those of Socrates (whom he never associates, even by a hint, with the Pythagoreans) and Cratylus. The theory in its developed form he regards as resembling Pythagoreanism in many respects. But so far as this is due to the direct influence of the Pythagoreans, that influence must have been brought to bear at a date subsequent to the original formation of the theory. This, at any rate, is the natural conclusion from Aristotle's words.

What, then, are we to make of the relation of the theory to that of the Pythagoreans, of the Ideas as numbers, of the analysis of the Ideas into their στοιχεῖα? It would be impossible to deal with these questions in detail here, and we are only concerned with them so far as they throw a light on the question of the origins of the theory. But we are at least in a position to answer the question whether Aristotle knew of an earlier or a later theory of Ideas, and whether we are to regard the belief that the Ideas were numbers merely, in Professor Burnet's words, as 'a senile aberration' of Plato's. It is clear that Aristotle knows nothing of a definite change in Plato's views in the sense that he adopted one view at one time, and subsequently came to believe that this was wrong and substituted a different view for it. On the other hand, the account, as here interpreted, does strongly suggest that he knew something about developments in the view, that Plato raised and answered certain further questions beyond the views that he first arrived at. Indeed, we should hardly need an Aristotle to tell us this. It would indeed be strange if this or any other theory sprang at one moment full-armed from the head of its creator, leaving no further problems which could be raised about it. We are almost bound to believe that the theory developed, that further questions were asked and answered about it as time went on. But this, of course, is a very different thing from believing that the theory

[1] See the passage in the *Poetics* (1449b 10) and Bywater's note on it for evidence that ἀκολουθεῖν does not necessarily imply succession in time.

changed and that definite parts of it were ever abandoned as false.

If the foregoing arguments are sound, Aristotle's account appears as consistent and intelligible, and it must be taken as serious and important evidence in any consideration of the question. The great question remains of the bearing of this evidence on the interpretation of our other sources of information, Plato in particular. No one would claim that Aristotle is an infallible witness ; and certainly, if his evidence seemed in contradiction to an explicit statement of Plato's, we should have to reject it or interpret it in a sense which would bring it in accord with this other evidence. But when the interpretation of Plato's statements is difficult or disputed, it does not seem an excessive claim to make that that interpretation should be adopted which is in closest accord with the natural meaning of Aristotle's words.

I should not pretend to claim any particular novelty for any of the above arguments. Indeed, it is probably impossible at this time of day to say anything absolutely novel on Platonic or Aristotelian questions. But as controversies on these questions are continually taking a slightly different form there would seem to be a place from time to time for a recapitulation of familiar evidence and old arguments. And that is the most that this paper can claim to have done.

# APPENDIX III

## SOCRATES AND PLATO IN POST-ARISTOTELIAN TRADITION

*[Reprinted with some alterations from ' The Classical Quarterly,' October, 1924, and January, 1925.]*

In a previous article, I have attempted to summarize the evidence of Aristotle about the relations of Socrates and Plato in the development of the theory of Ideas. It may be of interest now to carry the inquiry further, and to see whether writers later than Aristotle have anything of importance to say about the whole question of the general intellectual relationship between the two men. In particular we must inquire whether or how far they regard or say anything to lead us to regard the Dialogues of Plato as a record of Plato's own thought or as a biographical account of the thought of Socrates or—a third possibility—as both at the same time. And, in addition to this, we shall have to attempt some estimate of the value, if any, which we can put upon such statements—an estimate which would depend in its turn on our answer to the question how far they had access to original sources of information no longer extant.

We can think of two possible sources from which information might be derived which would help us to judge about the historical character of Plato's portrait of Socrates. One would be Plato himself, so far as information could have been derived from him personally apart from a reading of his published works ; and the other would be independent accounts of Socrates by others who knew him personally. But on looking into the evidence we find that the information which can be traced to the latter source is extremely slight, so slight indeed as to be almost non-existent. It will be convenient, therefore, to consider it first and get it out of the way before going on to the first source, which is by far the more important.

Of these independent accounts of Socrates we have, of course, extant in a complete form only the *Memorabilia* and the other Socratic writings of Xenophon. Xenophon is quoted freely by later writers, both for sayings of Socrates and for incidents of his life. But as he founded no school and left no tradition behind him, we know as much about his evidence as the later writers, so that he does not fall within the scope of the present discussion. The question of interest for us is whether we can find in these later writers any trace of an independent source of information about Socrates outside of both Xenophon and Plato. And we can say at once that the traces are of the scantiest. The only sources quoted are Aeschines and Antisthenes, both of whom are quoted by Athenaeus as late as the latter half of the second century A.D.[1] Antisthenes alone of the two founded a school, which might possibly have preserved such a tradition.[2] The story of Zeno's first introduction to Crates the Cynic (Diog. Laert. VII, 3) suggests, as Zeller pointed out, that the Cynic school made some sort of claim to have preserved the true Socratic tradition. So that it is just possible that fragments of this may have come down through Zeno to the Stoic school, besides the information that he gained from his Academic teachers. But this is purely problematical, and no conclusion can be based on such a bare possibility. Aeschines' dialogues appear to have had a high reputation as a true portrait of Socrates, and we have considerable fragments of his *Alcibiades* still extant. It cannot be said that these throw any light on our particular problem. But we can see from Diogenes (II, 20 ; III, 36) that there were writers such as Idomeneus of Lampsacus, an historian of the end of the fourth century B.C., author of a book περὶ τῶν Σωκρατικῶν, who seem to have been concerned to 'write up' Aeschines as the true Socratic, at the expense of Plato.

The corrections of Plato which we can derive from these sources are, however, quite apart from their doubtful historical value, extremely small in amount. In any case, being mainly concerned with questions of the incidents of Socrates' life, they do not concern us here. And we can dismiss at the same time the other attacks on Plato's account of these that we find in Athenaeus, attacks which do not from any point of view deserve much discussion. In general, Plato seems to have been accepted as a safe authority for the facts of Socrates' life, though he is not often quoted as such, either Xenophon or some unnamed writer being more frequently used.

We must, however, recognize that there is some trace, scanty though it is, of an attempt to correct Plato's account of Socrates from other sources. We need not linger over the stories which represent Socrates himself as objecting to the portrait that Plato drew of him (e.g. Diog. Laert. III, 35 ; *Vita Anon. Plat.*, ed. Didot, p. 7). It is very doubtful whether any of the dialogues were written during the lifetime of Socrates. But there is a passage of more serious interest which refers to the general range of his interest

---

[1] Aeschines' works were still extant as late as the time of Philostratus (about A.D. 200). See Krauss' introduction to the Teubner edition of the fragments of Aeschines, p. 28.

[2] I have left this sentence as it stood in the original article. But see Chapter XII above for the necessary qualifications of it.

in philosophical questions.  Sextus Empiricus (*Adv. Logic.*, 371, 372) asserts that Socrates was only interested in ethical matters according to τοὺς ἄλλους αὐτοῦ γνωρίμους, whereas Plato ascribes to him an interest in all branches of philosophy, and represents him as interested in definitions and virtues and laws and constitutions and the universe (κόσμος).[1]   He seems to refer to the *Timaeus* as his authority for the last point, which shows that he is not dealing so much with questions of definite views ascribed to Socrates, as with the kind of thing that would interest him.  The value of the statement depends largely, of course, on the authorities to which Sextus is referring.  He quotes Timon of Phlius—not a very reputable witness—as denouncing Plato for this, and it is possible that he was relying for his statement on Timon alone.  Of the writers personally acquainted with Socrates he mentions only Xenophon, but there seems no reason to doubt that he could have had access to the works of other writers such as Aeschines or Antisthenes.

This, then, is the most that we can say—and that only very tentatively and hesitatingly—that it is probable that these writers did not represent Socrates as discussing the kind of questions or putting forward the kind of views that some of the Platonic dialogues ascribe to him.  If this were absolutely proved, however—and it certainly is not—it would not take us very far.  It would merely be negative evidence, and as such would not be conclusive.  For there might have been sides of Socrates which he did not show them, or which they did not wish to record.  At the most their silence on these points would be a fact which called for some explanation.  We cannot, however, assert with any confidence that they were silent on these points.  And, in general, we have to recognize that there is next to no Socratic tradition in later times independent of that which comes to us through Plato.

We turn, then, to the tradition, such as it is, which comes down from Plato himself, through those who knew him personally such as Aristotle, Theophrastus, Speusippus, Xenocrates, and Hermodorus.  I have argued in the previous article that these men must at the very least have received personally from Plato the general information about his intentions in writing the dialogues.  Particularly, if the dialogues were not intended to represent his own view at all, but to be purely a biographical portrait of Socrates, that fact must have been perfectly well known to them, and must in all human probability have been handed on by them to their successors.  They must also have been accurately informed about at least Plato's own idea of his general philosophical relations with his predecessors, particularly Socrates.  We have, then, to trace

---

[1] With this cf. the passage from Dionysius of Halicarnassus quoted by Krauss (*op. cit.*, p. 19) : οἱ τῶν ἠθικῶν διαλόγων ποιηταὶ ὧν ἦν τὸ Σωκρατικὸν διδασκαλεῖον πᾶν ἔξω Πλάτωνο ς κ.τ.λ. The extant fragments of Aeschines certainly bear this out.

the passage of the information that they possessed down the different streams of the traditions of the schools. And let us start, not with the Academy, but with the school in which the study of the history of philosophy was first systematically developed. The Peripatetics had just the same access to the fountain-head as the Academy, and they would be much more likely to have recorded the information that came down to them.

*The Peripatetic Tradition.*—Even if we had access to all those works which are no longer extant, it is almost certain that none would give us more or more reliable information than Aristotle. In my previous article I have discussed the interpretation of his evidence as given in the *Metaphysics*, and have argued that there is really no reasonable doubt that he believed the most striking metaphysical theory put into the mouth of the Socrates of the dialogues to have been the discovery of Plato, and not to have been thought of by Socrates at all, though his influence started Plato on this line of investigation. In support of this, I quoted the ancient commentators, who certainly take Aristotle to mean this, whether they agree with him or not. To the evidence of Alexander, the Pseudo-Alexander, and Syrianus there quoted, may be added that of Joannes Philoponus (*De Aet. Mundi,* II, 2). It is true that he seems to suppose that Aristotle is suggesting that Plato misunderstood Socrates, which is, of course, out of the question. But he leaves no doubt that he takes Aristotle to mean that Socrates did not believe in any ἰδέαι beyond or different from the sensible particulars ((Σωκράτους . . . τὰς ἐν τοῖς αἰσθητοῖς κοινότητας ζητοῦντός τε καὶ ὁριζομένου κ.τ.λ.).

If the first history of Philosophy written, the Φυσικῶν δόξαι of Theophrastus, had survived in its entirety, we might have more definite statements on the subject. But, as a matter of fact, an examination of the available evidence makes it very doubtful whether Theophrastus has any more to tell us than Aristotle. It must be remembered that he was writing a history of opinions on questions of physical science, and it is quite possible that Socrates was never mentioned by him. In the Doxographies none of the definite opinions on individual questions are ascribed to Socrates. The Ideas, the tripartite division of the soul, the idea of the soul as self-mover, of which we hear first in the *Phaedrus,* are all ascribed to Plato, without mention of Socrates.[1]

It is true that in the introductory summaries something is said of him both by Hippolytus and Galen, but only in general terms, while he is never mentioned subsequently by either of them in connexion with any particular opinions. The actual passages are as follows :

[1] Diels is clearly right in regarding the mention of Socrates in the Pseudo-Plutarch as a later interpolation. It does not occur in the parallel passages in Stobaeus (see Diels, pp. 14, 287).

Hippolytus (Diels, *Dox. Graec*, p. 567) : Ὁ μὲν οὖν Σωκράτης γίνεται
Ἀρχελάου τοῦ φυσικοῦ ἀκροατής · ὃς τὸ γνῶθι σαυτὸν προτιμήσας καὶ μεγά-
λην σχολὴν συστήσας ἔσχε πάντων τῶν μαθητῶν ἱκανώτερον τὸν Πλάτωνα,
αὐτὸς μὲν μηδὲ σύγγραμμα καταλιπών. ὁ δὲ Πλάτων τ ῆ ν π ᾶ σ α ν
α ὐ τ ο ῦ σ ο φ ί α ν ἀ π ο μ α ξ ά μ ε ν ο ς συνέστησε τὸ διδασκαλεῖον
μίξας ὁμοῦ φυσικὴν ἠθικὴν διαλεκτικήν.

ἀπομαξάμενος suggests, perhaps, rather a general influence than
the adoption of any particular view, and the last clause certainly
ascribes to Plato the union of the three branches of Philosophy.
But it must be remembered that this is one of the passages in
Hippolytus where, according to Diels, he is drawing on a source
much inferior to that which he uses in other passages. (See
Diels, p. 153.)

Galen begins with a comparatively long introduction in which he
explains that Socrates was the first to treat Philosophy as a guide
to human life, while earlier speculation had dealt entirely with
physical questions. Then comes the usual historical summary in
which, after mentioning Archelaus, he goes on :

οὗπερ Σωκράτης ἀκροατὴς καταστὰς πολλοῖς καὶ τῶν ὕστερον γεγονό των
καὶ τῶν κατ' αὐτὸν αἴτιος τοῦ φιλοσοφεῖν εἰλικρινῶς γέγονε καὶ τοὺς ἐπιγε-
νομένους σχεδὸν ἅπαντας ὡς εἰπεῖν φιλοσοφίας ἐπιθυμητὰς ἀπέφηνε . . .
Πλάτων τοίνυν μάλιστα διενηνοχὼς τῶν ἄλλων ἐπὶ φιλοσοφίαν ἐλθόντων, ὡς
ἄν φαίη τις, ἀ ν ε π ί φ θ ο ν ο ν τ ὴ ν Σ ω κ ρ α τ ι κ ὴ ν μ α ρ τ υ -
ρ ί α ν π α ρ ε σ χ η κ ὼ ς τῆς ἀρχαίας λεγομένης Ἀκαδημίας κατῆρξε.

It is impossible to say how far this vague phrasing implies an
identity of particular views. Here, also, there is no further mention
of Socrates in the accounts of the views held by different thinkers on
particular questions.

Now these passages clearly tell us very little. But, little as it
is, a glance at a further quotation may make us suspect that it is
more than Theophrastus himself thought it necessary to tell us.
In Simplicius' commentary on Aristotle's *Physics* there is the following passage (Simplicius, *In Phys.*, VI, v. 20–25 ; Diels, *Dox. Gr.*, p.
484) :

Ὁ μέντοι Θεόφραστος τοὺς ἄλλους προϊστορήσας ' Τούτοις ' φησίν, ' ἐπι-
γενόμενος Πλάτων τῇ μὲν δόξῃ καὶ τῇ δυνάμει πρότερος τοῖς δὲ χρόνοις
ὕστερος καὶ τὴν πλείστην πραγματείαν περὶ τῆς πρώτης φιλοσοφίας ποιησά-
μενος ἐπέδωκεν ἑαυτὸν καὶ τοῖς φαινομένοις ἁψάμενος τῆς περὶ φύσεως
ἱστορίας, ἐν ᾗ δύο τὰς ἀρχὰς βούλεται ποιεῖν κ.τ.λ.

This is a direct quotation, and it is clear that it is the first mention of Plato in the historical account. Here, at any rate, there is
no statement about the influence of Socrates, or of any of his predecessors, on Plato. Nor does the tone in which Plato is contrasted
with these predecessors suggest that his admired master, Socrates,
is one of those to whom allusion is made here. After this introduction Theophrastus goes straight on to a statement of Plato's own
views—a statement, incidentally, which, as Diels points out (p. 485,

n. 1), appears to be drawn directly from Aristotle's account in the *Metaphysics*. The natural conclusion seems to be that Theophrastus tells us certainly no more about Socrates than we can learn from Aristotle, and very likely nothing about him at all. On the other hand, he tells us a good deal about Plato's views. Most of his information here is about his views on physical questions, mainly drawn from the *Timaeus*. But, so far as we can rely on the accounts in the Doxographies, certain views on important subjects, which Socrates is represented as holding in the dialogues, are by Theophrastus ascribed to Plato without mention of Socrates.

In a much later Peripatetic author, Aristocles of Messene, the teacher of Alexander of Aphrodisias, we find an historical account which has been thought to ascribe to Socrates a much greater share in the formation of Plato's views, at any rate in the Theory of Ideas, than this other evidence would suggest. The extant remains of this writer begin with an account of Plato and what he owed to former writers. The actual words referred to are :

Οὐχ ἥκιστα δὲ καὶ Σωκράτης, αὐτὸ δὴ τὸ λεγόμενον, ἐγένετο πῦρ ἐπὶ πυρί, καθάπερ αὐτὸς ἔφη Πλάτων. εὐφυέστατος γὰρ ὢν καὶ δεινὸς ἀπορῆσαι περὶ παντὸς ὅτουοῦν, ἐπεισήνεγκε τάς τε ἠθικὰς καὶ πολιτικὰς σκέψεις, ἔτι δὲ τὴν περὶ τῶν ἰδεῶν, πρῶτος ἐπιχειρήσας ὁρίζεσθαι · πάντα δὲ ἐγείρων λόγον καὶ περὶ πάντων ζητῶν, ἔφθη τελευτήσας.

Burnet (*Plato's Phaedo*, p. xlvii) characteristically asserts that this is ' the true Peripatetic interpretation ' of Aristotle's account. But he offers no arguments in support of this view. On the face of it, it does not appear to be an interpretation of Aristotle's account at all, but an account given by Aristocles himself, with no indication at all of the authority on which it is based. As an interpretation of Aristotle's words it seems to me absolutely impossible, and in direct contradiction to the interpretations of all other commentators.[1] At the best it is couched in very vague and general terms, and altogether I can see no reason for attaching much value to it as an indication of the teaching of Aristotle or his immediate successors.

Before leaving the Peripatetic tradition, there is still something to be said about their account of the ethical views of Socrates and Plato. There are familiar statements in the *Nicomachean Ethics* to the effect that Socrates believed that virtue was knowledge, and that ἀκρασία was impossible. And there are similar statements in the *Eudemian Ethics*. Now such assertions could quite naturally be made about the Socrates of the *Protagoras*, or indeed of most of the earliest dialogues. But equally certainly they could not be

[1] That is, if it is to be taken as Professor Burnet understands it. But I should be inclined to question his interpretation. To say that Socrates introduced investigation about the Ideas by being the first person who tried to define seems to me to say no more than Aristotle says, and to fall far short of asserting that Socrates believed in the Ideas.

made of the Socrates of the *Republic* or the *Phaedrus*, or even of the *Meno*. It has, however, been argued that these assertions are only intended to apply to Socrates, the dramatic figure in some of these earlier dialogues, who is selected as a suitable example of a particular view which Aristotle is anxious to deal with. But it is difficult to maintain this interpretation in view of the much more definite statements on the same subject in the *Magna Moralia*. This is, of course, a later work of the Peripatetic school.[1] But it is none the less strong evidence for the tradition that springs from Aristotle himself. We have the authority of Burnet (*The Ethics of Aristotle*, p. xi) for saying that it cannot be later than the third century B.C., and that it ' is, therefore,' in his words, ' evidence of the school tradition at a time when there was still a school with a living tradition.'

The passage in question occurs in the brief historical sketch at the beginning (*Magna Moralia*, I, i, 5–7). Socrates, we are told, τὰς γὰρ ἀρετὰς ἐπιστήμας ἐποίει. This, the author argues, involves that αἱ ἀρεταὶ πᾶσαι κατ' αὐτὸν ἐν τῷ λογιστικῷ τῆς ψυχῆς μορίῳ, which in fact means, he goes on, doing away with the unreasoning part of the soul altogether, and therefore doing away with πάθος καὶ ἦθος. Plato, as contrasted with this, διείλετο τὴν ψυχὴν εἴς τε τὸ λόγον ἔχον καὶ εἰς τὸ ἄλογον ὀρθῶς, καὶ ἀπέδωκεν ἑκάστου ἀρετὰς προσηκούσας. This the author approves. But he objects to the further developments of Plato's views, in that they confuse virtue with τὴν πραγματείαν τὴν ὑπὲρ τἀγαθοῦ. There is no need, he argues, to connect questions about virtue with questions about Being and Truth : for they have nothing in common. This is as clear a statement as we could have that views of the kind put into the mouth of the Socrates of the *Republic* and the *Phaedrus* were not the views of the historical Socrates, but were a development of Plato's. And it is clear that the Peripatetic school of this period had, or thought they had, an established tradition of interpretation of the Platonic dialogues, and that on the basis of this they thought themselves justified in ascribing the views put into the mouth of the Socrates of some of the most important dialogues to Plato and in expressly distinguishing them from the views of the historical Socrates. Nor does there seem any good reason for doubting that this tradition went directly back to Aristotle himself.

This is the extent of the recorded evidence of the Peripatetic school. We cannot tell with any certainty how much further information can be traced back to the same source. It was among the Peripatetics that the writing of histories of philosophy first developed, and the countless later biographers and doxographers

---

[1] Mr. Ross, our chief English authority on Aristotle, appears to have changed his view on this point, and in the introduction to his *Selections from Aristotle* regards the *Magna Moralia* as a genuine work of Aristotle.

traced a great deal of their material back to them. Besides Theophrastus, another pupil of Aristotle's, Dicaearchus, seems to have been a voluminous writer, and to have been much used by later writers. He wrote, among other things, a περὶ βίων, which is quoted five times by Diogenes. But nothing is quoted from him by name which has any bearing on our subject. We turn, then, to the other great school which was in direct contact with Plato, his own foundation, the Academy.

*The Tradition of the Academy.*—The Academic tradition, from which one might naturally hope to receive the fullest and most reliable information on the subject, proves on investigation to be extremely disappointing. And the reason for this is clear. The Peripatetic school became more and more identified with the study of the history of philosophy, so much so that in later years the term Peripatetic became almost identical with historian of philosophy, while their contributions to positive philosophical theory are of small importance. The Academy, on the other hand, from the very beginning showed itself interested in finding out what the truth was rather than what this or that philosopher thought about it. The immediate successors of Plato, it is true, had something to say about his life, though very little of this has come down to us, and nothing which has any bearing on the subject. But their real interest lay in the development of their own views, and we know from Aristotle that on important subjects (e.g. the relations of the mathematical to the ideal numbers) they differed from the views of their master. In later years, of course, the Academy departed from Plato's teaching still more widely, and became for a time the great Sceptical school.

There appears a momentary tendency to a different line of activity in the person of Crantor, a pupil of Xenocrates, who is described by Proclus (*Comm. in Tim.* 20D) as the first Platonic commentator. He wrote a commentary on the *Timaeus*, and his opinions on several points in the interpretation of that dialogue are quoted by Plutarch and Proclus. He seems to have derived hints from Xenocrates, although on important points he differed from him (see Plutarch, *De An. Procr. in Tim.* 1012D). But we have no record of any other commentary of his, and no quotation preserved which has any direct bearing on the subject. It is perhaps worth mentioning the remark of his quoted by Proclus (*loc. cit.*), ὅς [Crantor] δὴ καὶ σκώπτεσθαι μέν φησιν αὐτὸν [i.e. Plato] ὑπὸ τῶν τότε, ὡς οὐκ αὐτὸν ὄντα τῆς πολιτείας εὑρετήν, ἀλλὰ μεταγράψαντα τὰ Αἰγυπτίων, an allusion to the stories of Solon and the Egyptians in the *Timaeus*. There would hardly have been much point in the sarcasm unless Plato had claimed, or was supposed by his contemporaries to claim, originality in the political theories of the *Republic*. But, as evidence, this does not amount to much. And after this we have no sort of evidence from the Academy on the subject for about two centuries.

We meet the Academy next in the person of Cicero. Cicero is known to have studied there, and his philosophical works are recognized to be, in the main, translations or summaries of Greek originals. Among these originals two of the most important are Clitomachus and Antiochus, who both in their time taught in the Academy. Large passages in Cicero's works have been traced directly to them. But, mixed up with this, there are considerable portions which go back to Stoic or Epicurean originals, and it is not always easy to be certain about which is which. In all cases, however, we have to remember that the philosophers quoted were primarily interested in establishing their own views, and that they usually tried to interpret Plato so as to be able to claim his authority in support of these. This obviously weakens their claim to be taken as serious evidence. They may, of course, have had some kind of traditional or written evidence on which they based what they said of him. And it is not likely that there was any strong and definite evidence of this kind which directly contradicted their account. But that is the most we can say.

We find, then, throughout, the reference to Plato of most of the views most commonly associated with his name. Thus in passages derived most probably from Antiochus (*Post. Acad.* 30–32), the belief in the ἰδέαι 'iam a Platone ita nominatam,' is given as among the opinions which his followers received from him, as also is the distinction between knowledge and opinion. Or in the passage probably derived from Clitomachus (*Prior Acad.* 124) the tripartite division of the soul is referred to him. Again we find that the words of Socrates in the dialogues are constantly quoted as evidence of Plato's views. A particularly obvious case is a remark like 'ex quo illa ratio nata est Platonis, quae a Socrate in Phaedro explicata' (*Tusc. Disp.* II, 53). But it must be observed that he also at times uses the dialogues as authority for the opinion of Socrates. Thus in the *Posterior Academics* Varro (who represents Antiochus) states that Socrates was interested in matters of conduct, and that he inculcated virtue, 'ut e Socraticorum libris maximeque Platonis intellegi potest.' We find the same lack of definiteness on this point when Cicero himself is putting the sceptical position in arguments probably taken straight from Clitomachus' writings. Thus he suggests in the *Posterior Academics* that Plato really had no positive opinions, because he argues on both sides in his writings. And again (*Prior Acad.* 74) he says, firstly, that so many dialogues have been written at length which make it certain that Socrates held knowledge to be impossible. And he goes on to argue that Plato would not have developed the consequences of this view in so many books if he had not believed in it himself. He concludes with the curious remark, 'Ironiam enim alterius [i.e. Socrates], perpetuam praesertim, nulla fuit ratio persequi.' If this really represents Clitomachus' arguments it will hardly increase our respect for his clearness of thought. But the whole treatment is typical of the results produced by the tendency of the time to manipulate the historical evidence in the interests of some particular philosophical view.

But there are certain statements of a more general character which show a much more definite view on one historical point. This will be clear from three quotations. The first is from the *De Finibus*, where the information is probably to be traced to Antiochus. ' Nisi enim id faceret, cur Plato Aegyptum peragrauit ut a sacerdotibus barbaris numeros et caelestia acciperet ? Cur post Tarentum ad Archytam ? Cur ad reliquos Pythagoreos, Echecratem, Timaeum, Arionem Locros, ut, cum Socratem expressisset, adiungeret Pythagoreorum disciplinam *eaque, quae Socrates repudiabat*, addisceret ? ' (*De Fin.* V, 87). With this may be associated the statement in *Post. Acad.* I, 15–18, which is to be referred to the same original authority. Socrates, it is explained here, did not arrive at any positive views or lay down any dogmas. It was the influence of Plato on the Academy and the Peripatetics which led to the formation of a regular system of philosophy, a result which Socrates would not have desired.

Our second quotation is from the *Tusculan Disputations*, where Cicero is supposed to be using a Stoic original, possibly Posidonius. ' Platonem ferunt, ut Pythagoreos cognosceret, in Italiam uenisse, et didicisse Pythagorea omnia primumque de animorum aeternitate non solum sensisse idem, quod Pythagoram, sed rationem etiam attulisse ' (*Tusc. Disp.* I, 32).

Finally, we have the most definite statement of all, in the *De Republica* (I. 10), which comes most probably from the Stoic, Panaetius. Scipio is there represented as making the usual assertion that Socrates was exclusively interested in matters of human conduct. Tubero replies that he cannot understand how this tradition has come down. For no one gives us fuller information about him than Plato, and he represents him as interested, not only in these matters, but also in ' numeros et geometriam et harmoniam . . . Pythagorae more.' Scipio replies that this is so. But after Socrates' death, Plato travelled in Italy and came into contact with the Pythagoreans, and bought the books of Philolaus. ' Itaque cum Socratem unice dilexisset eique omnia tribuere uoluisset, leporem Socraticum subtilitatemque sermonis cum obscuritate Pythagorae et cum illa plurimarum artium grauitate contexuit.'

We here get a clear expression of a definite view. The Socratic and the Pythagorean influences on Plato are sharply distinguished and even opposed. Some of the most characteristic views put into the mouth of the Platonic Socrates are declared to be derived from the latter of these two sources, not from the historical Socrates at all. So the portrait of Socrates in the dialogue is definitely represented as being entirely unhistorical in important particulars, the figure of Socrates being used as the mouthpiece of Plato for the expression of views which Socrates himself never held. This is one of the most striking pieces of evidence that we have so far found. There can be no doubt about the meaning of the opinions expressed. But, unfortunately, there can be no such certainty about their historical value, or about their ultimate origin. Certain facts may, however, be noted which have some bearing on these points.

We must observe, to begin with, that this view seems to be part of a Stoic tradition ; for even Antiochus was only half an Academic. This, however, does not tell against it, at any rate by comparison with the Academy of the day, which had departed from the original thought of Plato at least as far as any other school had. But where does the Stoic tradition come from ? It would be tempting to trace back the view of Socrates to a Cynic tradition, going back through Crates to Antisthenes. But such temptations must be resisted in the entire absence of all positive evidence.

It is perhaps more probable that something came down from the Academy in earlier times. Both Zeno and Chrysippus, the ' second founder ' of Stoicism, studied there at one period of their .lives. Some statements, such as that which is repeated more than once that Socrates was only interested in matters of conduct, seem to refer us back to the familiar passage in Aristotle's *Metaphysics*. On the other hand, the source of the statements about the origin of Plato's belief in immortality, cannot be looked for there. The story of the purchase by Plato of the books of Philolaus comes from Aristoxenus (see Burnet, *Early Greek Philosophy*, p. 324), and may have been suggested to him by the last of the Pythagoreans whom he knew. They may also have been responsible for the statements about the belief in immortality. But we cannot say that with any certainty, any more than we can say from what source the definite statements come which oppose Plato's dogmatism to Socrates' scepticism. Of course there is nothing impossible in the idea that the same piece of information may have come through more than one channel. All that we can say with any plausibility is that there were various pieces of information from various sources that by the time of Cicero, or more strictly by the time of his Greek originals, had become welded into one tradition common to all the schools. On the special question of the tradition of the Academy all that we can say is that there was probably no definite. tradition or no published information which positively contradicted this account, and that some items in the account may have been part of the original tradition of that school.

*The Platonic Commentators.*—After Cicero the Academy is no more than a few names to us for nearly five centuries. The nearest that we get to contact with it in this period is in the writings of Plutarch. He was himself a student there, and was well read in the books of Plato and the commentaries thereon.

There is no direct statement on our special subject to be found in Plutarch. But we have plenty of evidence to show how he regarded the Platonic writings. And the first point that emerges beyond a shadow of doubt is that he regarded the dialogues throughout as direct evidence of Plato's own views. It is unnecessary to go through all the countless passages in which opinions expressed by Socrates in the dialogues are quoted as Plato's. Almost all the dialogues are used. And it is not a question merely of a casual ' as Plato says '. We get reference to τοῖς Πλάτωνος ἐν Γοργίᾳ καὶ Πολιτείᾳ δόγμασι (I, 87, 25,[1] Quomodo Adolescens Poetas Audire Debeat ?). After referring to Plato's views on immortality, he gives his evidence of these, φησὶ γὰρ ὁ παρὰ τῷ Πλάτωνι Σωκράτης (I, 295, 12, Cons. ad Apoll.). He quotes the well-known passage from the Phaedo as Plato's criticism of Anaxagoras (III, 135, De Def. Orac.). Most clearly perhaps of all in the De Animae Procreatione in Timaeo he uses several of the dialogues as evidence of Plato's view of the soul. When one of these appears to be in contradiction with the account in the Timaeus he labours to reconcile them, without a hint that he had ever considered the possibility that the Phaedo, for instance, represented Socrates' views, and not Plato's at all.

It is much less easy to say how far he regarded the dialogues as evidence about Socrates. They are rarely quoted for anything to do with him. Xenophon is used more frequently, and many of the stories come from unnamed sources. But he seems to accept the dialogues as historically correct in any statement about incidents in Socrates' life. In the Platonicae Quaestiones he discusses why Plato in the Theaetetus represents Socrates as saying that the god told him to practise midwifery, but forbade him to bear himself. He suggests that the intention of this is to ascribe the critical and dialectical method to Socrates. But he concludes the discussion with the assertion that Socrates had no positive opinions of his own and did not teach any. The same assertion is made in the Aduersus Coloten (VI, 441), though he does imply there that Plato and Socrates thought that there was a sensible and an intelligible world. This last point, however, does not commit him to much. And if the assertion about Socrates' lack of positive opinions represents his considered view, and if, as we have seen to be the case, he thinks that Plato had positive opinions and that these could be found in the dialogues, the conclusion is obvious. But the first condition is far less certainly fulfilled than the second.

After Plutarch we do not come into contact with the Academy again until we reach the age of the commentators in the fifth and early sixth centuries A.D. Incomparably the most important of

[1] The references are to the volume, page, and line of the Teubner edition of Plutarch's Moralia.

these is Proclus. But we have also the commentary on the *Phaedrus* by Hermias, his contemporary and fellow-student under Syrianus at Athens, and several commentaries by the younger Olympiodorus, a writer probably of the later part of the sixth century, who is supposed to have been teaching at Alexandria at a date subsequent to the closing of the Academy. There are also several commentaries on Aristotle by writers of the same school and period, of whom Simplicius is the last and certainly the ablest.

It must be confessed that these Platonic commentaries are not very inspiring reading. And the great bulk of them, being concerned with the interpretation of the text of the dialogues, have nothing of direct bearing on our subject. But we may note first, what emerges with absolute clearness, that all these commentators throughout assume that they are expounding writings in which Plato's own philosophy is to be found. Olympiodorus continually pauses in his exposition of the *Phaedo* to point out some particular δόγμα Πλατωνικόν which is illustrated there. Hermias expounds the theory of the soul in the *Phaedrus* as Plato's, illustrating it by reference to other dialogues, including the *Laws*. Proclus throughout quotes the dialogues for Plato's views. But quotation is really unnecessary, as the fact is so obvious throughout. Perhaps the clearest illustration of this is when Proclus quotes with approval the statement of Iamblichus about τοῖς δέκα [1] διαλόγοις, ἐν οἷς οἴεται τὴν ὅλην τοῦ Πλάτωνος περιέχεσθαι φιλοσοφίαν (Proclus, *In Alcib.*, ed. Creuzer, I, 11), of which the *Alcibiades* is put first. And the contents of these ten are really summarized once more in the *Parmenides* and the *Timaeus* (Proclus, *In Tim.*, ed. Teubner, I, 13).

It is clear beyond a doubt that all the commentators regard the dialogues as expressing Plato's own views. How, then, do they regard the figure of Socrates in them ? The most direct information about this is a passage in the *Prolegomena in Platonis Philosophiam* of Olympiodorus. In speaking of the characters of the dialogues he says : Ταῦτα δὲ τὰ πρόσωπα οὔτε πάντη κέκτηνται τὸ ἱστορικόν · οὐ γὰρ ἂν καὶ τὰ μικρότατα εἶχεν ἱστορῆσαι ὁ Πλάτων, οἷον ὅτι συνέκαμψε τὸ σκέλος ὁ Σωκράτης · ἀλλ᾽ οὔτε πάντα πλασματώδη ἐστὶν τὰ περὶ τὰ πρόσωπα · οὐ γὰρ ἂν ἐκέκτηντο τὸ ἀληθές, ἀλλὰ τὰ εἰς ἑνὸς πράγματος ἀπόδειξιν συντείνοντα. λέγει δ᾽ ὁ Πλάτων δίκην τῶν γραφέων ἐκλεγομένων τὰ ἐπιτήδεια χρώματα πρὸς ἑνὸς εἴδους γραφήν. This is the most definite statement that we have, but it is not very illuminating, and might be open to varying interpretations. It says nothing directly about the opinions put

---

[1] Proclus seems to imply that the ten excluded the *Timaeus* and the *Parmenides*. Olympiodorus (*Prolegomena*, § XXVI) quotes Iamblichus as mentioning twelve dialogues, and gives the list : *Alcibiades, Philebus, Gorgias, Phaedo, Cratylus, Theatetus, Phaedrus, Symposium, Timaeus, Parmenides, Laws, Republic*. But he adds the last two as an afterthought, because ' certain people ' wish to include them.

into the mouths of the characters. But on the whole it is doubtful whether it would allow opinions to be put into their mouths which they had never held at all. The last sentence would rather suggest that Plato would allow himself no more than the liberty to select from the opinions actually held by them those which he himself agreed with and wished to enforce in the particular dialogue.

If this is so, it would follow that, according to these writers, the views put into the mouth of Socrates in the dialogues would be views which he actually held and in which Plato also believed. And this is in fact the impression that we get in general from the commentaries. It is true that very often, when the views are mentioned as those of Socrates, he may be quoted simply as a dramatic character in the dialogue. This explanation would be more doubtful when the view is mentioned as being held by Socrates without special reference to the particular dialogue and confirmed by quotations from other dialogues, which happens more than once. There are, however, three passages in the commentary of Proclus on the *Parmenides*, where he is definitely giving an historical account, which place the matter beyond a doubt. I will give them in full, giving reference to the book of Proclus' commentary, and to the volume and page of Cousin's edition.

(1) Book II (IV, 55) : A reference to the two schools of Italian and Ionian philosophy; then, Σωκράτης δὲ καὶ Πλάτων, ἀμφοτέρων μετασχόντες, τελειοῦσι μὲν τὴν καταδεεστέραν φιλοσοφίαν, ἐκφαίνουσι δὲ τὴν ὑψηλοτέραν, καὶ τοῦτο καὶ ὁ Σωκράτης ἐν Φαίδωνι δηλοῖ, ὅτι πρότερον μὲν φυσιολογίας ἦν ἐραστής, ὕστερον δὲ ἐπὶ τὰ εἴδη καὶ τὰς θείας τῶν ὄντων αἰτίας ἀναδεδράμηκεν.

(2) Book II (IV, 149): ἦν μὲν γὰρ καὶ παρὰ τοῖς Πυθαγορείοις ἡ περὶ τῶν εἰδῶν θεωρία, καὶ δηλοῖ καὶ αὐτὸς ἐν Σοφιστῇ τῶν εἰδῶν φίλους προσαγορεύων τοὺς ἐν Ἰταλίᾳ σοφούς, ἀλλ᾽ ὅ γε μάλιστα πρεσβεύσας καὶ διαρρήδην ὑποθέμενος τὰ εἴδη Σωκράτης ἐστὶν κ.τ.λ.

(3) Book III (V, 4) : καὶ δεῖ λαβεῖν ἐκ τούτων ἐχεγγυωτέρων ὄντων, ὅτι ἄρα οὐ μόνον τῶν ὁριστῶν ἔσχεν ἔννοιαν ὁ Σωκράτης, ἀλλὰ καὶ αὐτῶν τῶν χωριστῶν εἰδῶν · οὐδ᾽, ὡς Ἀριστοτέλης φησίν, ἐπήχθη ἂν εἰς τὴν ἐκείνων θέσιν ἐκ τῆς περὶ τοὺς ὁρισμοὺς διατριβῆς, ἀλλ᾽ ὅτι διὰ θείαν ὄντως ὁρμήν, καὶ ταῖς ἰδέαις αὐτὸς ἐπέβαλεν. This last passage is perhaps the most striking. For it shows Proclus arguing against Aristotle (for the first sentence also is clearly directed against Aristotle's account in the *Metaphysics*) about Socrates' opinions, and using the evidence of the dialogues as the basis of the argument. The three passages together are decisive.

This being the case, we have to ask how much authority this opinion of Proclus and his contemporaries has. We have found no such definite opinions on the subject in any earlier writers. What we have found tends, if anything, in the other direction. Had Proclus access to reliable testimony from the earliest days of the Academy on which he based his view ? He quotes none, at

15*

any rate, though from the last passage it is clear that he knew that there was another view.    There is, however, a passage in Syrianus's commentary on Aristotle's *Metaphysics* which may possibly throw some light on the kind of argument which appealed to these later Platonists in arriving at this conclusion.    Syrianus was the head of the Academy, the teacher both of Proclus and Hermias, and himself a commentator on Plato.    The passage occurs in the commentary on Book M, 1078b.    Syrianus is objecting to the whole of Aristotle's account of the matter.    He denies that there is any truth in the assertion that Socrates did not separate the universal from the particular, and that Plato introduced a new development into the doctrine.    He points out that the Socrates in the dialogues certainly separates the universal.    And Plato, he says, was δίκαιος καὶ ἀξιοπιστότατος ἁπάντων τὰ Σωκράτους ἡμῖν ἀπαγγέλλειν · οὔθ' ὁ παρ' ἐκείνου τὴν φιλοσοφίαν ὑποδεξάμενος ἢ π α ρ έ β η ἄ ν τ ι τ ῶ ν ὑ π ὸ τ ο ῦ δ ι δ α σ κ ά λ ο υ δ ι α τ ε τ α γ μ έ ν ω ν ἢ παραβαίνων αὐτῷ ἐκείνῳ περιετίθει τὰ μηδὲν αὐτῷ προσήκοντα δόγματα.    Syrianus is familiar with the earlier Platonic commentators.    And in a polemical passage it is natural to suppose that, if he had any early authority to bring against Aristotle, he would have quoted it.    It looks much more as if his sole reason for contradicting Aristotle was his own sense of what was fitting in the relations of teacher and disciple.    We may perhaps see in this a characteristic of an age when philosophy was coming more and more to be regarded not as a matter for free inquiry and argument, but as a revelation of truth to be preserved and handed on to successive generations.[1]    It is quite consistent with this that, in point of fact, the original authority should be explained and interpreted in some cases out of all recognition.    In fact, that would be the natural result of this attitude.

All this will help us in deciding the extremely important question of the amount of weight that modern students of Plato should attach to the interpretations of the commentators of this age.    Was there, as some modern scholars seem to suppose, an established tradition of interpretation in the Academy, going ultimately back to Plato himself?    An examination of the evidence hardly supports that view.    We have plenty of references throughout Proclus and the others to serious differences of opinion among Platonic commentators, and it is difficult to find traces of a single established and authoritative interpretation either before or after his time.    Olympiodorus refers more than once to difference of interpretation between him and Damascius (see e.g. *In Alcib.*, ed. Creuzer, pp. 4, 126 ; and

---

[1] I do not wish to be taken as denying the real originality of the best of the later neo-Platonists.    But it is significant that, on the whole, they appear to be anxious to deny their own originality, and to claim that they are merely repeating the thought of Plato.

p. 110 for differences between Proclus and Iamblichus). It is also important to note the other commentators to whom reference is made by name. They go back as far as Xenocrates and Crantor, and the significance of the references to these will have to be considered directly. But after this there is a great gap. The earliest references after these are, I think, to Posidonius (Proclus, *In Parm.* VI, 25, 36 ; *In Tim.* 40 A.B., ed. Teubner, III, 125 ; Hermias, *In Phaedrum* 245c, ed. Couvreur, p. 102), a jump of two hundred years. After this there are one or two references to Dercyllides, of the time of Tiberius, and one or two mentions of Plutarch of Chaeronea in the commentary on the *Timaeus*. And this is all for a space of a century and a half, at any rate so far as we know anything about the authors quoted. And those whom we cannot identify are few and infrequently quoted.

The second century A.D. seems to have been a great age of Platonic commentary.[1] Of the writers quoted by Proclus and the other commentators we can assign with reasonable certainty to this century Gaius, Albinus, Harpocration, and Numenius, who are mentioned by Proclus as among τῶν Πλατωνικῶν οἱ κορυφαῖοι (*In Remp.*, ed. Teubner, II, 96). There is also Atticus, the teacher of Harpocration, and perhaps Severus, while a little later there are Longinus and Origenes, the contemporaries of Plotinus. All these are quoted frequently, and it is probably to the commentators of this period that Proclus refers as οἱ παλαιοί or οἱ πρεσβύτεροι. At any rate, we may judge so by a passage in the commentary on the *Timaeus* (*In Tim.*, ed. Teubner, III, 234), where he writes : ὥσπερ οἱ παλαιότεροι . . . τοὺς 'Αττικοὺς λέγω καὶ 'Αλβίνους καὶ τοιούτους πάντας. They are contrasted here with οἱ περὶ Πορφύριον. Porphyry is evidently regarded by Proclus as having begun a new epoch in Platonic interpretation. In one passage he puts him above all other Platonic commentators. And he quotes him far more frequently than any other, except Iamblichus and his own master, Syrianus.

These facts tell very strongly against the idea of a continuous tradition of Platonic interpretation going back to the early Academy. They suggest rather that little, if any, of the tradition on the subject goes back further than the second century A.D. And if we can judge by the commentators quoted, the centre of the study was not in the Academy or in Athens at all, until Plutarch, the son of Nestorius, and his pupil, Syrianus, revived the predominance of Athens in the fifth century A.D. Between Crantor and Syrianus the history of Platonic commentary in the Academy is a blank as

---

[1] The anonymous commentary on the *Theaetetus*, of which portions have been preserved, is probably to be assigned to this period. It is generally supposed to be a production of a member of the school of Gaius.

far as our recorded knowledge goes.[1]  These conclusions are confirmed if we examine the scanty references in the commentaries to
the work of these first commentators.  Crantor, we are told, was
the first Platonic commentator.  But there is no record of any
commentary of his except on the *Timaeus*.  And the sole reference
to that commentary that we find in Proclus is to the story already
referred to above.[2]  Plutarch, however, refers at much greater
length to his explanations of the dialogue, but it is not always
perfectly clear how far the views that are ascribed to him are his
interpretation of what Plato meant or what he thought himself.
There is still more uncertainty about this in the case of Xenocrates,[3]
whose views are quoted several times by Proclus, and frequently
by Plutarch.  He is quoted by the latter as representing one of the
two opposing views about the nature of the soul, while the other
is represented by Crantor, so that if we are to suppose that they
are discussing what Plato thought and meant, we see as early as
this diametrically opposed views about the interpretation of the
dialogue.  This could hardly have been possible if there had been
any authoritative interpretation which had come from Plato himself.
We reach, then, these conclusions about the early beginnings
of Platonic commentary.  Plato himself certainly never used the
dialogues as textbooks nor expounded them systematically in the
Academy.  At the very most all that can have been derived from
him would have been stray hints on the interpretation of isolated
points.  Xenocrates, if he expressed opinions on the interpretation
of the dialogues at all,[4] handed down no more than similar stray
hints.  Crantor only wrote on the *Timaeus* ; he is never quoted for
any other dialogue.  There is no evidence that his successors ever
expounded Plato's dialogues at all ; they were more interested in
the development of their own philosophy, and they only used
Plato's writings, if at all, to find this philosophy in them.  So the
conclusion of the whole matter is that there is no authoritative
tradition of interpretation of the dialogues going back to Plato

[1] The suggestion put forward by one scholar, that Gaius was the
head of the Academy, has absolutely no evidence at all in its support.

[2] Taking this into account, we may well doubt whether Proclus
had ever himself seen the commentary of Crantor, or whether it was
extant in his time at all.

[3] I suspect in Plutarch the first signs of the tendency that we have
already observed in later writers—the tendency, that is, to assume
that if Xenocrates held certain views himself, he must necessarily
have ascribed them to his master.

[4] The remarks of his quoted by Plutarch and Proclus on the *Timaeus*
might have been his own opinions.  But Olympiodorus refers to what
looks like a definite piece of explanation by him of the meaning of
φρουρά in the *Phaedo* (Olympiodorus, *In Phaed.*, ed. Teubner, p. 85).
We are not told from what work this passage is quoted.

himself, and very little, if any, going back beyond the second century A.D. It follows from this that the later commentators have no kind of authority for us beyond what they owe to their own natural intelligence and learning, and we are under no obligation to accept any explanation or interpretation of theirs which does not appeal to us as reasonable.

*The Biographies and Doxographies.*—Our consideration of the Platonic commentaries has taken us on to the last years of pagan philosophy. There remains to consider one class of writings, of which the bulk that has come down to us dates from that earlier century in which, as we saw, such a large portion of Platonic commentary was composed. That is the lives of Plato and the introductions to and summaries of his philosophy, of which several have come down to us. Of these we have a life of Plato and a summary of his doctrines by Apuleius. This dates from about the middle of the second century A.D. ; and of approximately the same period we have an introduction to Plato's dialogues by Albinus of Smyrna, whom we have already met in Proclus' list of the chief Platonic commentators. To the same author we must ascribe an account of Plato's doctrines headed in the manuscripts by the name of Alcinous. It is now generally accepted that this name is an error for Albinus,[1] and that the account of the doctrines is by the same author as the introduction. Probably from the beginning of the following century we have the compilation of Diogenes Laertius, which includes, of course, much older material. There is an anonymous life of Plato of uncertain date, and at the end of the period we find a life of Plato and prolegomena to his philosophy by Olympiodorus, of which we have already spoken.

The lives of Plato may be dismissed briefly. The same incidents and statements are found in all of them, though Diogenes is fuller and contains a certain amount that is not found in the others. This account is also of more interest than the others, in that it gives the authority for many of the statements. He mentions about twenty different authors, some of them more than once. The earliest of them are Speusippus, who is quoted (probably at second or third hand) for the rumours about Plato's miraculous birth, and Hermodorus, who is the authority for the statement—omitted in the other biographies—about Plato's sojourn with Euclides at Megara after the death of Socrates. Dicaearchus and Aristoxenus, both of them pupils of Aristotle, are quoted more than once. But the author most frequently quoted of all is Favorinus, who wrote in the second century A.D.

Compare now the two earlier lives—those of Apuleius and Diogenes.. The former is much the shorter, and every statement of fact

---

[1] This was first shown by J. Freudenthal, *Hellenistische Studien* III. : *Der Platoniker Albinos und der falsche Alkinoos.*

in it is also in Diogenes, though generally in a fuller, and once or twice in a slightly different, form.    But it is noteworthy that the great majority of the statements which these two have in common are given by Diogenes without the reference to any authority by name.    And these statements are very often about quite small details, such as the assertion, which appears in all the lives, that Plato's first visit to Sicily was undertaken for the purpose of seeing the volcanoes.[1]    We are probably safe in assuming, then, that they both were using the same original work, but that Diogenes supplemented it by extracts from other writers.    What this original work was need not be discussed here.    It is certainly not an authority of any great weight.

There are two statements, one each in Diogenes and Apuleius, which bear slightly on our subject.    Apuleius, after his account of the early influences on Plato, goes on : ' Nam quamuis de diuersis officinis haec ei essent philosophiae membra suscepta, naturalis a· Pythagoreis, [dialectica] rationalis . . . atque moralis ex ipso Socrate fonte, unum tamen ex omnibus et quasi proprii partus corpus effecit,' etc. (Apuleius, De Platone, 187).    There is a lacuna after ' rationalis ' : ' ab Eleaticis ' has been conjectured.    Apuleius ascribes to them an important influence on Plato in the preceding passage.    Diogenes expresses himself on somewhat similar lines, but with certain differences : Μῖξίν τε ἐποιήσατο τῶν τε ῾Ηρακλειτείων λόγων καὶ Πυθαγορικῶν καὶ Σωκρατικῶν.  Τὰ μὲν γὰρ αἰσθητά, καθ᾽ ῾Ηράκλειτον · τὰ δὲ νοητά, κατὰ Πυθαγόραν · τὰ δὲ πολιτικά, κατὰ Σωκράτην ἐφιλοσόφει.    It will be observed that they agree in distinguishing and contrasting the Socratic and Pythagorean influence, and in ascribing to the former only the moral and political views of Plato.    For the rest, the statement of Apuleius clearly rests on an inference from the Timaeus, and (if ' ab Eleaticis ' is correct) from the Sophist and Parmenides ; while the account of Diogenes very obviously goes straight back once more to Aristotle in the Metaphysics.    To the same source, somewhat elaborated, may be traced another incidental remark of Diogenes (III, i, 56).    After a comparison with the history of the drama, he goes on : οὕτως καὶ τῆς φιλοσοφίας ὁ λόγος.  πρότερον μὲν ἦν μονοειδής, ὡς ὁ φυσικός · δεύτερον δὲ Σωκράτης προσέθηκε τὸν ἠθικόν · τρίτον δὲ Πλάτων τὸν διαλεκτικόν, καὶ ἐτελεσιούργησε τὴν φιλοσοφίαν.

We turn, then, to the doxographies of Plato, the introductions to his dialogues, and the accounts of his philosophy.    Besides the authors already mentioned, we have fragments, preserved by Eusebius, of the writings of Atticus, Severus, and Numenius, whose names we have already met in the writings of Proclus.    But, with

[1] It has been suggested that this is an inference from the description of volcanic phenomena in the Phaedo.    This is quite possible.    But it is not likely that the inference would have occurred independently to several authors.

one exception, there is nothing in these which has much bearing either direct or indirect on our subject. The exception is an interesting quotation from Numenius (*Fragmenta Phil. Graec.*, ed. Didot, Vol. III, p. 154, fr. 1). He is explaining how the different disciples of Socrates came to hold views entirely opposed to each other.. This happened, according to him, because each of them only attended to one of the different elements that Socrates combined in his philosophy. ὁ δὲ Πλάτων Πυθαγορίσας (ᾔδει δὲ τὸν Σωκράτην μηδαμόθεν ἢ ἐκεῖθεν ταῦτα καὶ τοιαῦτα εἰπεῖν τε καὶ γνόντα εἰρηκέναι), ὧδε οὖν καὶ αὐτὸς συνεδήσατο τὰ πράγματα κ.τ.λ. This is striking, because not only does it assume definitely that Plato followed Socrates in his views, but it also equally definitely connects Socrates' views with those of the Pythagoreans. It is, I think, the only passage where this connexion is unequivocally asserted, though there are hints of it in Plutarch. Otherwise, as we have seen, the prevalent view is directly opposed to any idea of such a connexion. Numenius does not give any earlier authority in support of his account, and it is perfectly possible that it is purely his own idea. He is certainly an original, even eccentric, exponent of earlier philosophies. Himself a Pythagorean rather than a Platonist, his aim seems to have been to trace back Greek philosophy to the wisdom of the East, introduced into Europe by Pythagoras. He is the author of the well-known saying, Τί γάρ ἐστι Πλάτων ἢ Μωύσης ἀττικίζων;—a remark which hardly tends to establish our confidence in his judgement.

We turn, then, to the accounts of Plato's philosophy which have been preserved to us in their entirety. Of these we have one by Albinus, including the Introduction to the dialogues, one by Apuleius, and at least three, probably four, different accounts in Diogenes Laertius. Of these last, the first is ascribed to a certain Alcimus, who gives a brief account of Plato's views in the course of an argument directed to show that they were largely borrowed from Epicharmus. We then have an elaborate introduction to the study of Plato, containing a discussion of the dialogue form, of the order and arrangement of the dialogues, and other similar points. This is presented in a comparatively literary form, and is clearly the work of Diogenes himself, or of the author on whom his work is based. There is then a brief and badly arranged account of Plato's views, which is almost certainly by a different hand from this introduction. Finally, we have an extraordinary list of διαιρέσεις of every imaginable kind of thing, which is given as Plato's on the authority of Aristotle. This last is of no value and no interest to us.

The evidence of Alcimus, on the other hand, is of extreme interest. We are told nothing about him here, except that this passage is taken from the first of four books πρὸς Ἀμύνταν. On the basis of this he has been identified (by Schwartz in *Pauly-Wissowa*) with a Sicilian historian of this name, who was probably a younger contemporary of Plato's. If this be so, this is one of the earliest accounts of Plato's philosophy that we possess, and it is of great interest as showing the kind of knowledge of this philosophy that was possessed by those outside of Plato's own school. It is a brief and compressed account, obviously only a selection from what Alcimus said, though what is given purports to be his exact words. Without going into it in detail, we can say that the whole of it could be derived from the dialogues. Nor are there any signs of some dialogues being considered of superior authority to others. The distinction between αἰσθητόν and νοητόν, between γένεσις and οὐσία, the world of flux and the eternal Forms, are the common property of all the dialogues from the *Phaedo* to the *Timaeus*. We also have the doctrine of Reminiscence, though in a distorted form, and the expressions μετέχειν and παραδείγματα to describe the relation between the Forms and the things of sense. The whole account is clearly derived straight from the dialogues, and from no other sources.

The other passages in Diogenes and the works of Albinus and Apuleius present some nice problems in ' Quellenforschung '. A comparison of parallel passages shows in the first place that Apuleius and Albinus are clearly using the same source for their accounts of the doctrine. In the introduction to the dialogues there are passages almost verbally the same in Albinus and Diogenes,[1] though there are many passages in each with no parallel in the other. And finally there is a passage in Albinus's account of the doctrine which very closely resembles, sometimes in the actual words and phrases, a passage preserved by Eusebius from Arius Didymus, a writer of uncertain date.

The most varied conclusions have been drawn from this and other evidence about the original sources of these authors. They need not however detain us here. The important point to notice is that a careful examination of these accounts shows that the authors relied almost entirely on the dialogues for their account of Plato's philosophy. Further, they apparently regarded all the dialogues as of equal authority. The *Timaeus* certainly is quoted much more frequently than any other dialogue : the first part of Apuleius's account, for instance, is based on it alone. But that is natural, because it is the only dialogue which deals at length with subjects such as the creation of the world and the nature of physical processes, in which these later writers ·were particularly interested. But there is no evidence that the other dialogues were not con-

---

[1] This seems to me to tell strongly in favour of the view that Diogenes is a mere scissors-and-paste compilation, and that the more continuous passages are not his own work but taken over *en bloc* from some other writer.

sidered as equally authoritative expressions of Plato's thought. Considerable use is also made of the *Republic* and the *Phaedo*, both of which Albinus uses as his sources for Plato's arguments in favour of the immortality of the soul. And there are throughout many traces of dependence on other dialogues. Nor are there any signs that any other source of information about Plato was recognized. The additions to be found in these writers are clearly later developments under Stoic, Peripatetic, or other influences, generally, it is true, to be found implicitly, if not explicitly, in Plato's writings. A typical instance of the way these later developments are foisted on Plato is to be found in Albinus. He attributes certain logical doctrines to Plato, which, as formulated, are clearly of a later date. And he supports this attribution by illustrating from Plato's dialogues the different kinds of argument which these views distinguished and classified.

It is curious that, though Aristotelian and pseudo-Aristotelian doctrines are sometimes ascribed to Plato, Aristotle's own account of Plato's views does not seem to have been used by these writers to modify or supplement the information that can be derived from the dialogues. The commentators on Aristotle do, of course, know of his contributions to our knowledge on this point. But there is no sign that they regarded it as in any way correcting or modifying what could be learnt from the dialogues which they quote freely for Plato's views. It is from these commentators that we get our only hint of other authoritative sources of information about Plato besides what we can get from Aristotle and the dialogues. Simplicius twice mentions a work of Hermodorus about Plato, which he quotes for certain views of his about the division of existing beings into καθ' αὐτά and πρὸς ἕτερα and further developments of this. It is to be observed that this book was evidently not extant in the Academy in the time of Simplicius. He does not claim to have seen it himself, but quotes Porphyry as the authority, who in his turn quotes it from a work of Dercyllides on the philosophy of Plato. This, incidentally, is but one more instance of how complete the break is between the Academy of the neo-Platonists and the Academy of its first founders.[1] In any case, the information that Hermodorus has to give, though in a small degree it supplements, cannot be said in any way to modify the information that we can derive from the dialogues. Porphyry himself points out the close connexion between what we find in this passage and what we can derive from the *Philebus*. Except for these passages and the one historical statement in Diogenes I can find nothing in later writers which is derived from Hermodorus.

[1] In particular it throws some light on the contents of that library of the Academy to which these commentators had access, on the strength of which some modern writers seem prepared to treat them as almost first-hand authorities on Plato.

There remains now to give a brief account of what is said by Albinus and Diogenes in the way of introduction to the dialogues, and with that our long task will be concluded. There is little of any great interest to us to be extracted from these passages, except the fact, already abundantly clear, that they regarded the dialogues as containing the philosophy of Plato. It may be of interest to quote the definition of the dialogue, which is given in almost verbally the same form by our two authors, who thus clearly took it as an accepted account from an earlier writer : Ἔστι δὲ διάλογος [οὐκ ἄλλο τι ἢ λόγος, Albinus] ἐξ ἐρωτήσεως καὶ ἀποκρίσεως συγκείμενος περί τινος τῶν φιλοσοφουμένων καὶ πολιτικῶν [πραγμάτων, Albinus] μετὰ τῆς πρεπούσης ἠθοποιίας τῶν παραλαμβανομένων προσώπων καὶ τῆς κατὰ τὴν λέξιν κατασκευῆς (Diogenes Laertius, III, i, 48). The words πρεπούσης ἠθοποιίας do not imply any great degree of historical accuracy. Albinus explains them subsequently as meaning that the philosopher in the dialogue should always be represented as speaking with a noble simplicity and love of truth, while to the sophist should be attributed τὸ ποικίλον καὶ τὸ παλίμβολον καὶ τὸ φιλόδοξον, and the ἰδιωτικός should also speak according to character. This does not tell us very much, nor does the discussion of the classification and arrangement of the dialogues add anything to what we know already.

There are, however, definite statements found in Diogenes alone, which, if he were a much more valuable authority than he really is, would almost settle the whole question. The first is a brief remark in the life of Socrates to the effect that Plato ἃ Σωκράτης ἀρνεῖται, περὶ τούτων αὐτὸς λέγει, καίπερ ἀνατιθεὶς παντα Σωκράτει. A fuller and more definite statement occurs in the life of Plato. There he refers to the old controversy, which we have already met with in Cicero, whether Plato was a dogmatist or a sceptic. This controversy evidently began as soon as the Academy became affected by the sceptical doctrine. And even a writer as late as Olympiodorus feels it necessary to refer to it and to argue the point (Olymp., *Proleg. in Platon. Phil.* X, XI). Diogenes entirely rejects the sceptical interpretation of the dialogues, and sums up thus (III, i, 52) : Καὶ περὶ μὲν τῶν αὐτῷ δοκούντων ἀποφαίνεται διὰ τεττάρων προσώπων, Σωκράτους, Τιμαίου, τοῦ Ἀθηναίου ξένου, τοῦ Ἐλεάτου ξένου. Εἰσὶ δ' οἱ ξένοι οὐχ, ὥς τινες ὑπέλαβον, Πλάτων καὶ Παρμενίδης, ἀλλὰ πλάσματά εἰσιν ἀνώνυμα. Ἐπεὶ καὶ τὰ Σωκράτους καὶ τὰ Τιμαίου λέγων Πλάτων δογματίζει. This is a pretty definite statement, which certainly represents the established critical opinion in the time of Diogenes. We find it expressed by Aelius Aristides (*Orat.* XLVI), who says of Plato ἄλλα μυρία δήπου διεξέρχεται ἐπί τῷ Σωκράτους ὀνόματι περὶ ὧν ὁμολογεῖται μηδὲν ἐκεῖνον πραγματεύεσθαι. And it goes back earlier still. Sextus Empiricus (*Pyrrh. Hyp.* I, a, 33) mentions the controversy and this particular view, which he refers to in almost the same words (ἀποφαίνεται διὰ Σωκράτους ἢ Τιμαίου ἤ τινος τῶν τοιούτων). He ascribes it to Aenesidemus,[1] whom he quotes as one of the leading figures in the controversy. This takes us back to early in the first century B.C. But it is doubtful if we can trace it much further. This particular formulation of the view is clearly a product of the sceptical controversy. Its value as evidence of earlier opinion is, then, mainly negative. What it does suggest most strongly is that there cannot have been in existence any decisive evidence in favour of an opposite view. And this, as we have already seen, is a characteristic of a great part of our evidence.

'This long and, it must be confessed, rather tedious investigation is now concluded. I cannot claim to have discussed or even examined every existing piece of evidence on the subject. To make that claim it would be necessary to have examined every allusion to Plato or Socrates in the whole of the later Greek literature. In that vast field there are no doubt many such passages which have escaped my notice, though I have, of course, examined many more than I have thought necessary to discuss here. But I think that at least I have examined all the most important authorities and discussed the more striking statements.

What, then, are the general conclusions which can be drawn from this investigation? We can say, in the first place, that there is practical unanimity among all later writers that the dialogues represent Plato's own thought. They are invariably quoted as evidence for this, and the views with which we are familiar in the dialogues are regularly ascribed to Plato. The theory which is most frequently associated with his name is the doctrine of the Forms, and after that we probably hear most about the tripartite division of the soul. But almost every view that is put into the mouth of Socrates in the dialogues is at one time or the other ascribed to Plato. And there is absolutely no hint that the dialogues are ever considered as being purely biographical in character or as having any other purpose than the inculcation of views which the author believed to be true. There is no such general agreement about the extent to which the dialogues present an historical picture of Socrates. They seem to be generally accepted as an accurate representation of his personal characteristics, and also as evidence, so far as they go, for incidents in his life. But it is much more doubtful how far they are taken as representing the philosophical views which he actually held. There is much less said than we might have hoped on the question. Some statements are ambiguous, some seem pretty definitely to imply that the dialogues are not to be taken as representing the actual views of Socrates, while others seem to imply even more definitely that they are. But it

---

[1] The name of Aenesidemus in this passage is a conjectural emendation, originally made by Fabricius, for an otherwise unknown name in the MSS. But the conjecture is almost certainly right, and has been universally accepted.

is to be remarked that the most definite statements in this latter sense come from the latest writers.   We may note in passing that there is next to no evidence to connect Socrates with the Pythagoreans ; in fact, most of the evidence, such as it is, is rather the other way.

About the worth of all this evidence it is hard to arrive at a definite conclusion.   Little or none of it can be traced back with certainty to an earlier source of any real authority, except to the passages in Aristotle which are still extant.   And certainly we have nothing which we can possibly set up in rivalry to his account. Indeed the evidence, such as it is, confirms this account and leaves us with much the same impression that we derive from that source.

# I. INDEX OF AUTHORS QUOTED

*[References to individual works are only given for a few of the most important authors, of whom more than one work is quoted by name.]*

239

# II. GENERAL INDEX

241